CHICAGO
Special
EVENTS
Sourcebook

The comprehensive guide to locations in
Chicago and suburbs for MEETINGS, PARTIES,
WEDDINGS, and other SPECIAL
OCCASIONS

EDITED BY LINDA LUTTON

CHICAGO
REVIEW
PRESS

Library of Congress Cataloging-in-Publication Data
Chicago special events sourcebook : the comprehensive guide to locations
in Chicago and suburbs for meetings, parties, weddings, and other
special occasions / edited by Linda Lutton.
    p. cm.
  Includes index.
  ISBN 1-55652-394-7
  1. Chicago (Ill.)—Guidebooks. 2. Chicago Region (Ill.)—Guidebooks
I. Lutton, Linda.
  F548.18 .C4568 2001
  917.73'110444—dc21

Prices and facilities are subject to change. We have made every effort to
make this book as accurate as possible at the time of publication. Please
call locations to get current information.

To update your listing or to be considered for the next edition, please write to
the *Chicago Special Events Sourcebook* Editor in care of Chicago Review Press.

The author and the publisher of this book disclaim all liability incurred in
connection with the use of the information contained in this book.

Front cover photograph: Field Museum
Back cover photographs: clockwise from left: South Shore Cultural Center,
Four Seasons Hotel, Chicago, Bella Vista Fine Arts Gallery, Ghost Bar,
Museum of Science and Industry, Nine, Grillroom Chophouse, & Wine Bar.
Cover design: Rattray Design
Interior design: Mel Kupfer

Published by Chicago Review Press, Incorporated
814 North Franklin Street
Chicago, Illinois 60610
ISBN 1-55652-394-7
Printed in the United States of America
5 4 3 2 1

CONTENTS

INTRODUCTION

Whether you're planning a company outing for 1,000, a wedding reception for 100, or a holiday celebration for a few, this directory will help you find the perfect location for your special event. With more than 300 detailed listings to the best places in Chicago and the surrounding suburbs, you'll find a site that is perfect for every occasion.

Full of unique venues, this book will inspire even the most seasoned event planner. Have you ever thought of having a company product kick-off in the First Feet exhibit room at the Scholl College of Podiatric Medicine? How about a rehearsal dinner aboard *Chicago's First Lady*? Buddy Guy's Legends would be an ideal spot for a 40th birthday party—everyone can join the guest-of-honor in singing the blues. Or how about inviting employees to play a game of Whirlyball? It's a great exercise in teamwork that could also be pretty entertaining. In addition to information on unusual party and meeting sites, more traditional venues, such as hotels, conference centers, banquet halls, and restaurants are included.

Each listing combines a description of the site with information on its capacity, rental fees, catering guidelines, equipment availability, menu prices, amenities, and restrictions. When available, fax numbers, E-mail addresses, and Web sites are included. Capacity is listed as banquet (round tables), reception (a combination of standing area and tables), theater-style, or classroom-style. Keep in mind that tables and chairs can be arranged in a variety of ways, depending on the site. The capacity will vary according to your seating needs.

To help you find the ideal venue more quickly, each chapter is devoted to a particular type of site: banquet rooms, museums, hotels, etc. Indexes list venues with special features such as outdoor facilities, kid-friendly venues, and places that can accommodate more than 500 guests. A Chicago-area map and a listing of venues by location will help you find a site in any part of town.

For information on catering companies, entertainers, florists, and other services that will contribute to the success of your event, we've added a resource advertising section at the back of the book. (Please note that the location listings are completely independent of the advertising section. The locations did not pay to be in this book.)

Once you've selected a venue, we suggest that you call the contact to determine availability and schedule a site visit. The information in this book was verified before going to press. However, prices and menus often change in this business so be sure to double-check the details. Many venues are extremely flexible; their goal is to accommodate you. Let them know your budget and your needs. Then ask how they can accommodate you.

Finding the perfect location for your event can be a time-consuming task. In compiling the sites listed in this book, we've done some of the legwork. Now you will be able to focus on the details. And you just might even have time to enjoy the party!

CHICAGO
EVENTS
Special
Sourcebook

ACTIVITIES AND GAME AND SPORT CENTERS

Arlington Park

Comiskey Park

Dave & Buster's

Enchanted Castle Restaurant &
 Entertainment Center

FAO Schwarz

Fox River Games Paintball Sports

Hawthorne Race Course

Hoops The Gym

Hoops The Gym–Stadium Club

Lakeview Baseball Club

Lucky Strike, The

Medieval Times Dinner &
 Tournament

North Beach Chicago

Odeum Sports & Expo Center

Pirates' Cove Theme Park

Rainbow Falls Water Theme Park

Ravinia Festival

Six Flags Great America

Southport Lanes and Billiards

Sportsman's Park

Stadium Club at Wrigley Field

WhirlyBall

Windy City Fieldhouse

ARLINGTON PARK

EUCLID AVENUE AT WILKE ROAD
ARLINGTON HEIGHTS, IL 60006
(847) 385-7500
WWW.ARLINGTONPARK.COM
E-MAIL ABYCZYNSKI@ARLINGTONPARK.COM

CONTACT Allison Byczynski, exposition
manager
BEST FEATURE World-renowned elegant
entertainment facility.
BEST PARTY Off-season events.
CAPACITY 300 banquet, 1,000 reception; 450
10x10 foot trade show booths.
RENTAL FEE Main building, $11,000 per day;
parking lots, $2,000–$6,000.
HOURS Available November through May.
PARKING $6 per car; valet obtainable.

Courtesy of Arlington Park

Arlington Park has long been admired
as a premier thoroughbred racecourse.
Set among immaculately landscaped
grounds, this sprawling white grandstand makes an elegant and unique setting for a black-tie dinner and dance.
Enjoy cocktails on the spacious brick-
paved patio overlooking the flower-
decked European-style paddock where
famous thoroughbreds have paraded for
more than 70 years. Then, head up the
marble Grand Staircase bordered by
indoor waterfalls to the second level
where you can enjoy dinner and dancing. More than 40,000 square feet of
space makes this a perfect location for
public expositions.

Arlington Park is available from November through May for expos or Ride
and Drives (there are two large parking
lots available.) The site is handicapped
accessible and has audio-visual equipment available.

COMISKEY PARK

333 W. 35TH STREET
CHICAGO, IL 60616
(312) 335-5045, FAX (312) 664-6822

CONTACT Cari Frankenstein
BEST FEATURE Two locations overlooking
the field.
CAPACITY The Stadium Club, 325 banquet,
650 reception; Terrace Suites, 50–400.
RENTAL FEE The Stadium Club, food and bev-
erage minimum; Terrace Suites, $73–$100
per person, inclusive.
HOURS The Stadium Club, year around, on
nongame days; Terrace Suites on game
days only.
PARKING Lot near entrance. No charge for
Stadium Club; maximum $10 charge for
Terrace Suites.

Courtesy of Comiskey Park

Whether you choose to host your event
in the sophisticated Stadium Club or in
the casual Terrace Suites, you're sure to
throw a home-run party. The Stadium
Club, a multilevel dining room and bar
area with a breathtaking view overlooking the field, is available on non-game
days throughout the year. The two
Terrace Suites feature an outdoor patio
and are available on game days throughout the season. In-house event planners
will take care of all of the details, from
customized menus to entertainment
and décor.

Both sites are catered by Levy Restaurants with a wide variety of menu
selections for you to choose from. Both
sites are handicapped accessible, and
audio-visual equipment is available.

Dave & Buster's

1030 N. Clark Street
Chicago, IL 60610
(312) 943-5151, fax (312) 943-4686
www.daveandbusters.com

Contact Special Events Department
Best Features Video games, bowling, virtual golf, billiards, and more.
Capacity Viewpoint 1, 25–45; Viewpoint 2, 30–100; Viewpoint 3, 30–65; Executive Billiard, 25–45; The Showroom, up to 200; Oak Room, 30–140.
Rental Fee Viewpoint 1, $30/hour; Viewpoint 2, $60/hour; Viewpoint 3, $40/hour; Executive Billiard, $60/hour; no charge for other rooms.
Discounts Special rates on D&B PowerCards, which are good for play on 250 games.
For the Kids No unattended minors are allowed. All minors must leave by 10 P.M.
Hours Sunday–Tuesday, 11:30 A.M.–midnight; Wednesday–Saturday, 11:30 A.M.–1 A.M.
Parking Valet; nearby parking garages offer a discounted rate with validation.

Photograph by Steve Matteo

Imagine 200 state-of-the-art computer games, simulators, and games of skill all under one roof and you have Dave & Buster's—a bar/restaurant that features entertainment for the young-at-heart. Explore the video game options with a PowerCard, good for play on most games. (The cards are available at a discount rate for special events.) This site offers 60,000 square feet of great food and great fun.

Dave & Buster's has an array of menu selections. Texas BBQ, Fiesta Party, and D&B Italian Feasts are just a few of the buffets to choose from. Only bakery-bought cakes may be brought in. Buffets range from $11.95–$29.95 per person. There are three bar options to choose from: open bar, drink tickets, and cash bar. The site is handicapped accessible and has audiovisual equipment available.

Enchanted Castle Restaurant & Entertainment Center

1103 S. Main Street
Lombard, IL 60148
(630) 953-7860, fax (630) 953-2453

Contact Scott Nowo, sales representative
Best Features Movie 'n Motion theater ride, laser tag, bumper cars, indoor miniature golf, Wally Wizard and the Singing Dragon Show, and video karaoke.
Capacity Entire facility, 2,000 reception; Four dining rooms combined, 625 banquet.
Rental Fee Various food and entertainment packages.
For the Kids Special areas just for kids: Castle Corral and ImaGYMnation Station Adventure Playland.
Hours Sunday–Thursday, 11 A.M.–10 P.M.; Friday and Saturday, 11 A.M.–midnight.
Parking Free lot.

The largest entertainment complex in Chicago and surrounding suburbs, the Castle features 46,000 square feet of food and fun for all ages. Experience the ride of your life on the Race Movie 'n Motion Theatre ride with six different adventures, challenge friends or coworkers in a game of Q-Zar Laser Tag, race on the Virtual Speedway, and enjoy more than 280 sports and games, plus indoor golf, bumper cars, and more. The Murder Mystery Dinner Theatre and creativity seminars are also available.

Casual dining includes hot appetizers, salads, king-size sandwiches, fresh pastas, and deep-dish pizza. Beer and Wine available. Staff party planners will arrange custom menus and theme events. A sound system, podium, large screen TVs, and audiovisual equipment are on hand.

Courtesy of Enchanted Castle Restaurant & Entertainment Center

FAO Schwarz

840 N. Michigan Avenue
Chicago, IL 60611
(312) 587-5000, fax (312) 587-0318
www.fao.com
E-mail faochicago@fao.net

Contact Anthony Beguhl, event manager
Best Features Talking tree, gravity loop, clock tower.
Capacity All three floors, 1,200 reception; 450 banquet.
Rental Fees Breakfast starting at $2,200; evenings, $5,000–$13,500.
For the Kids Birthday parties and sleepovers with characters such as Barbie, Raggedy Ann, Raggedy Andy, or Bobby the Toy Soldier.
Hours Day receptions, Sunday 9 A.M.– 11 A.M., Monday–Saturday 8 A.M.–10 A.M.; evening receptions, after store closing.
Parking Three nearby garages.

The fun and games begin as soon as you get past the gigantic waving bear, where

a 22-foot clock tower welcomes you to a world of toys. Cross the xylophone bridge, pass the talking tree, then check out the country's only "great swoop gravity loop," where balls swoosh overhead to 280 feet per second. This ultimate location for after-hour functions isn't just for kids. FAO Schwarz offers the opportunity to celebrate in a fun-filled, unique ambiance that's sure to please guests of all ages.

The staff will tailor the store to suit any event by dressing as storybook characters and decorating around a theme. All food and drink must be served by an approved caterer. A list of preferred caterers is provided. Service equipment and audiovisual equipment must be brought in. FAO Schwarz is handicapped accessible.

Courtesy of FAO Schwarz

Fox River Games Paintball Sports

1891 N. Farnsworth Avenue
Aurora, Illinois 60505
(630) 585-5651, fax (630) 585-5657
www.foxpaintball.com

Contact Group reservations
Best Features Build teamwork, tactics, and communication.
Best Party Company outings.
Capacity Nearly any size group.
Rental Fees Average cost for 4–7 hours of paintball is $35–$45 per person, or $5–$10 per hour.
Discounts Pay entire game fee 30 days in advance and get a 10 percent discount; special rates off-peak (Nov. 17–Dec. 31).
For the Kids Players must be 13 years old to participate.
Hours Office hours: Monday–Friday 11 A.M.– 7 P.M.; Saturday 11 A.M.–6 P.M.; closed Sunday. Field hours: Saturday and Sunday 8 A.M.–4 P.M.; weekdays by reservation only.
Parking Plenty available.

Courtesy of Fox River Games Paintball Sports

Paintball is an excellent way to teach teamwork, foster communication, encourage competition, or just blow off a little steam. Players under eighteen must have a notarized and signed parent consent form. Game rates are set up with a base fee of $250 that covers 16– 20 players, field use for the entire day, tracer pump gun rental, free CO_2 propellant for all guns, goggles/face protection, and staff to run the games. The

base fee also guarantees that your event will be private. You must purchase paintballs separately and they run from $8 for 100 paintballs to $99 for 1,800. Bring Ziplock bags to carry the paintballs. No outside paintballs are allowed.

You can have your event catered, bring your own food, or choose from Fox River's concession stand. Fox River requires that you bring your own drinking water.

HAWTHORNE RACE COURSE

3501 S. LARAMIE AVENUE
STICKNEY/CICERO, IL 60804
(800) 780-3986, FAX (708) 780-3755
WWW.HAWTHORNERACECOURSE.COM

CONTACT Caryl Meadows, director of sales
CAPACITY Clubhouse, grandstand, and center fields, 75,000; Gold Cup Dining Room, 750; Terrace area, 800; Derby Room, 350; Turf Club, 300; VIP Room, 30 banquet.
RENTAL FEE Prices based on food and beverage consumption during racing season; there is a rental fee in the off-season.
HOURS Thoroughbred races run from July 1–November 28, post time 1 P.M. Dates subject to change. Space is available anytime during the off-season and by arrangement during nonracing hours in season.
PARKING On-site parking for 3,500 cars.

Courtesy of Hawthorne Race Course

Hawthorne Race Course offers a wide variety of accomodations and amenities for your business and social events. The facility is completely glass-enclosed and climate-controlled, and features 800 televisions on site, plus other audiovisual equipment.

The VIP Room offers the best view of the finish line and has the most personalized service for $30 per person including food, beer, and wine. The Gold Cup Dining Room has tiered seating and TV monitors for a great view from every seat. Entrées start at $8.95 and include clubhouse admission, racing program, name in the daily program, and winner's circle picture. The Turf Club and Derby Room are private banquet rooms. During the off-season, the facility is available for picnics, concerts, and festivals in the center field as well as banquets and trade shows. Hawthorne Race Course is handicapped accessible.

HOOPS THE GYM

1001 W. WASHINGTON BOULEVARD
CHICAGO, IL 60607
(312) 850-4667, FAX (312) 850-0364

CONTACT General manager
BEST FEATURE Spacious basketball gymnasium.
CAPACITY Gym, 250 banquet, 400 reception; Party room, 50 banquet, 100 reception.
RENTAL FEE Varies depending on size and nature of the event.
FOR THE KIDS Parties for kids range from $250 for 15 kids to $375 for 33–40 and are based on a 2-hour party with 1½ hours on the court and ½ hour in the party room.
HOURS Flexible, 24 hours a day, seven days a week.
PARKING On street; valet also available.

Courtesy of Hoops The Gym

Score with a party at this sports facility where guests can play a little b-ball, then head to the party room for dinner or a drink. This bright gymnasium is approximately 5,000 square feet and is designed for basketball, but can also be used for volleyball and other sporting and special events. The adjacent party room combines with the gym to create a great site for anything from an intimate dinner to a rowdy children's party to a company "team-building" event.

An approved caterer can supply the food or you may bring your own eats. Liquor can only be served with proper license and insurance. The party room features a fully equipped kitchen. Tables and folding chairs are provide for up to 75 people, but linens, china, and flatware must be brought in. The gym and party room have separate sound systems. All areas are handicapped accessible. No smoking is allowed.

HOOPS THE GYM

Stadium Club

1380 W. RANDOLPH STREET
CHICAGO, IL 60607
(312) 850-4667, FAX (312) 850-0364

CONTACT General manager

BEST FEATURE 27,000-square-foot private basketball gymnasium.

CAPACITY Gym, 400 banquet or reception; mezzanine-level party room, 50 banquet, 100 reception; Skydeck, 100 banquet, 150 reception; Skybox, 16 banquet, 25 reception.

RENTAL FEE Varies depending on size and nature of event.

FOR THE KIDS Parties for kids range from $250 for 15 kids to $375 for 33–40 and are based on a 2-hour party with 1½ hours on the court and ½ hour in the party room.

HOURS Flexible, 24 hours a day, seven days a week.

PARKING 45-car parking lot; ample street parking.

Courtesy of Hoops The Gym

This 27,000-square-foot private sports facility is an expansion of the original concept. This location features a three-court gymnasium with 30-foot ceilings, state-of-the-art lighting, professional stereo and audio system, as well as a first-floor party room and mezzanine level skydeck—all with views of the courts. The first floor party room features oak floors and track lighting and the sky-deck area has a large, carpeted room.

You can bring in your own food or hire an approved outside caterer. Liquor is allowed with appropriate licensing and insurance. Both event spaces have fully equipped kitchens with ample counter and refrigerator space. Tables and chairs are provided for up to 100 people, but linens, china, and flatware must be brought in. The entire facility is handicapped accessible. Lockers and locks are provided and towel service is available for a fee. There is no smoking allowed.

LAKEVIEW BASEBALL CLUB

3633 N. SHEFFIELD AVENUE
CHICAGO, IL 60613
(773) 935-1880, FAX (773) 935-2101
E-MAIL LVBC@LAKEVIEWBASEBALLCLUB.COM

CONTACT Judy Jordan, administrative director

BEST FEATURE Rooftop view of Chicago Cubs games.

CAPACITY Entire club, 140; Club room, 50; Rooftop deck, 50 banquet plus 40 upper deck seats.

RENTAL FEE $15,250 for food and beverages and exclusive use of facility for up to 140 people (club membership required); approximately $115 per person for smaller groups.

HOURS Available to members year-round.

PARKING Public lots; street. Strict neighborhood parking restrictions apply for night games.

This nonprofit, private membership club is located next to Chicago's historic Wrigley Field and offers an excellent

Courtesy of Lakeview Baseball Club

view of the playing field. The 3,000-square-foot facility has three separate levels of entertainment options. The club room has four large windows, a kitchen, bar, and buffet counter. The rooftop deck (464 feet from home plate) is higher than any of the other Sheffield decks, providing the best view of the field. The deck has covered bleachers as well as an upper deck that seats 40. There are TV monitors and space for live entertainment in both clubhouse and deck.

To rent the club you must be a member—individual, $250; executive, $500; or corporate, $800. Food and beverages are supplied by the club. Audiovisual equipment must be brought in. The club is not handicapped accessible.

The Lucky Strike

2747 N. Lincoln Avenue
Chicago, IL 60614
(773) 472-1601
www.theluckystrike.com

Contact Kim Veber, director of special events; or Claire Perry or Heather Zomer, special events sales managers

Best Features Eight vintage bowling lanes, six regulation-size pool tables.

Capacity Both private rooms, 75–200; Single rooms, 20–80; entire facility, 400.

Rental Fee Single private room, $295–$395; both private rooms, $590–$1,000; entire facility, determined on a per-case basis.

Hours Monday–Friday, 5 P.M.–2 A.M.; Saturday, noon–3 A.M.; Sunday, noon–1 A.M.; other times by arrangement.

Parking Street; valet by request.

The Lucky Strike has revolutionized bowling and billiards by housing both in a swank, trendy, multiroom bar and restaurant with decor reminiscent of the

Courtesy of The Lucky Strike

early 1920s. The high, pressed-tin ceiling, vintage French advertisements on the walls, art-deco light fixtures, and red and black checked floor, make this anything but your typical bowling alley or pool hall. The single private room includes four lanes of bowling, one pool table, nine tables, and a buffet area. With the rental of both private rooms, your guests can use eight lanes of bowling, one pool table, 15 tables, buffet area, and bar.

The restaurant provides all food and beverage. A variety of bar and buffet options are available, including a burger and chicken sandwich buffet, a Southwestern buffet, a pizza buffet, and an Italian buffet. The Lucky Strike is handicapped accessible. Staff can arrange for audiovisual equipment.

Medieval Times Dinner & Tournament

2001 N. Roselle Road
Schaumburg, IL 60195
(847) 882-0555 or (800) 544-2001
www.medievaltimes.com

Contact Group Sales

Capacity Grand Ceremonial Area, 1,426 banquet; Hall of Stallions, 200 banquet, 400 reception; Hall of Arms, 300 banquet, 400 reception; Knight Club, 216 banquet, 275 reception; King's Corner, 25 banquet, 36 reception.

Rental Fee None for private areas with the purchase of drink-and-appetizer package.

For the Kids Group rates for matinees.

Hours Flexible. Call for regular show times.

Parking Free lot on premises.

This dinner theater is a journey back to the glory of the Middle Ages. Guests enter the castle tower and enjoy a two-

Courtesy of Medieval Times Dinner & Tournament

hour spectacle of knights in shining armor performing feats of arms and horsemanship. The action takes place in the Grand Ceremonial Arena. Private areas are curtained-off sections of the foyer surrounding the arena. The facility is handicapped accessible. There is an overhead projector and screen on-site, and a podium and microphone are also available.

During the performance, you will enjoy a four-course banquet, served in the true medieval style—without utensils. Admission includes dinner, soft drinks, show, tax, and gratuity. Rates vary.

North Beach Chicago

1551 N. Sheffield Avenue
Chicago, IL 60622
(312) 266-7842, fax (312) 266-8762
www.northbeachchicago.com

Contact Sharon Kraus, event coordinator
Best Features Sand volleyball, nine-hole miniature golf, bowling.
Best Party Corporate family picnic with live Calypso band, face painter, tarot card reader, and volleyball tournament.
Capacity Private party areas, 30–1,200.
Rental Fee Based on food and beverage consumption.
For the Kids Kid's parties are allowed during the daytime only.
Hours Flexible.
Parking Valet; limited street parking.

Sand volleyball, bowling, nine-hole miniature golf, Ping-Pong, pool, air hockey, darts, and many other games are all located under one roof. This 20,000-

Courtesy of North Beach Chicago

square-foot sports bar offers plenty to keep your guests occupied; no boring small talk or yawns here. There are several private or semiprivate rooms available so that you can rent a portion of the bar or the entire facility. The site is handicapped accessible.

Food and beverages are provided by North Beach. Combination food and bar packages start at $22 per person. You may hire your own entertainment and bring in decorations. The event staff will offer assistance if you are interested, and can arrange for rental of audiovisual equipment. There are also two locations in the western suburbs.

Odeum Sports & Expo Center

1033 N. Villa Avenue
Villa Park, IL 60181
(630) 941-9292, fax (630) 832-9183
www.odeumexpo.com
E-mail odeum1@aol.com

Contact Mike Arndt
Best Party Screamfest.
Capacity 600 banquet, 5,200 theater.
Rental Fee Based upon space type.
Discounts Multiple-day discounts.
For the Kids Soccer parties on weekends from November to March.
Hours Office: 9 A.M.–5:30 P.M.
Parking Free spaces for 2000.

With over 85,000 sq. feet of flexible trade show and event space, the Odeum is the perfect location for concerts, corporate meetings, and other large events. The suburban facility is conveniently located in the heart of DuPage County and is surrounded by hotels, restau-

Photograph by John T. Merkle, courtesy of Odeum Sports & Expo Center

rants, and shopping malls, with major airports and highways within ten miles.

The Odeum Sports and Expo Center is the home of Screamfest, ECW Wrestling, and one of the largest arts and crafts shows in the Midwest. The Odeum is handicapped accessible, and in-house audiovisual equipment is available.

PIRATES' COVE THEME PARK

LEICESTER AND BIESTERFIELD ROAD
ELK GROVE VILLAGE, IL 60007
(847) 437-9494

CONTACT Theme park manager

BEST FEATURE Children's theme park for ages 2–9.

CAPACITY Corporate rentals can accommodate up to 850 guests. Smaller parties including birthday parties and day-care center rentals are welcome.

RENTAL FEE Varies according to the size of the party.

DISCOUNTS Available for large group rentals.

FOR THE KIDS Excellent site for children's parties.

HOURS Open June 1 through Labor Day. Monday–Friday, 11 A.M.–5 P.M.; Saturday–Sunday, 10 A.M.–4 P.M.; Monday–Wednesday, evening hours 6 P.M.–8 P.M. Birthday parties can be held in the evenings.

PARKING Available next to the park.

Courtesy of Pirates' Cove Theme Park

For a celebration with children in mind, try the Pirates' Cove Theme Park. It is designed to stimulate and encourage children's imaginations. The park features an old-fashioned carousel, an authentic 18th-century pirate ship for kids to climb on and explore, a jungle cruise ride, and Misty, the smoke breathing dragon. There is also the Castle of Camelot with its maze of tunnels, nets, tires, and tubes; the 60-foot cable slide; or the bumper boats on the refreshing Pebble Pond. Pirates' Cove Theme Park is the perfect place to entertain groups of children, or to bring out the child in adults. In addition to children's events, the park can accommodate weddings or company picnics.

There are concessions, souvenirs, clean restrooms, diaper changing tables, and drinking fountains available.

RAINBOW FALLS WATER THEME PARK

LIONS DRIVE AND ELK GROVE BOULEVARD
ELK GROVE VILLAGE, IL 60007
(847) 437-9494

CONTACT Aquatic manager

BEST FEATURE Water theme park for all ages.

CAPACITY A 5.5-acre park, can accommodate up to 999 people.

RENTAL FEE Depends on size of party and package selected.

DISCOUNTS Available for group rentals.

FOR THE KIDS Children's parties welcome.

HOURS Monday–Thursday, 10 A.M.–7:30 P.M.; Friday, 10 A.M.–6:30 P.M.; Saturday–Sunday, 11 A.M.–5 P.M.

PARKING Adjacent lot.

Rainbow Falls offers five-and-a-half acres of wet and dry attractions in an aquatic recreation theme park setting. The park features a three-story water fun house, three heart-stopping water slides that spill into a large L-shaped pool, a 300-foot water tube ride, a junior water slide, and a wading pool for younger children. When you're ready to dry off, there's a miniature golf course surrounded by hilly terrain, rock formations, waterfalls, and a beautiful landscape.

Feed your hunger on tasty treats like pizza and popcorn from the concession stand, or hop aboard the Mississippi paddle boat for a relaxing lunch. Restrooms, showers, and a clothing check are available.

Courtesy of Rainbow Falls Water Theme Park

RAVINIA FESTIVAL

400 IRIS LANE
HIGHLAND PARK, IL 60035
(847) 266-5000, FAX (847) 433-7983
WWW.RAVINIA.ORG

CONTACT Shana Hayes, director of sales

BEST FEATURE Open air concerts.

BEST PARTY Chicago Symphony Orchestra in its summer residence at Ravinia.

CAPACITY Northern Tent, 80; Ameritech Tent, up to 200; Sante Fe Railway Tent, 120; Ravinia Tent, 200, 300, or 400.

RENTAL FEES Tent rental requires purchase of concert tickets. Tickets range from $15–$60 per person. Private parties receive 20 percent discount on most concerts. Tent rental fees vary. Catering is additional.

FOR THE KIDS Lawn-catered children's parties during Saturday morning Kraft Kids Concerts (performances begin at 11 A.M.).

HOURS June–Labor Day: Monday–Saturday, 5 P.M.–midnight; Sunday, 4 P.M.–midnight.

PARKING Lot, $5 per car; free park 'n' ride shuttle service.

Courtesy of Ravinia

Ravinia Festival, a scenic 36-acre woodland setting complete with lush landscaping, floral plantings, and sculptures, offers a variety of event entertaining options: lawn-catered parties, pre- and post-concert catered tent parties, and the individual Instant Ravinia lawn chair/gate pass/box dinner package. During the summer season, audiences can enjoy nightly performances including more than 20 concerts by the famous Chicago Symphony Orchestra.

Ravinia's tents are catered exclusively by Gaper's. The Levy Restaurants offer menus for lawn catering. Lawn chairs and side-tables can be rented for group lawn parties. Arrange audiovisual equipment through the caterer. The location is handicapped accessible.

SIX FLAGS GREAT AMERICA

542 N. ROUTE 21
P.O. BOX 1776
GURNEE, IL 60031
(847) 625-7518, FAX (847) 249-1782
WWW.SIXFLAGS.COM

CONTACT Kris Ellsworth, special events coordinator, at (847) 625-7520

BEST FEATURES Exhilarating rides and family fun.

BEST PARTY Gotham Gala, a black-tie dinner for 1,000.

CAPACITY Entire theme park, 10,000 plus during Spring and Fall only; several theaters, 1,000–3,500; Picnic grove, 100–10,000 banquet; seven theme areas with restaurants of varying capacities.

RENTAL FEE Call for details.

DISCOUNTS Call for details.

FOR THE KIDS Could there be a better place for a kid's party?

HOURS Park is open late May–September, and in October for a Halloween extravaganza, Fright Fest. Hours vary.

PARKING $8 per vehicle, buses with at least 25 people park at no charge.

Six Flags with its 100 rides, shows, and attractions, is equipped to handle spectacular special events—everything from entire park buyouts to theme parties, picnics, or black-tie galas. Although Six Flags is known for its roller coasters (it has eight!) don't overlook the magic shows, live music shows, Great Russian Circus spectacular, full-scale steam-engine train, or the children's entertainment area. In addition, there are high-action stunt shows and IMAX films shown on the park's seven-story screen.

Six Flags' catering staff can prepare anything from hors d'oeuvres to multicourse, theme dinners in the private picnic area. Standard group packages are available for groups of 20 or more, but catered events require a minimum of 100 guests.

Courtesy of Six Flags Great America

SOUTHPORT LANES AND BILLIARDS

3325 N. SOUTHPORT AVENUE
CHICAGO, IL 60657
(773) 472-1601
WWW.SOUTHPORTLANES.COM

CONTACT Kim Veber, director of special events; or Claire Perry or Heather Zomer, special events sales managers
BEST FEATURES Four hand-set vintage bowling lanes, six regulation-size pool tables.
CAPACITY Private room, 20–80.
RENTAL FEE $295–$395.
HOURS Monday–Friday, flexible; Saturday, 12 P.M.–3 A.M.; Sunday, 12 P.M.–1 A.M.
PARKING Street parking; valet upon request.

Courtesy of Southport Lanes and Billiards

Southport Lanes and Billiards is truly a Chicago original. This bar/bowling alley will transform your guests back in time for a fun-filled evening of bowling, pool, and delicious food. Features include an antique bar and an original 1920s mural. The four vintage bowling lanes are still set by hand. The private room includes four lanes of bowling, a pool table, and buffet area. The room rental fee includes pin setters and score-keepers. The bar area and pool hall are open to the public during private parties and cannot be rented separately.

Southport Lanes provides all food and beverages. Bar packages are available. Southport Lanes and Billiards can arrange for audiovisual equipment. The site is handicapped accessible.

SPORTSMAN'S PARK

3301 S. LARAMIE AVENUE
CICERO, IL 60804
(773) 242-1121, EXT. 392,
FAX (708) 652-9897
WWW.SPORTSMANSPARK.COM; SEE ALSO
WWW.CHICAGOMOTORSPEEDWAY.COM

CONTACT Sandra Reinhart or Kate McGregor, sales representatives
BEST FEATURE Multipurpose facility featuring thoroughbred horse racing and auto racing.
CAPACITY Sportsman's Club, 500 banquet, 1,000 reception; Gold Club dining room, 450 banquet; skyboxes, 42 each.
RENTAL FEE Most packages include food, admission, seating, parking, racing program, and photo in the winner's circle; prices start at $7.95 per person and vary depending on the season.
HOURS Year-round, days and evenings.
PARKING Horse racing, free lot or valet (recommended); auto racing, various locations and prices.

During the summer Sportsman's Park offers the excitement of auto racing and during the spring thoroughbred racing provides the entertainment. This is the perfect place for an exhilarating and memorable social or corporate meeting or fundraiser, and a great place to celebrate birthdays or weddings. Packages are available for groups of 20 or more and include dinner, admission, racing program, race named in the group's honor, photo in the winner's circle, room rental, and parking. Impressive skyboxes overlook the finish line and are the perfect choice for smaller groups.

Sportsman's Park is available year-round for track rental or for hosting expositions, concerts, and banquets. The facility is handicapped accessible, and rental of audiovisual equipment can be arranged.

Courtesy of Sportsman's Park

STADIUM CLUB AT WRIGLEY FIELD

1060 W. Addison Street
Chicago, IL 60613
(312) 335-5045

Contact Cari Frankenstein, event planner
Best Feature Located inside Wrigley Field.
Capacity Entire facility, 350 banquet, 250 reception; conference room, 50.
Rental Fee Must meet food and beverage minimum.
Hours On nongame days only.
Parking Lot available for $68 per event.

Tucked under the right field grandstands at Wrigley Field, the Stadium Club is available for private events throughout the year. Although there is no view of the field, there is plenty of baseball memorabilia and Cubs paraphernalia. The main dining room has a hardwood floor that is great for dancing. An exposed brick wall covered with the famous Wrigley Field ivy defines the casual bar area. Down a set of stairs is the Dugout, a long spacious room that can be used in addition to the main dining room or as a separate function room. The site is handicapped accessible.

Levy Restaurants caters all events. You may choose from a variety of casual buffets or a formal multicourse dinner complemented by a superb selection of wines. The Stadium Club has some audiovisual equipment and can arrange for additional equipment.

Courtesy of Stadium Club

WHIRLYBALL

1880 W. Fullerton Avenue
Chicago, IL 60614
(800) 894-4759 or (773) 486-7777
800 E. Roosevelt Road
Lombard, IL 60148
(800) 894-4759 or (630) 932-4800
www.whirlyball.com

Contact Events coordinator
Capacity Chicago, 20–1,000; Lombard, 20–400.
Rental Fees *Chicago*, Monday–Thursday, $170 per court hour; Friday–Sunday, $190 per court hour. *Lombard*, Monday–Thursday, $150 per court hour; Friday–Sunday, $170 per court hour.
For the Kids The Lombard location is a fun kid's party place.
Hours *Chicago*, Monday–Friday, 10 A.M.– 2 A.M.; Saturday, 12 P.M.–3 A.M.; Sunday, 12 P.M.–2 A.M. *Lombard*, Sunday–Friday, 12 P.M.–midnight; Saturday, 12 P.M.–1 A.M.
Parking *Chicago*, small free parking lot and street parking *Lombard*, free parking lot.

Courtesy of WhirlyBall.

WhirlyBall is a combination of lacrosse, hockey, basketball, and high-tech bumper cars. Since WhirlyBall is a new sport, everyone will have the same skill level, making the game that much more fun. WhirlyBall's private rooms are perfect for birthday celebrations, corporate outings, or other intimate gatherings. Your guests will find plenty to keep them entertained. In Chicago there are three WhirlyBall courts; Lombard has two courts. Both facilities feature pool tables, dart boards, video games, and foosball. The Chicago facility, a sports bar, also has three 10-foot video walls so you can watch any ball game.

Catering packages are only available for parties of 20 of more. The site is handicapped accessible. Let the events coordinator know at least one week in advance if you need to rent audiovisual equipment for your event.

WINDY CITY FIELDHOUSE

2367 W. LOGAN BOULEVARD
CHICAGO, IL 60647
(773) 486-7421, FAX (773) 486-7865
WWW.WINDYCITYFIELDHOUSE.COM
E-MAIL ERIC@WINDYCITYFIELDHOUSE.COM

CONTACT Eric DeLau, special events director
BEST FEATURES Creative packages, from black-tie galas to outdoor summer picnics.
CAPACITY Entire facility, 2,500 banquet, 3,500 meeting/reception; conference room, 100 banquet, 180 meeting/reception; mezzanine, 100 banquet, 180 meeting/reception.
RENTAL FEE Call for a quote.
FOR THE KIDS Birthday parties, bar/bat mitzvahs with action-packed games supervised by experienced staff.
HOURS Flexible.
PARKING Free lot for 200+; valet available.

Courtesy of Windy City Fieldhouse

Windy City Fieldhouse is Chicago's premier team building and entertainment company, and features incredible special events. Packages are customized for corporate outings, theme parties, outdoor picnics, holiday parties, scavenger hunts, block parties, and more. Customers can create a unique event or select from a multitude of existing packages. Event managers will handle all the details—from transportation to catering.

The facility features a kitchen and has a list of preferred caterers, or you can bring in your own with no extra charge. A complete rental program is available for linens, tables, chairs, decorations, and audiovisual support. The facility is handicapped accessible and is located just 10 minutes north of the Loop.

BALLROOMS, BANQUET ROOMS, AND RECEPTION HALLS

Ashton Place

Barn of Barrington, The

Bristol Court Banquets and Catering

Broadway United Methodist Church

Chantilly Banquets

Chateau Bu-Sché

Concorde Banquets

DiNolfo's Banquets

Elmcrest Banquets by Biancalana

Garden Chalet

Garden Manor

Garden Terrace

Garden Terrace Banquets at the Jack A. Claes Pavilion

Garden Walk

Grace Place: Grace Episcopal Church of Chicago

Great Hall of Café Brauer, The

Grove Banquets, The: Schwaben Center

Hoosier Grove Barn Banquet Facility

Kissane Banquet Hall

Lakeview Rooms at Park Center, The

Lido Banquets

Logan Square Auditorium

Mar Lac House

Marshall Field's

Maxim's: The Nancy Goldberg International Center

Monastero's Ristorante and Banquets

North Shore Lights at Hotel Morraine

Pitzaferro's Banquets

Rosewood Restaurant and Banquets

Royal Gardens

Scandinavian Club

School of the Art Institute of Chicago, The

Second Unitarian Church

Sovereign, The: Grand Ballroom

Unity Temple

William Tell Restaurant and Banquets

Willowbrook Ballroom & Banquets

ASHTON PLACE

341 WEST 75TH STREET
WILLOWBROOK, IL 60514
(630) 789-3337, FAX (630) 789-3331
WWW.ASHTONPLACE.COM
E-MAIL INFO@ASHTONPLACE.COM

CONTACT Joan Paganini, office manager
BEST FEATURE Multifunctional banquet, meeting, and tradeshow facility.
BEST PARTY Chrysler Ride and Drive.
CAPACITY Four rooms, up to 1,200 banquet.
RENTAL FEES Meeting rooms are $55 per hour with meal, $75 per hour without; the entire facility is $220 per hour with meal, $300 per hour without; conference room and Executive Suites are $25 per hour.
DISCOUNTS 15 percent discount available Fridays and Sundays for weddings.
HOURS Flexible.
PARKING Lot for 500 cars.

Courtesy of Ashton Place

Ashton Place is one of the western suburb's premier banquet facilities, where you can surround yourself in elegance. Ashton Place is easily accessible from downtown, the suburbs, or the airports. Upon entering Ashton Place, you and your guests will be greeted with a captivating two-story foyer, accented with cascading staircases and dazzling crystal chandeliers. Ashton Place exudes elegance and charm. The facility offers more than 14,000 square feet of meeting and exhibition space; a large overhead door makes it easy to bring in and out large equipment, and the site is handicapped accessible.

All catering is provided by Ashton Place's award-winning chef. Professional event coordinators will work with you to plan your event, including a custom menu. Audiovisual equipment, data lines, and electrical service make this facility state-of-the-art, whether your group is 25 or 1,200.

THE BARN OF BARRINGTON

1415 S. BARRINGTON ROAD
BARRINGTON, IL 60010
(847) 381-8585, FAX (847) 381-8591
WWW.BARNOFBARRINGTON.COM

CONTACT William Vaughn
CAPACITY Crown Room, 200 banquet; Great Hall, 140 banquet; smaller additional private party rooms.
RENTAL FEE Based on food and beverage consumption.
HOURS Office, Monday 9 A.M.–3 P.M.; Tuesday–Thursday 9 A.M.–9 P.M.; Friday 9 A.M.–5 P.M.; Saturday 10 A.M.–4 P.M.
PARKING Adjacent lot.

The Great Hall at The Barn of Barrington is part of the original structure that was built 125 years ago. With its 40-foot ceiling and 12-foot stained-glass rose window, the room imparts a Gothic feel. Private dining areas for parties of 20–100 include the Baronial Chamber, the Architect's Loft, the Sunken Dining Room, the Solarium, and the Vintage Room. Larger events for up to 200 guests are held in the Crown Room. The site is handicapped accessible.

The Barn will handle food preparation. Luncheon banquets are $12–$40 per person and dinners are $19.95–$65 per person. Luncheon package includes a five-course candlelight menu. A six-course wedding reception package with a four-hour open bar is $42–$88 per person. Floral centerpieces and floral cake top are provided by The Barn for the six-course package. Audiovisual equipment is available for a fee.

Photograph by Jan Ingve & Associates, courtesy of The Barn of Barrington

BRISTOL COURT BANQUETS AND CATERING

828 E. RAND ROAD
MT. PROSPECT, IL 60056
(847) 577-6055, FAX (847) 577-6358

CONTACT Catering consultant
BEST FEATURES Seventeen-foot ceilings; marble dance floor.
CAPACITY Two ballrooms, combined 625 banquet, 800 reception.
RENTAL FEE Negotiable.
DISCOUNTS Friday and Sunday parties; afternoon events.
HOURS Daily, 9:30 A.M.–8 P.M.
PARKING Lot for 300 cars.

Specializing in wedding receptions, Bristol Court is also a great location for meetings, seminars, reunions, retirement parties, and more. The main ballroom has 17-foot ceilings and is decorated in burgundies, teals, and grays.

One of the neatest things about this site is the marble dance floor that will help your waltz look effortless. The three-story foyer complete with a balcony and a staircase, is the perfect spot for picture taking, greeting your guests, or tossing the bridal bouquet. The site is handicapped accessible.

All food preparation is done on-site by Bristol Court. Menu items range from herb roasted chicken to Tournedoes Diane to African lobster tail. A dinner package includes seven-course dinner, four hours of open bar with premium liquors, wine or champagne toast, cake, fresh flowers, and bridal and hospitality suites. Packages start at $42 per person. Audiovisual equipment must be rented.

Courtesy of Bristol Court Banquets and Catering

BROADWAY UNITED METHODIST CHURCH

3344 N. BROADWAY
CHICAGO, IL 60657-3520
(773) 348-2679, FAX (773) 348-2521

CONTACT Gregory Dell, pastor
BEST FEATURE Large, inexpensive hall.
CAPACITY Reception hall, 120 banquet, 150 reception; Wesley Room, 25 banquet; choir room 25 banquet; library, 15 banquet; nursery, 12 banquet.
RENTAL FEE Sanctuary, $150; reception halls, $100; other rooms, $25.
HOURS Flexible.
PARKING Street or small adjoining lot.

Courtesy of Broadway United Methodist Church

The original church at this site burned down in 1983, and a new brick replacement was built in 1988. Geared toward the community, this is a popular site for support groups, meetings, and theater group rehearsals. There is also a reception hall where wedding receptions or other larger events may be held. The sanctuary is available for meetings, but not for parties.

You may choose a caterer or bring your own food. The reception hall has a kitchen with two microwaves and a refrigerator. Another smaller kitchen with three ovens is available for the meeting rooms. Tables, chairs, and coffee makers are available, but linens, china, and utensils must be brought in. A podium and easel are on hand and you may bring in other meeting equipment. There is no smoking or alcohol allowed. The church is wheelchair accessible.

CHANTILLY BANQUETS

5412 S. LaGrange Road
Countryside, IL 60525
(708) 354-8884, fax (708) 354-8887

Contact Loula Stolis, owner; or Phyllis Holleman, director of catering

Discounts Wedding for Ann Jillian's daughter; fundraiser with Mike Ditka.

Capacity Three rooms combined, 750 banquet, 1,500 reception.

Rental Fee Based on food and beverage consumption.

Discounts Weddings on Fridays and Sundays.

Hours Monday–Friday 10 A.M.–7:30 P.M.; Saturday and Sunday, 11 A.M.–5:30 P.M.

Parking Free for 600+.

Courtesy of Chantilly Banquets

People who appreciate antiques and a touch of Old World charm will be delighted to host an event at Chantilly. Framed with beautiful staircases, the lobby leaves a good first impression and is an excellent spot for wedding photos. There are three banquet rooms: the Callalily, the Bouquet, and the Primrose. The rooms have Venetian chandeliers, a large marble dance floor, a built-in oak bar, and cascading staircases. Private bridal quarters complete with a bathroom are located upstairs. Chantilly is handicapped accessible.

Chantilly caters all events. Prices start at $4.75 per person for breakfast, $8.95 per person for a luncheon, $11.95 per person for dinner. Wedding packages start at $33 per person. Chantilly specializes in weddings, but they are also available for any other special occasion. The site can facilitate rental of audiovisual equipment.

CHATEAU BU-SCHÉ

11535 S. Cicero Avenue
Alsip, IL 60803
(708) 371-6400, fax (708) 371-3836
www.chateaubusche.com

Contact Special events coordinator

Best Feature Unique country club setting.

Capacity Tamerlane Room, 370 banquet; Crystalane Room, 350 banquet; Westminster Ballroom, 450 banquet.

Rental Fee Call for details.

Hours Monday–Friday, 9 A.M.–9 P.M.; Saturday–Sunday, 10 A.M.–6 P.M.

Parking Ample space.

Courtesy of Chateau Bu-Sché

Nestled on 30 acres of impeccably landscaped grounds, this banquet facility has been completely renovated into a beautiful antebellum-style structure complete with white columns and a carport. The Chateau features classic architectural accents, dramatic lighting, marble flooring, a massive fireplace, and an impressive two-and-a-half-story ceiling. Two banquet rooms lead into an amazingly elegant atrium area that can be used year-round and is perfect for wedding receptions and formal galas.

The Chateau caters all events. Dinners range from $30–$42 per person. Tables, chairs, linens, and flowers are provided. A bridal suite is available. There is a CD/cassette sound system, but additional audiovisual equipment must be rented.

CONCORDE BANQUETS

20922 N. RAND ROAD
KILDEER, IL 60047
(847) 438-0025, FAX (847) 438-5068
WWW.CONCORDEBANQUETS.COM

CONTACT John Kalyviaris
BEST FEATURE Fountain with swans and gazebo.
CAPACITY 20–1,000.
RENTAL FEE Based on food and beverage consumption for banquets.
HOURS Flexible.
PARKING Free lot.

Courtesy of Concorde Banquets

The Concorde is a contemporary banquet facility with an exceptional atrium assembly area and elite banquet rooms decorated with soft pastel colors, elegant high ceilings, brass chandeliers, beveled mirrors, and granite and porcelain dance floors. The Concorde's picturesque grounds provide the perfect backdrop for wedding photos and feature a small pond and fountain complete with white swans and a romantic gazebo. In addition to hosting elegant wedding receptions, the Concorde specializes in corporate affairs. The facility is handicapped accessible.

The Concorde handles all food and beverage preparation on-site; a variety of menu options are available. Staff can custom design a package to meet your specific social or business needs. Complete party packages range from $41–$52 per person. Discounts are available during off-peak days, months, and hours. The Concorde can arrange to bring in audiovisual equipment upon request.

DINOLFO'S BANQUETS

9425 W. 191ST STREET
MOKENA, IL 60448
(708) 479-1919, FAX (708) 479-0187
7941 W. 47TH STREET
MCCOOK, IL 60525
(708) 442-6969, FAX (708) 442-7016

CONTACT Sales manager at either location
BEST FEATURE Winding oak staircase.
CAPACITY 900 banquet, 1,000 reception.
RENTAL FEE Call for rates.
DISCOUNTS Friday and Sunday evening events.
HOURS Office: Monday–Friday 11 A.M.– 8 P.M.; Saturday and Sunday, 11:30 A.M.– 4 P.M.
PARKING Lot on-site.

Photograph by Joe Venckus, courtesy of DiNolfo's Banquets

This family owned and operated banquet facility has been in business since 1976. They offer spacious and elegant accommodations for wedding receptions, company banquets, and special events of all kinds. As you enter one of the four banquet rooms, you will note the high ceilings, shining brass chandeliers, marble bar areas, and the hardwood parquet dance floor. A final special touch is the winding oak staircase that leads the bride and groom from their private bridal room down into the party to begin an evening to remember.

DiNolfo's caters all events. A party package includes a five-and-a-half-hour reception, wedding cake, wine during dinner, four-hour open bar, flowers at each table, linen napkins and tablecloths, and use of bridal room. This package starts at $39.95 per person. (Service fees and taxes are included in the per person rate.)

ELMCREST BANQUETS BY BIANCALANA

7370 W. GRAND AVENUE
CHICAGO, IL 60607
(708) 453-3989, FAX (708) 453-4365
WWW.ELMCRESTBANQUETS.COM

CONTACT Al Biancalana, president
BEST FEATURE Centrally located, new facility.
CAPACITY Grandview Ballroom, 450 banquet; Tuscany Room, 110 banquet; Grandview East, 275 banquet; Grandview West, 140 banquet.
RENTAL FEE Call for rates.
DISCOUNTS Weekdays, Friday, and Sunday.
FOR THE KIDS Children's parties are half price.
HOURS Office: Monday–Friday, 10 A.M.– 9 P.M.; Saturday and Sunday, 11 A.M.–5 P.M.
PARKING Valet; ample street parking.

Elmcrest Banquets, in its west suburban setting, combines superb cuisine, an elegant decor, and many years of experience to make your event a success. The

Photograph by J & J Photography, courtesy of Elmcrest Banquets

Grandview Ballroom is decorated in off-white and features a gleaming white dance floor. It can be divided into the Grandview East and West rooms for smaller events. The Tuscany Room also has a predominately off-white decor. In the foyer there is a staircase that is an excellent spot for photographs. Although Elmcrest specializes in wedding receptions and grand galas, they can also accommodate your next seminar, sales meeting, or corporate function. The facility is handicapped accessible.

Elmcrest will cater all events. Lunches start at $11.95 per person during the week and at $15.25 per person on weekends. Wedding dinner packages including a four-hour premium bar and a bridal suite start at $39 per person. They will customize a menu to fit your needs and your budget. Audiovisual equipment is provided on a rental basis.

GARDEN CHALET

11000 S. RIDGELAND AVENUE
CHICAGO, IL 60482
(708) 361-0400, FAX (708) 361-0478
WWW.GARDENCHALETBANQUETS.COM

CONTACT Regina Fischer, banquet manager
BEST FEATURE Great outdoor facility.
CAPACITY Main dining room, 300 reception; Garden Room, 125 banquet; outside area, 75 banquet.
RENTAL FEE None with food and beverage package.
DISCOUNTS January–March.
HOURS Flexible.
PARKING Free on-site.

The Garden Chalet has two beautiful banquet rooms to host any type of function. The Garden Room is a warm, intimate setting with two cozy fireplaces and a separate bar and restroom. It is ideal for small weddings, anniversary parties, and bridal and baby showers. The main dining room has a

Courtesy of Garden Chalet

dramatic cathedral ceiling and a wonderful outdoor patio. The patio features a colored waterfall and a gazebo that is an excellent spot for an outdoor wedding ceremony.

No outside caterers are allowed. The Chalet's catering staff will work with you to determine a menu. Packages range from $19.50–$29 per person. Package prices include a family-style or plated dinner, 3½- to 4½-hour bar, wedding cake, hors d'oeuvres, candle centerpieces, color linens, and champagne toast. All audiovisual equipment must be brought in.

Garden Manor

4720 W. Armitage Avenue
Chicago, IL 60639
(773) 736-1131, fax (773) 889-8794
www.gardenbanquets.com

Contact Walter or Scott Saranecki
Best Feature Garden-like setting with large dance floor.
Capacity Sherwood Room, 450 banquet; additional room, 150 banquet.
Rental Fee Based on food and beverage consumption.
Discounts For afternoon and Friday and Sunday parties.
Hours Monday–Friday, 10 A.M.–10 P.M.; Saturday and Sunday, noon–6 P.M.
Parking Three adjacent free lots.

The plain, white exterior of the Garden Manor's Sherwood Room is in stark contrast to the fairytale world of garden courtyards within. Realistic plaster trees sparkle with little white lights and vines hanging from trellises sur-

Courtesy of Garden Manor

round a black and white checkered dance floor. The overall effect of this banquet facility is one of romance, right down to the heart-shaped mirrors in the private bridal suites. The dining area has acoustical tiles and carpet, which make for easier conversation. The facility is handicapped accessible.

Saranecki Brothers Continental Catering supplies all food and beverages. Wedding packages range from $26.50–$65 per person, including liquor. Without liquor, packages start at $13.95. They will provide flowers and wedding cakes or you may bring your own.

Garden Terrace

6330 W. Irving Park
Chicago, IL 60634
(773) 736-1131, fax (773) 889-8794
Mailing Address:
4720 W. Armitage
Chicago, IL 60639
www.gardenbanquets.com

Contact Walter or Scott Saranecki
Best Feature Outdoor garden wedding ceremony site.
Capacity One room, 250 banquet; second room with outdoor garden, 150 banquet.
Rental Fee Included with food and beverage package.
Discounts On Fridays and Sundays and in the afternoons.
Hours By appointment.
Parking Free in adjacent lots.

Easily accessible from the Kennedy Expressway and located across from Chicago's Merrimac Park, these two indoor garden-like facilities are

Courtesy of Garden Terrace

divided by a solid wall, making them soundproof. Each room has a separate entrance and separate bathrooms. The East Room features a Monet-inspired outdoor enclosed garden, complete with an arched wooden bridge. This area is perfect for nuptial vows or dramatic photographs. Both rooms have lifelike trees and vines that hang from trellises. The site is handicapped accessible.

All food is prepared by Saranecki Brothers Continental Catering that has 55 years of experience. Custom menus range from ethnic food to vegetarian. Wedding packages are $26.50–$65 per person. Without liquor, meal packages start at $13.95 per person and a cash bar can be arranged. Flowers and wedding cakes are provided or you may bring your own.

GARDEN TERRACE BANQUETS

at the Jack A. Claes Pavilion

ELK GROVE PARK DISTRICT
1000 WELLINGTON AVENUE
ELK GROVE VILLAGE, IL 60007
(847) 228-3524, FAX (847) 228-3520
WWW.GARDENTERRACEBANQUETS.COM

CONTACT For the Garden Terrace Banquets, Tony Paluch, banquet manager; for the Jack A. Claes Pavilion, Leslie DeMoss, pavilion manager

CAPACITY Banquet room, 220 banquet, 250 theater.

RENTAL FEE Varies depending on event.

DISCOUNTS Friday and Sunday wedding discount packages available.

FOR THE KIDS A 28-foot carousel; theme parties such as a splash party complete with an indoor water slide, a dance party with costumes, a sport party in the gym.

HOURS Flexible.

PARKING Lot on-site.

Courtesy of Garden Terrace Banquets

The Garden Terrace Banquet facility with two large rooms and a smaller adjacent room can be used for an elegant wedding or business meetings and seminars. A landscaped patio is adjacent to the banquet hall and makes a great setting for cocktails. The Carousel Room contains the pavilion's 28-foot carousel, and is available for showers, wedding receptions, and kid's parties. There are two gymnasiums, an indoor and outdoor pool, gazebo, TV studio, and fitness center.

Food choices range from a simple continental breakfast to an elegant gourmet dinner. You can provide your own licensed caterer, but they will need to fill out a catering permit. Tables and chairs are available. Linens, china, and ice are available for an additional charge. Outside caterers must provide all serving equipment. A projector TV and VCR with a five-foot screen, overhead projector, Kodak Carousel projector, audio cassette player, screens, microphones, easels, and podium are provided for a minimal charge.

GARDEN WALK

3705 W. FULLERTON
CHICAGO, IL 60639
(773) 736-1131, FAX (773) 889-8794
MAILING ADDRESS:
4720 W. ARMITAGE
CHICAGO, IL 60639
WWW.GARDENBANQUETS.COM

CONTACT Walter or Scott Saranecki

BEST FEATURE Large private bridal suite.

CAPACITY Banquet room, 350 banquet.

RENTAL FEE Based on food and beverage consumption.

DISCOUNTS Afternoon, Friday, and Sunday specials.

HOURS Open daily, by appointment.

PARKING Free lot across the street.

The exterior of this banquet site is somewhat uninviting, with bright green neon that outlines a white stucco facade. However, the interior gives a much different impression. The garden-like banquet room is both warm and

Courtesy of Garden Walk

romantic. There are six large lifelike trees that glow with twinkling lights. Hand-laid stone walls and mirrors decorate the border, and the large dance floor crowns the center of the room. The overall effect is exceedingly romantic. The expansive private bride's room includes two dressing rooms and flowered rattan couches.

The Saranecki Brothers Continental Catering caters all events at the Garden Walk. Their chefs will prepare custom menus, including vegetarian, ethnic, or special diet foods. Wedding packages range from $26–$65 per person. Without liquor, meal packages start at $13.95 per person. Flowers and wedding cake are provided or you can bring your own. Privacy is assured because the site is not open to the public; only one event is scheduled at a time. The facility is handicapped accessible.

GRACE PLACE

Grace Episcopal Church of Chicago

637 S. DEARBORN STREET
CHICAGO, IL 60605
(312) 922-1426, FAX (312) 922-7119
WWW.GRACECHICAGO.ORG

CONTACT Patricia Mosley, church administrator
BEST FEATURE Postmodern space convenient to the Loop.
CAPACITY Meeting/party room, 150; sanctuary, 150; lower level, 50.
RENTAL FEE Vary per function.
HOURS Daily, except Sunday, 9 A.M.–5 P.M.
PARKING Paid lots.

Courtesy of Grace Place

Grace Place, the Grace Episcopal Church Community Center, is located in a renovated printing house in the heart of Printer's Row in the South Loop. The main floor features natural oak woodwork, a black and white checkered floor flooded with plenty of light, and teal and gray carpeting. The first floor and basement have meeting spaces and the sanctuary on the second level is also available for certain events. The sanctuary won a Chicago Architecture Foundation award for renovations. The site is handicapped accessible.

All food and drink must be catered. There is a small kitchen that can be used for preparation, but is not good for cooking. Tables and chairs are available. There is no food allowed in the sanctuary. There is no audiovisual equipment available.

THE GREAT HALL OF CAFÉ BRAUER

2021 N. STOCKTON DRIVE
CHICAGO, IL 60614
(312) 742-2400, FAX (312) 664-6822

CONTACT Elyse Weiss, sales manager
BEST FEATURE Prairie-style atrium overlooking Lincoln Park lagoon.
CAPACITY Entire site, 300 banquet, 500 reception, 325 theater.
RENTAL FEE Daytime, $1,200; evenings Monday–Thursday, $1,800; Friday, $3,000; Saturday, $3,500; Sunday, $3,000.
FOR THE KIDS In conjunction with Lincoln Park Zoo, packages available for kids' parties.
HOURS Closes at midnight; will stay open until 2 A.M. for $500.
PARKING Valet for $500 flat fee; in addition to flat fee, $7 per car required.

Courtesy of The Great Hall of Café Brauer

Nestled on the shore of Lincoln Park's south lagoon, the Great Hall of Café Brauer has been restored to its early 20th-century splendor. The stunning view of the park, lagoon, and city skyline will enhance any event. The Great Hall is ideal for a wide variety of catered and corporate receptions, including weddings, charitable events, and press conferences. Recognized by the National Register of Historic Places, the Great Hall features a dramatic skylight, polished hardwood floors with oak trim, rook-wood-style glazed tile murals, and leaded glass and bronze light fixtures. Weather permitting, the outside Loggia area can be used for a cocktail party under the stars or a casual picnic.

Select a caterer from their preferred list. There is a fully equipped kitchen but all equipment must be brought in, including tables and chairs.

THE GROVE BANQUETS

Schwaben Center

301 WEILAND ROAD
BUFFALO GROVE, IL 60089
(847) 541-1090

CONTACT Luana Schardt, banquet coordinator
BEST FEATURES Brass chandeliers, 15-foot ceiling, large oak bar adjacent to dining room.
CAPACITY Wallenborn Room, 350 banquet; Club Room, 60 banquet.
RENTAL FEE Based on food and beverage consumption.
DISCOUNTS Weekdays and Sundays.
HOURS Open daily, 11 A.M.–2 A.M.
PARKING Available on grounds.

This one-story brick building was built in1982 by two German-American Clubs; the Schwaben Athletic Club and the Schwaben Verein. The entrance and hallways are laid in brick-patterned

Courtesy of Grove Banquets

ceramic tile. The atmosphere of the Wallenborn Room is warm and comfortable, with its neutral decor, brass chandeliers, large dance floor, and beautiful oak bar adjacent to the dining room. The Club Room has wood paneling, a small bar, and walls decorated with photos of the Schwaben Center's winning soccer teams. Large picture windows overlook the green soccer fields.

The center provides all food and beverages. Wedding packages start at $33 per person, including tax and gratuity. Packages include a four-hour open bar, unlimited champagne, complimentary hors d'oeuvres during cocktail hour, color-coordinated napkins and flowers for all guest tables. Lunches start at $12 per person, including tax and gratuity. Rooms are also available weekdays for meetings.

HOOSIER GROVE BARN BANQUET FACILITY

STREAMWOOD PARK DISTRICT
700 W. IRVING PARK ROAD
STREAMWOOD, IL 60107
(630) 372-7275 EXT. 120 OR 121,
 FAX (630) 372-1893
WWW.STREAMWOODPARKDISTRICT.ORG

CONTACT Carol Green, Barn supervisor
CAPACITY Main floor, 100 banquet; loft, 30 banquet; outdoor gazebo, 50.
RENTAL FEE Call for rates.
HOURS Sunday–Thursday 8:30 A.M.–12 A.M.; Friday and Saturday 8:30 A.M.–1 A.M.
PARKING Lot for 175 cars.

The Hoosier Grove Barn is owned and operated by the Streamwood Park District and is located within the 19-acre Hoosier Grove Park. This park features a turn-of-the-century one-room schoolhouse museum, a farmhouse, a horse

Courtesy of Hoosier Grove Barn

barn, and other small buildings that create a charming atmosphere and a perfect backdrop for pictures. A beautiful gazebo ideal for group gatherings and wedding ceremonies is located next to the 2,000-square-foot Barn. The character of the original 1888 structure has been retained and the sophisticated,

rustic atmosphere welcomes guests.
  A list of preferred caterers is provided, but you may bring in your own caterer. Kitchen privileges are allowed and liquor package information is available. Hoosier Grove Barn is handicapped accessible. Audiovisual equipment is available.

KISSANE BANQUET HALL

5106 W. IRVING PARK ROAD
CHICAGO, IL 60641
(773) 282-6106, FAX (773) 282-2207

CONTACT Party consultant
CAPACITY 70 banquet with dance floor, 100 banquet without dance floor.
RENTAL FEE Based on food and beverage consumption.
HOURS Flexible.
PARKING 10-car free lot; street.

Photograph by Steve Matteo

Run by a catering company, this small storefront banquet hall is bright and cheerful. The decor is mostly done in whites and mauves with wall-to-wall plum carpeting.

The catering company operates out of the two adjacent storefronts and provides all food service. The chef can prepare a menu to suit just about any occasion. There are seasonal specials and theme menus such as the Luau or the Western Ho-Down. Prices are budget-friendly, ranging from $9.95–$11.95 per person for lunch and $16.95–$19.95 per person for dinner. Prices include a four-hour open bar. Cash bars are not permitted. A minimum of 30 people is required to rent the room. You must provide your own flowers but Kissane will create a cake according to your specifications.

THE LAKEVIEW ROOMS AT PARK CENTER

2400 CHESTNUT AVENUE
GLENVIEW, IL 60025
(847) 657-3206

CONTACT Sandy Dixon, Manager of Center Operations
BEST FEATURE Splendid views of Lake Glenview in Gallery Park.
CAPACITY 60–230 banquet, 85–310 theater.
RENTAL FEE Call for rates.
HOURS Monday–Thursday, 5 P.M.–10:30 P.M.; Friday, 5 P.M.–Midnight; Saturday–Sunday, 8 A.M.–Midnight.
PARKING Adjacent free lot.

Courtesy of the Lakeview Rooms at Park Center

Whether you're celebrating a special occasion, planning a corporate function, or hosting a meeting for your group, the Lakeview Rooms at Park Center offer the perfect setting for almost any gathering. Available for rental individually or as a three-room suite, each room is richly appointed with elegant lighting, wall-to-wall carpeting, floor-to-ceiling windows, and state-of-the-art sound system.

The Lakeview Rooms feature a 17' x 30' stage perfect for entertainment or presentations as well as a 15' x 20' dance floor. Outside the Lakeview Rooms, overlooking Lake Glenview, is a patio ideal for cocktail functions. There is a separate bride's room just steps away from the banquet rooms. A variety of AV equipment is also available for rental. There is a commercial-grade kitchen, and a list of recommended caterers is available to assist you in planning your event.

LIDO BANQUETS

5504 N. MILWAUKEE AVENUE
CHICAGO, IL 60630
(773) 763-1408, FAX (773) 763-3101

CONTACT   Joseph Marchetti
BEST FEATURE   Marble dance floor.
CAPACITY   250 banquet.
RENTAL FEE   None with food and beverage
  package.
HOURS   Monday–Thursday, 6:30 P.M.–9 P.M.;
  Friday–Sunday, noon–5 P.M.
PARKING   Two lots.

Courtesy of Lido Banquets

Established in 1968, the family-owned Lido Banquet Hall boasts an inviting, warm atmosphere and a friendly staff. In the last few years the facility has been completely remodeled. Elegant crystal chandeliers hang over a huge marble dance floor and the surrounding mirrors reflect the dim light. The light wood and soft colors contribute to the warm atmosphere. There is only one banquet room at this site, so your event is guaranteed to be private.

All food is prepared on-premise. The menu features traditional northern Italian dishes, but the chefs will prepare dishes to suit your occasion. Packages range from $15–$32 per person.

This does not include tax or the 15 percent service charge, which is less than many banquet facilities. Entertainers and audiovisual equipment must be brought in. The site is handicapped accessible.

LOGAN SQUARE AUDITORIUM

2539 N. KEDZIE BOULEVARD, SUITE 15
CHICAGO, IL 60647
(773) 252-6179, FAX (847) 564-9218

CONTACT   Iliana Rozemberg, manager
BEST PARTY   Casting of Muhammad Ali
  movie.
CAPACITY   500+.
RENTAL FEES   Variable, depending on date
  and time.
HOURS   Flexible.
PARKING   Self-park lot.

Courtesy of Logan Square Auditorium

The Logan Square Auditorium's renovated, turn-of-the-century ballroom almost glows in the dark, with its tall, arched windows overlooking the boulevards of Logan Square. The large hall is perfect for receptions, meetings, dances, weddings, bar/bat mitzvahs, theatrical rehearsals, or performances. Building features include dark wood paneling, detailed plasterwork, wall sconces, dimmable lighting, a small balcony near the entryway topped with gold American eagles, and a light, sanded dance floor.

Bring your own caterer or we will help you arrange one. Tables, chairs, portable bars, stage, refrigerators, food warmers, ice, and full kitchen are provided.

Mar Lac House

104 S. Marion Street
Chicago, IL 60302
(708) 848-4636, fax (708) 848-2678
www.marlacbanquets.com
E-mail banquets@prodigy.net

Contact Michael Fabbri, Lou Fabbri, or Bob Norton

Best Feature Historic theater.

Capacity Marina Room, 500 banquet or reception; Warrington Room, 100–300 banquet.

Rental Fee Based on food and beverage consumption.

Discounts Available on weekdays and Sundays.

Hours Monday–Friday evenings; Saturday or Sunday anytime.

Parking Self-parking for 200; valet.

Courtesy of Mar Lac House

While Mar Lac opened as a banquet facility in 1958, its historical significance dates back to the turn of the last century. The former Warrington Opera House, opened to the public in October 1902, is currently the Warrington Banquet Room. The elegant stage, balcony, and the 24-foot ceiling remain, while a 32-foot bar has been added to the rear of the room. In 1962 a second banquet room, the Marina Room, with curved staircases, arches, columns, and crystal chandeliers was added on the upper level. The two banquet rooms are operated completely independent of each other including separate bars, restrooms, coat checks, and kitchens.

The Mar Lac House provides all food and beverage. There are a variety of menu options available for hors d'oeuvre receptions, lunches, and dinners. Book well in advance. Both rooms are wheelchair accessible. Audiovisual equipment must be brought in.

Marshall Field's

111 N. State Street
Chicago, IL 60602
(312) 781-3697, fax (312) 781-3702

Contact Catering manager

Best Feature A piece of Chicago history.

Capacity Walnut Room, 450 banquet, 850 reception; Wedgwood Room, 130 reception; Archives, 350 reception; Meeting Center, 25–125 classroom; Event Center, 450 banquet, 850 reception; 7 on State, 650 banquet, 1,000 reception.

Rental Fee Depends on type of event and food and beverage consumption.

Hours Flexible.

Parking Nearby garage.

Marshall Field's now has a half dozen special-event rooms that are ideal for everything from a fashion show to a wedding reception to a business luncheon. The Walnut Room features a three-story atrium and a view of State Street, while the Event Center features views of downtown Chicago. In the Archives guests can mingle among Marshall Field's historic artifacts, and 7 on State occupies the entire seventh floor of the historic Marshall Field's store.

Talented professional chefs prepare your food using the finest regional and seasonal ingredients with an emphasis on visual presentation. An experienced staff of catering professionals will work with you to create a menu to match your style, taste, and budget. Marshall Field's staff is ready to coordinate all aspects of your event including location, food, flowers, decor, and beverage and wine service. Everything from tables, chairs, linens, glassware and more will be taken care.

Courtesy of Marshall Fields

MAXIM'S

The Nancy Goldberg International Center

24 E. GOETHE STREET
CHICAGO, IL 60610
(312) 642-7000, FAX (312) 744-9629
WWW.CITYOFCHICAGO.ORG/CULTURALAFFAIRS/
MAXIMS.HTML

CONTACT Jane Northway, director
CAPACITY Entire venue, 135 banquet, 175 buffet, 200 reception; Private Wine Room, 12 banquet.
RENTAL FEE $3,000 weekends, $2,500 weekdays; Private Wine Room, $500.
HOURS Daily, flexible.
PARKING Street parking is limited; arrangements can be made for additional parking.

Courtesy of Maxim's

Located in the midst of Chicago's Gold Coast, Maxim's offers an elegant, intimate setting for special occasions of all kinds. Opened in 1963 as Maxim's de Paris, it was a replica of the famous art nouveau Parisian restaurant, from the famed scroll work and plush red banquettes to the glistening inlays of brass and stained glass. Formal dining rooms, a bar, and a dancing room provide flexibility for wedding receptions, benefits, or galas.

Bring your own caterer; a fully equipped kitchen is available for set-up and staging. Two pianos are available. There is a microphone and sound system, but additional equipment must be brought in. Maxim's is handicapped accessible.

MONASTERO'S RISTORANTE AND BANQUETS

3935 W. DEVON AVENUE
CHICAGO, IL 60659
(773) 588-2515, FAX (773) 588-2112
WWW.MONASTEROS.COM

CONTACT Maria Monastero or Penny Ioannou, catering directors
BEST FEATURE Versatility, affordability, and central location.
CAPACITY Botticelli Room, 300 banquet; Gina's Banquet Room, 200 banquet; Garden (atrium), 110 banquet; Rose Room, 70 banquet.
RENTAL FEE None, based on food and beverage consumption.
HOURS Tuesdays–Sundays, 7 A.M.–1 A.M.
PARKING Free on-site or complementary valet.

Courtesy of Monastero's Ristorante and Banquets

With four entirely private rooms, Monastero's is the perfect location for all kinds of events, from corporate meetings or parties to sophisticated banquets or wedding extravaganzas. The Garden features skylights and fresh greenery, while the Botticelli Ballroom boasts a private foyer that opens into a magnificent Rennaisance-style dining room. The facility is handicapped accessible.

Monastero's offers a range of creative or traditional menu options, from boneless chicken breast marsala to beef tenderloin Wellington. Complete packages including open bar, dinner, wine, specialty cake, and tax and gratuity start at $35 per person. Monastero's is centrally located between Chicago's Loop and North Shore and easily accessible from I-94/Edens expressway.

NORTH SHORE LIGHTS AT HOTEL MORRAINE

700 N. SHERIDAN ROAD
HIGHWOOD, IL 60040
(847) 433-6366, FAX (847) 433-6378
WWW.NORTHSHORELIGHTS.COM

CONTACT Robert and Tanya Wehrle, owners
BEST FEATURE European elegance.
CAPACITY Bannockburn Ballroom, 350; Glencoe Room, 130; Club and Emelia, 70.
RENTAL FEE Based on food and beverage consumption.
FOR THE KIDS Bar/bat mitzvahs.
HOURS Daily, 9 A.M.–Late.
PARKING Easily found near building.

Courtesy of North Shore Lights at Hotel Morraine

North Shore Lights can design an event that reflects the clients personal tastes and preferences, including candle-lit dinners served by white gloved butlers. As you enter this boutique hotel you are greeted by a breathtaking lobby with original Morraine furniture, and a picturesque winding staircase.

The hotel offers a wide selection of appetizing and expertly prepared cuisine, served by an attentive staff. Its ballrooms are accented with crystal chandeliers, marble dance floors, fireplaces, and high ceilings, and can accommodate from 20 to 500 guests.

PITZAFERRO'S BANQUETS

6755 W. DIVERSEY AVENUE
CHICAGO, IL 60707
(773) 237-9700, FAX (773) 237-5365
WWW.PITZAFERROS.COM
E-MAIL INFO@PITZAFERROS.COM

CONTACT Banquet consultant
CAPACITY Crystal Room, 300 banquet; Piccolo Room, 75 banquet.
RENTAL FEE None.
HOURS Tuesday–Sunday, flexible.
PARKING Complimentary valet parking.

Courtesy of Pitzaferro's Banquets

This banquet space has a modern feel with soft grays, black lacquer accents, and art deco. There are two rooms available for your function. The Crystal Room has a polished porcelain dance floor, and several mirrors decorate the walls. The smaller Piccolo Room also has a dance floor and a similar decor.

Pitzaferro's gourmet chefs cater all events. Dinner packages range from $29.99–$52 per person and include tax and gratuity. A special events menu is offered Monday through Thursday, evenings and afternoons, for $13.50–$22.50 per person. Pitzaferro's offers a variety of continental cuisines, or can work with you to custom design your menu. Wedding packages include four-hour open bar, complete seven-course dinner, unlimited wine with dinner, cake service, champagne toast, ice sculpture, and bride's room.

Rosewood Restaurant and Banquets

9421 W. Higgins Road
Rosemont, IL 60018
(847) 696-9494, fax (847) 696-9499
www.rosewoodrestaurant.com

Contact Jim Mandas, owner
Best Feature Convenient to O'Hare Airport.
Capacity Ballroom, 300 banquet, 500 reception; Fireplace Room, 100 banquet, 150 reception.
Rental Fee None.
Discounts Weddings on Friday and Sunday nights receive special pricing.
Hours Monday–Friday 11 A.M.–11 P.M.; Saturday 4 P.M.–11 P.M.; Sunday 4 P.M.–10 P.M.
Parking 300-car garage and valet.

The Rosewood's richly decorated banquet rooms can accommodate intimate rehearsal dinners or bridal showers for 50, or a more lavish reception for 300. The Ballroom has a modern feel with a square-paneled ceiling, square chandeliers, and mirrored walls. There is a nice-sized dance floor and a raised area for the head table. The Fireplace Room has an elegant, comfortable atmosphere and is appropriate for business meetings or smaller events. The facility is handicapped accessible.

The Rosewood caters all events. The menu features prime steaks, fresh seafood, veal, or pasta. A wedding package starts at $44 per person. The package includes a five-course meal, four-hour open bar, wine with dinner, a wedding cake, formal tablecloths, candelabras at the head tables, and gratuity. The catering staff will help arrange musicians, florists, and additional decorations. Audiovisual equipment is available on site.

Courtesy of Rosewood Restaurant and Banquets

Royal Gardens

2515 N. Harlem Avenue
Chicago, IL 60707
(773) 736-1131, fax (773) 889-8794
www.gardenbanquets.com

Contact Walter or Scott Saranecki
Best Feature Indoor garden-like setting with a large dance floor.
Capacity Entire site, 350 banquet.
Rental Fee Based on food and beverage consumption.
Discounts Large group discounts; Friday and Sunday specials.
Hours Open daily by appointment.
Parking Free parking in adjacent lots.

Located in Chicago's Little Italy, this private wedding celebration facility is a romantic's delight. Lifelike tree branches sparkle with twinkling lights. Lush vines hang from trellises encircling the perimeter, and a highly polished dance floor shimmers in the center of the room. There is a private bridal suite with a chaise lounge sitting area that is surrounded by floor-to-ceiling mirrors.

Saraneki Brothers Continental Catering provides all food and beverage service. Custom menus are prepared by skilled chefs, and range from all ethnicities to vegetarian. Special diets are available from the two licensed dieticians on staff. Wedding packages range from $26.50–$65 per person. Without liquor, meal packages are available from $14.95 per person and a cash bar can be arranged. Flowers and a wedding cake are provided, or you can bring your own. Royal Gardens is handicapped accessible.

Courtesy of Royal Gardens

SCANDINAVIAN CLUB

2323 N. WILKE ROAD
ARLINGTON HEIGHTS, IL 60004
(847) 870-1710, FAX (847) 870-1745

CONTACT John Luyten, club general manager
BEST FEATURES Vaulted wooden ceilings and large oak dance floor.
CAPACITY Main dining room, 100 banquet; banquet hall, 300 banquet; bar with lounge, 100 reception.
RENTAL FEE Based on food and beverage consumption.
DISCOUNTS Available at certain times.
HOURS Wednesday–Saturday, 5 P.M.–1 A.M.; Sunday 11 A.M.–4 P.M.; other times by arrangement.
PARKING Ample free parking on premises.

Courtesy of Scandinavian Club

Surrounded by lush landscaping, the Scandinavian Club features rich heritage and warm charm throughout. The main dining room has a stone fireplace and walls that are decorated with Scandinavian antiques and pictures; fresh flowers and candles complete the atmosphere. Two double doors lead into the Freja's Sal, the main banquet hall. The hall has bright windows along the south wall, a vaulted wooden ceiling, and a large oak dance floor. The Saga Room is the main bar area and is decorated in burgundy wood paneling and carpet.

All food and beverages are provided by the club. Luncheons and dinners range from $10.95–$35.95 per person, with bar packages available. Complete wedding packages start at $25.95 per person. Podium, sound system, and movie screen are available.

THE SCHOOL OF THE ART INSTITUTE OF CHICAGO

112 S. MICHIGAN AVENUE
CHICAGO, IL 60603
(312) 345-3506, FAX (312) 541-8063
WWW.ARTIC.EDU

CONTACT Sales department
CAPACITY Ballroom, 350 banquet, 600 reception, 350 meeting.
RENTAL FEES Fees vary. Call for a quote.
DISCOUNTS For nonprofit organizations.
HOURS Daily, 8 A.M.–12 A.M.
PARKING Nearby garages.

Photograph by Don DuBroff, courtesy of School of the Art Institute of Chicago

Located steps from the Art Institute, Orchestra Hall, theaters, restaurants, and shopping, the restored 1927 American Renaissance style ballroom at the School of the Art Institute is a hidden architectural treasure, with marbelized columns, terrazzo dance floor, and baroque opera balconies.

Select a caterer from their list of approved caterers. Beverages are provided by the School of the Art Institute. The rental fee includes 300 chairs, twenty 36-inch round tables, thirty 72-inch rounds, and ten 8-foot banquet tables. There are lighting and sound systems, a projection booth, and a stage. The facility is handicapped accessible.

SECOND UNITARIAN CHURCH

656 W. BARRY AVENUE
CHICAGO, IL 60657
(312) 549-0260
WWW.ENTERACT.COM/~GOODNEWS/2U
E-MAIL TwoUOFFICE@AOL.COM

CONTACT Rick Latham, administrative manager

CAPACITY Sanctuary, 200 banquet, 300 reception; Palmer Room, 75 banquet, 150 reception; five meeting rooms, 5-50.

RENTAL FEE Sanctuary, $230; Palmer Room, $120; Sanctuary and Palmer Room combined, $300; meeting rooms, $30-$60.

HOURS Flexible.

PARKING Street; public garage nearby.

Designed in the Prairie style of architecture, the Second Unitarian Church is a simple, yet dignified setting for weddings, memorial services, benefits, and meetings. Charming characteristics of the sanctuary include leaded-glass windows, a high vaulted ceiling, sandy-colored brick walls, and hardwood floors. Large upholstered chairs, two grand pianos, and a podium are located in the rostrum. Movable padded chairs provide the main seating which can be creatively arranged. French doors separate the Sanctuary from the adjacent Palmer Room, which also has hardwood floors. The church has a backyard that is a nice location for photographs.

You may select a caterer. There is a large kitchen that is equipped with a refrigerator, stove, oven, sink, coffee makers, and microwave. Chairs and tables are available, but other serving and meeting equipment must be brought in. There is a microphone and speaker system available. The site is handicapped accessible.

Courtesy of Second Unitarian Church

THE SOVEREIGN

Grand Ballroom

1040 W. GRANVILLE
CHICAGO, IL 60660
(773) 274-8000

CONTACT Michael Restko, property manager

BEST FEATURE A landmark building.

BEST PARTY The setting for Liz Phair's rock video.

CAPACITY 75–250 banquet, 300 reception.

RENTAL FEE From $825, depending on type of function.

HOURS Flexible.

PARKING Public garage two blocks away.

For party planners who are searching for beauty and distinction, the Sovereign may be an ideal choice. The Sovereign Grand Ballroom has turn-of-the-century elegance. A reception area welcomes guests with a handcrafted serpentine bar reflected in art nouveau mirrors. The oval-shaped dance floor can be viewed from two balconies. A soaring domed ceiling is illuminated by an antique chandelier, which is the focal point of the room. The room's visual charm is supported by Corinthian-style columns, intricately decorated wall panels, and sconces which offer a wide range of light settings. Silver and white room accents make an ideal background for an endless array of party themes. The site is not handicapped accessible.

An off-premise caterer is necessary. Sovereign provides tables and chairs for up to 125. An insurance certificate is required. There are additional charges for event attendants and staff. Audio-visual equipment must be brought in.

Photograph by Val Studio Photography, courtesy of the Sovereign Grand Ballroom

UNITY TEMPLE

875 Lake Street
Oak Park, IL 60301
(708) 848-6225

Contact Church office
Capacity Temple (sanctuary), 425 theater; Unity House (fellowship room), 100 banquet, 225 reception.
Rental Fee $750 for use of Temple, $300 for use of the Unity House. Includes up to four hours, $75 each additional hour.
Hours Saturday, 10 A.M.–1 P.M. or 4 P.M.–7 P.M., until midnight for receptions; other times by arrangement.
Parking On street and in nearby lots.

A young Frank Lloyd Wright designed this site in 1905. Unity Temple is actually two buildings joined by a foyer—the Unity Temple and the Unity House. The sanctuary is located in the Temple and is ideal for concerts, weddings, or other religious services. The bright, airy interior with its glass ceiling and tiered seating stands in contrast to the massive, seemingly impenetrable, exterior. Wright named the sanctuary his "Jewel Box," because when you open the doors, the room seems to shine with light. After the service in the sanctuary, you can hold a reception in the Unity House. The site is handicapped accessible.

You should hire your own caterer. A working kitchen is available. The church has tables, chairs, and some audio-visual equipment. You must purchase special insurance if liquor is served. A grand piano and an organ can be rented. Audiovisual equipment must be brought in. If you are planning a summer event, you should note that there is no air-conditioning. The Temple embraces a wide range of events and commonly hosts gay and lesbian union services.

Photograph by Judith Bromley, courtesy of Unity Temple

WILLIAM TELL RESTAURANT AND BANQUETS

6201 Joliet Road
Countryside, IL 60525
(708) 352-1101, fax (708) 354-4241

Contact Banquet manager
Best Feature Old World European setting.
Capacity 10 banquet rooms, 30–400.
Rental Fee None for banquets, varies for meetings.
Hours Daily, flexible.
Parking Free lot.

William Tell offers more than 22,000 square feet of space spread throughout 10 banquet and meeting rooms. One of the most interesting rooms features a huge stone fireplace situated right in the middle of the room. Brass and glass chandeliers hang from high vaulted ceilings and a dark green and red carpet gives the room a cozy feel. Some-

Courtesy of William Tell Restaurant and Banquets

what in contrast to the rest of the room is the shiny white dance floor. However, when the room is decorated with white fabric draped across the ceiling beams, the dance floor blends very nicely.

The restaurant prepares all meals.

Breakfast, lunch, dinner, and party packages range from $8.95–$45 per person. They will customize a menu to suit your needs and the sales staff will work with you to arrange other amenities.

WILLOWBROOK BALL- ROOM & BANQUETS

8900 S. ARCHER AVENUE
WILLOW SPRINGS, IL 60480
(708) 839-1000, FAX (708) 839-1005
WWW.WILLOWBROOKBALLROOM.COM
E-MAIL DANCE@WILLOWBROOKBALLROOM.COM

CONTACT Toni Spero, banquet coordinator
CAPACITY Grand Ballroom, 500 banquet, 1,500 reception; Flamingo Room, 175 banquet; Willowbrook Room, 140 banquet; Arbor Room, 100 banquet; Bordeaux Room, 60 banquet; Club Oh Henry Room, 40 banquet, 50 reception.
RENTAL FEE Call for rates.
HOURS Daily until 12:30 A.M.
PARKING Adjacent free lot for 450 cars.

Courtesy of Willowbrook Ballroom & Banquets

The centerpiece of this historic complex is its distinct 1930s ballroom. The room is illuminated by original Spanish mission-style chandeliers and lanterns that line the room's silk-draped ceiling. Guests can dance the night away on the ballroom's famous "floating" dance floor. Here you'll also find a multitiered stage; a baby grand piano; an expert sound, light, and video system; plus a complete DJ booth. For smaller parties, the Willowbrook offers five adjoining banquet rooms. In addition, the ballroom's outdoor patio is perfect for cocktails, garden ceremonies, and wedding photos. The site is handicapped accessible. Some audiovisual equipment is available.

The Willowbrook provides all food and beverage service, with a banquet menu of classic favorites, plus the ability to custom-create menus to reflect the mood of an event. Dinners range from $15.50–$31.50 per person, with various bar packages available.

BARS AND NIGHTCLUBS

Big Chick's Uptown Bar:
 The Salon

Blue Chicago

Buddy Guy's Legends

Corner Pocket, The

Crobar Nightclub

Cubby Bear Bar & Grill

Cubby Bear Lincolnshire

Dick's Last Resort

Drink

Excalibur

Frank's

Ghost Bar

Hi-Tops

Kincade's

Metro

Neo

Nine

Philosofur's

Pops for Champagne

Prop House, The

Schuba's Tavern/Harmony Grill

Smart Bar

Tequila Roadhouse

Underground Wonder Bar

BIG CHICK'S UPTOWN BAR

The Salon

5024 N. SHERIDAN ROAD
CHICAGO, IL 60640
(773) 728-5511, FAX (773) 769-6677
E-MAIL BIGCHICK@CORE.COM

CONTACT Michelle Fire, events coordinator
CAPACITY The Salon, 40 banquet, 80–100 reception.
RENTAL FEE $50 room plus staff fee.
HOURS Not available Friday and Saturday after 10 P.M., Wednesday after 7 P.M., Sunday from noon–8 P.M.
PARKING Three small free lots on a first-come basis (second lot two doors south, third lot across alley); street parking.

A former beauty parlor, The Salon is adjacent to Michelle Fire's Big Chick's Uptown Bar. The space highlights include a swanky cocktail swirl inlaid tile floor, stage, and an eclectic art collec-

Courtesy of Big Chick's Uptown Bar

tion. According to the bar, this is the largest privately-owned, publicly-displayed art collection in Chicago.

There is an excellent sound system, a microphone, and two video monitors for your use. Choose between track lighting, stage lighting, or a disco dance floor atmosphere. Bring your own caterer. There is an adjacent kitchen for food preparation. Most events have a cash bar. Bartender fee is $10 per hour with a 5 hour minimum. The Salon is handicapped accessible.

BLUE CHICAGO

736 N. CLARK STREET
CHICAGO, IL 60610
(312) 642-6261, FAX (312) 642-6168
WWW.BLUECHICAGO.COM
E-MAIL BLUES@BLUECHICAGO.COM

CONTACT Patrick McCoy, general manager
BEST FEATURE Spotlight on blues musicians.
CAPACITY Entire club, 150 buffet, 200 reception.
RENTAL FEE Included with package price.
HOURS Daily, 8 P.M.–2 A.M.
PARKING Public lot next door.

Blue Chicago is a world-famous blues bar located in the River North area, steps away from the Magnificent Mile. The club spotlights professional Chicago blues musicians with female vocalists. The decor features hardwood flooring and exposed brick with award-winning original oil paintings of blues musicians by John Carroll Doyle. This is the perfect

Courtesy of Blue Chicago

site for a cocktail reception and buffet to celebrate a birthday, reward employees, or congratulate an engagement.

Blue Chicago will custom design the menu for your special events. Prices range from $50 per person for a cock-tail reception to $100 per person for a gourmet dinner buffet. These prices include the musical entertainers. The facility is handicapped accessible. Audiovisual equipment must be brought in.

BUDDY GUY'S LEGENDS

754 S. WABASH AVENUE
CHICAGO, IL 60605
(312) 427-0333, FAX (312) 427-1192
WWW.BUDDYGUYS.COM
E-MAIL ELIZABETH@BUDDYGUYS.COM

CONTACT Elizabeth Irvine, director of special events

BEST FEATURE One of the nation's premiere blues nightclubs.

CAPACITY Entire restaurant, 150 banquet, 400+ reception.

RENTAL FEE Varies depending on date and time.

DISCOUNTS Weeknight music discounts.

HOURS Monday–Thursday, 5 P.M.–2 A.M.; Friday, 4 P.M.–2 A.M.; Saturday, 5 P.M.–3 A.M.; Sunday, 6 P.M.–2 A.M.

PARKING Two pay lots adjacent to the club.

Photograph by Kate Hoddinott, courtesy of Buddy Guy's Legends

Owned by Grammy Award winner Buddy Guy, this well-known nightclub features the finest blues seven nights a week, down-home cooking, and a major archive of blues memorabilia. Legends has hosted parties for groups of all sizes, ranging from large functions for Fortune 500 companies to wedding receptions and other special events. The site is wheelchair accessible.

Legends is equipped with a state-of-the-art sound system, four pool tables, and a complete kitchen serving Louisiana-style soul food. House specialties include chicken and Andouille sausage jambalaya, BBQ ribs, and crawfish étouffée. In-house caterers provide all food and beverage. Dinner menu prices range from $10–$25 per person. Dinner, music, and bar packages can be arranged.

THE CORNER POCKET

2610 N. HALSTED STREET
CHICAGO, IL 60614
(773) 472-1601
WWW.THECORNERPOCKET.NET

CONTACT Kim Veber, director of special events; Claire Perry or Heather Zomer, special events sales managers

BEST FEATURE Nine regulation-size pool tables.

CAPACITY Private room, 20–70 reception; entire facility, 300.

RENTAL FEE Private room, $50–$75 per hour; entire facility, call for an estimate.

HOURS Flexible.

PARKING Street; valet parking available upon request.

Courtesy of Cable Studios, Inc.

Since it opened in 1989, The Corner Pocket has established itself as one of Lincoln Park's friendliest bars and pool halls. The cozy decor includes hardwood floors, brass light fixtures, Chicago historical memorabilia, and nine regulation-size pool tables. The private party room—perfect for small, casual gatherings—is complete with three pool tables, buffet area, and a foosball table. The site is wheelchair accessible.

The Corner Pocket offers an array of dinner buffets, including a burger and chicken sandwich buffet and a South-western-style buffet. You can begin the evening with Harry's Jumbo Buffalo Wings and end it with a mouthwatering dessert buffet. Prices range from $5.95 per person to $14.95 per person. Drink packages range from $15–$25 per person. Staff can arrange for audiovisual equipment.

CROBAR NIGHTCLUB

1543 N. KINGSBURY
CHICAGO, IL 60610
(312) 413-7000 OR (773) 486-4002
WWW.CROBARNIGHTCLUB.COM

CONTACT Special events coordinator
BEST FEATURE Rated one of the best sound and light shows.
CAPACITY Balcony/VIP, 75 reception; mezzanine, 100 reception; main floor, 150 banquet, 800 reception.
RENTAL FEE $500–$3,000 depending upon number of people, date, and time of event.
HOURS 9 P.M.–4 A.M.; other times by arrangement.
PARKING Valet; lot next door.

This futuristic, industrial warehouse will make your guests feel as if they've entered the movie set of *BladeRunner*. Overscale gears, stained-glass cathedral walls, water towers, and transformers loom over this larger-than-life theatrical space. The main room has one of the

Courtesy of Big Time Productions

largest club dance floors in the city and is dominated by a stained-glass "church" wall. High above the main room is the mezzanine. This enclosed balcony area has smoked glass windows that allow guests to see out into the club without the club looking back in. A full bar, intimate booths add a hip, clubby feel to this private space. The Crobar's

cushy backstage VIP area and VIP balcony overlook the stage and dance floor and can accommodate 100 guests.

The bar will cater your event or you may bring in an approved caterer. You must supply all serving equipment and linens. There is extensive audiovisual equipment available.

CUBBY BEAR BAR & GRILL

1059 W. ADDISON STREET
CHICAGO, IL 60613
(773) 327-1662, FAX (773) 472-7736
WWW.CUBBYBEAR.COM

CONTACT Susan Pierson, general manager
BEST FEATURES View of Wrigley Field; numerous TVs.
BEST PARTY WGN baseball opening day party.
CAPACITY Main floor, 800; Lower Deck (semi-private), 50; Upper Deck, 175; Skybox, 400.
RENTAL FEE Negotiable.
DISCOUNTS Negotiable for charity events.
HOURS Party facilities available anytime.
PARKING $20 for game days; $8 when there is not a game; negotiable for private events.

At the heart of Wrigleyville is the Cubby Bear, a bar and grill that features Cubs memorabilia and photos. The main

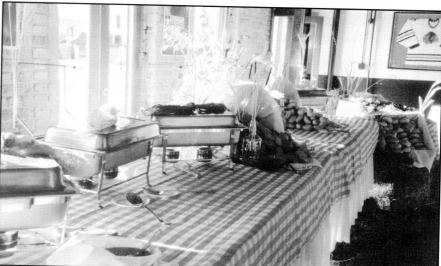

Courtesy of Cubby Bear Bar and Grill

floor has hosted such artists George Clinton, Johnny Cash, and Tito Puente. Upstairs are the exclusive Upper Deck party rooms. These rooms are complete with exposed brick, full-service bars, banquet capabilities, and a stunning view of Wrigley Field from several large picture windows. The Upper Deck also has its own sound system with a wide

variety of music selections.

All events are catered by the Cubby Bear. They will mix and match different food and beverage packages to meet your needs. They offer everything from ballpark fair to Southwestern buffets. There are several bar options: open, cash, or full service. The Cubby Bear is wheelchair accessible.

CUBBY BEAR LINCOLNSHIRE

21661 N. MILWAUKEE AVE.
LINCOLNSHIRE, IL 60069
(847) 541-4700, FAX (847) 541-4777
WWW.CUBBYBEAR.COM

CONTACT Mary Piekarski, corporate events manager

BEST PARTY Cheap Trick concert.

CAPACITY Parties of 20–1,500.

RENTAL FEE Variable, depending on date and time.

DISCOUNTS Daily food and drink specials.

FOR THE KIDS Call for details.

HOURS Sunday–Thursday, 11 A.M.–Midnight; Friday–Saturday 11 A.M.–2A.M.

PARKING Self-serve lot; valet available.

Courtesy of Cubby Bear Lincolnshire

The Cubby Bear Lincolnshire, a sports bar/restaurant/entertainment complex, has 30,000 square feet of space and is open seven days a week for lunch and dinner. On weekends, there are live concerts and can accommodate over 1,500 patrons. On Sundays during the football season we feature an "All You Care to Eat" brunch buffet with former Bears players as special guests. During baseball season, the Cubby Bear Lincolnshire will offer bus transportation, box lunches, game tickets, and a post-game party at the Wrigleyville location for corporations.

The Lincolnshire facility has 2 giant screens, 33 TVs, and seating for over 600 for lunch and dinner, plus 10 pool tables, 2 dartboards, and numerous arcade games for all ages. It is a perfect location to host private parties from 20 to 1,500.

DICK'S LAST RESORT

435 E. ILLINOIS STREET AT NORTH PIER
CHICAGO, IL 60611
(312) 836-4234, FAX (312) 836-7871
WWW.DICKSLASTRESORT.COM

CONTACT Cynthia, party planner/group sales

BEST FEATURE You choose the rowdiness level: 1 Alarm, 2 Alarms, or No Holds Barred.

BEST PARTY Bachelorette parties.

CAPACITY Main Room, 242 banquet; River Room, 85 banquet; Pool Room, 25–50; Cabana Room, 42 banquet; dock and veranda, 140 banquet.

RENTAL FEE None with food and beverage package.

HOURS Monday–Thursday, 11 A.M.–2 A.M.; Friday–Saturday, 11 A.M.–2 A.M.; Sunday, 10 A.M.–2 A.M.

PARKING Validated parking lot located at Illinois and McClurg Court.

Courtesy of Dick's Last Resort

If you're looking for a place that's wildly fun and rowdy, Dick's Last Resort should be your first resort. After all, their private party theme is "Shock your boss and friends and have a party at my place." You can control the level of your party's rowdiness by choosing either a 1-Alarm, for a pretty mild event; 2-Alarms, for a little more fun; or No Holds Barred, for an anything goes bash. There is live music every night.

Dick's menu consists of homestyle American dishes with a Cajun influence, like fried catfish, steamed crawfish, and BBQ ribs or chicken. They offer a Super Deluxe lunch package for a minimum of 8 guests for $15.25 per person. The Super Deluxe dinner package is $20.99 per person and includes meat, fish, salads, pasta, nonalcoholic beverages, tax, and gratuity. The site is handicapped accessible.

DRINK

702 W. FULTON STREET
CHICAGO, IL 60661
(312) 733-7800, FAX (312)733-8060

CONTACT Julie Zerega, corporate special
events director

CAPACITY Entire bar, 340 banquet, 1,200
reception; main room, 100 banquet, 250
reception; upper dining, 40 banquet, 50
reception; Psychedelic Room, 60 banquet,
300 reception; Moroccan, 90 banquet, 350
reception; VIP/Cigar, 50 banquet, 250
reception.

RENTAL FEE Negotiable.

HOURS Flexible.

PARKING Limited on street; nearby lots;
valet available.

Courtesy of Drink

The *New Yorker* described Drink by
saying, "If cocktail making is theater,
Drink is Broadway." Host an intimate
soiree in a glass-enclosed elevator
equipped with private bar. Enjoy fine
cigar selections and sip cognac on velvet
banquettes by the Cigar Room fireplace.
Sample from the 75 premium and
infused tequilas at the VIP Room's
Tequila bar. Enjoy a visual feast of color
in the Psychedelic Room with 40-foot
ceilings, a 32-foot stage, DJ booth, and
vodka bar. The Moroccan Room's dun-
geon door and Middle Eastern tenting
enclose an expansive video wall. Audiovisual equipment is available for rental.

Drink supplies all food and beverages.
Menu items include thin-crust pizzas,
salads, pasta dishes, and sandwiches.
All guests must be 21 years of age or
older. No outside DJs are allowed. The
club is handicapped accessible.

EXCALIBUR

632 N. DEARBORN STREET
CHICAGO, IL 60610
(312) 337-3836, FAX (312) 337-1836
WWW.ACEPLACES.COM

CONTACT Director of catering

BEST FEATURES Three dance floors, lighting,
and special effects.

CAPACITY Entire club, 3,000 reception;
Great Hall, 250 banquet, 1,000 reception;
Dome Room, 120 banquet, 400 reception;
Cabaret, 150 banquet, 250 reception;
Billiards Room, 30–125 reception; Game
Emporium, 30–60 reception.

RENTAL FEE $200–$1,000.

HOURS Daytime and weekend evenings
until 10 P.M.

PARKING Valet and nearby lots.

Originally built as the Chicago Historical
Society and now a landmark building,
Excalibur has consistently been voted
Chicago's #1 nightclub. Located in the
hot River North district, this 50,000-
square-foot entertainment
complex contains three floor
of nonstop fun. Club Aura is
an impressive multilevel
room, with a dance floor and
two balcony levels beneath a
huge painted dome. Modern
rock is played with occasion-
al live acts. The Cabaret features a Retro music format
with dancing to hits from the
60s, 70s, and 80s. There is
also a billiard room, a large
video game room, and in-
house DJ and video services.

A full-service banquet
kitchen will prepare your
customized meal and create
an innovative presentation
to fit your budget. No food
or liquor may be brought
in. The facility is handicapped accessible. Audiovisual equipment is available.

Courtesy of Excalibur

FRANK'S

2503 N. CLARK STREET
CHICAGO, IL 60614
(773) 549-2700

CONTACT Frank Mylander, owner
BEST FEATURE Beautiful woodwork through-
out.
CAPACITY Entire facility, 125 reception.
RENTAL FEE Varies.
HOURS Daily, 11 a.m–4 A.M.; open until
5 A.M. on Saturday.
PARKING Two nearby lots; street parking
available.

Courtesy of Frank's

Located in the heart of Lincoln Park, Frank's is a charming, neighborhood bar fashioned in the mood of a 1940s saloon. Its centerpiece is a 30-foot vertical cherry-wood, fully-stocked bar. Frank's specializes in serving up anything from a traditional gin martini to an ice-cold glass of beer. Pool table, six-foot screen TV, and a classic jukebox stock full of artists ranging from Frank Sinatra and Tony Bennett to Pearl Jam and Smashing Pumpkins adorns the rear of the bar.

Frank's boasts Chicago's friendliest bartenders and waitstaff who greet guests with a smile. All food and beverage is provided by the restaurant. Frank's is a unique place to host an intimate birthday party or a raging company holiday bash.

GHOST BAR

440 W. RANDOLPH
CHICAGO, IL 60606
(312) 575-9900, FAX (312) 575-9901

CONTACT Julie Zerega or Saskia Volkers
BEST FEATURE Super chic ultra-lounge.
CAPACITY 150 banquet, 200 reception.
RENTAL FEE Variable.
HOURS Variable.
PARKING Valet available.

Courtesy of Ghost Bar

Ghost Bar, on the upper level of Nine restaurant, is located in the Daniel Burnham-designed building now known as Randolph Place. This super chic ultra-lounge is seductively lit, incorporating hues of grays and greens. This dramatic background is perfect for high style events from cocktail and hors d'oeuvre receptions to formal plated dinners. Ghost Bar features intimate, custom-designed pod and suede banquette seating for receptions. For plated dinners, Ghost Bar transforms into an elegant dining room, and is handicapped accessible. Audiovisual equipment is available on a rental basis.

All food service is prepared in the Nine restaurant kitchen directly below Ghost Bar. The menu focuses on high-quality ingredients, with steaks and chops sharing the spotlight with fresh seafood and lighter fare. Classic cocktails plus specialty drinks such as fruit bellinis, cold sakes, and bottle service of frozen vodka are available, as well as an extensive wine list.

HI-TOPS

3551 N. SHEFFIELD STREET
CHICAGO, IL 60614
(773) 348-0009
WWW.HITOPSCAFE.COM

CONTACT Special events coordinator
BEST FEATURE Bird's-eye view of Wrigley Field.
CAPACITY Main floor, 300 banquet, 1,000 reception; Skybox, 150 reception.
RENTAL FEE $500–$2,000 depending upon number of people, time and day of event.
HOURS 11 A.M.–3 A.M., other times by arrangement.
PARKING On the street.

Courtesy of Big Time Productions

Conveniently located across from Wrigley Field, Hi-Tops sports bar lets your guests be part of the game any season, all year long. The main-floor area can accommodate large parties and features 40 TV monitors and seven giant screen TVs. There isn't a bad seat in the house. Located on the second floor is the Skybox, which offers a bird's-eye view of Wrigley Field. The facility is handicapped accessible. A wide array of audiovisual equipment is available, including microphones, projection TVs, and pull-down screens.

Whether it's a luncheon or dinner buffet, Hi-Tops menu has something for everyone. The restaurant caters all events and the staff will work with you to customize your menu.

KINCADE'S

950 W. ARMITAGE AVENUE
CHICAGO, IL 60614
(773) 348-0010, FAX (773) 348-8077
WWW.BARSONLINE.COM/CHICAGO/KINCADES

CONTACT Kevin Killerman, owner
BEST FEATURE Numerous TV sets.
CAPACITY Back room, 300; upstairs, 50; other rooms on a semiprivate basis.
RENTAL FEE No charge with purchase of package deals, otherwise negotiable.
DISCOUNTS Daily drink and food specials.
HOURS Sunday–Friday, 11 A.M.–2 A.M.; Saturday, 11 A.M.–3 A.M.
PARKING Street or valet.

Courtesy of Kincade's

With highlights such as shuttle service to all home Bears games, full satellite capability on four large TV screens and more than 60 monitors, five pool tables, and three Golden Tee golf games, Kincade's is a good choice for the sports fan. Originally a butcher shop in the 1940s, this popular bar with its oak paneling and forest green walls, still maintains an old-fashioned feel. The back room, the largest party room, features a private entrance, restrooms, pool tables, plenty of TVs, VCR hook-up, fireplace, high ceilings with skylights, and an island bar. Kincade's most recent addition is located upstairs, overlooking Armitage Avenue. The room can accommodate up to 50 people. For smaller events, the upper deck in the main bar can be reserved on a semiprivate basis.

There are several party packages available. Prices for three-hour unlimited drink packages are from $12–$30 per person. Food packages from light appetizers to five-course meals are available. There is no fee for the space; however, a minimum guarantee is required.

METRO

3730 N. CLARK STREET
CHICAGO, IL 60613
(773) 549-4140, FAX (773) 549-2688
WWW.METROCHICAGO.COM

CONTACT Mendy Medlin
BEST FEATURE Concert venue and dance club.
BEST PARTIES Concerts for Bob Dylan, Nirvana, and Smashing Pumpkins.
CAPACITY Entire club, 600 banquet, 1,100 reception, 200 theater.
RENTAL FEE Varies.
HOURS Varies depending on previously scheduled concerts. Generally not available Fridays and Saturdays.
PARKING On street; nearby lots.

Courtesy of Metro

Built in 1922 as a Swedish men's club, Metro is now a popular concert venue and hip site for your next private party of a thousand. The pillars on either side of the stage, the light fixtures, and the white and gold rococo trim are part of the original decor that has remained intact. The main stage area is perfect for dancing with hardwood floors and lots of space. There are two small areas on either side of the room that can be used for dining or cocktails. A bar is located on both floors of the club.

You should bring your own caterer, and be advised that there are no kitchen facilities at the club. All linens, serving equipment, and tables and chairs must be brought in with the exception of cocktail tables. Metro will provide the libations; drinks are $2–$4 each. They will arrange your musical entertainment, or you can hire your own band or DJ. The club is not handicapped accessible. No recording devices or cameras are allowed.

NEO

2350 N. CLARK STREET
CHICAGO, IL 60614
(773) 528-2622 OR (773) 486-4002

CONTACT Special events coordinator
BEST FEATURE Chicago's oldest dance club.
CAPACITY 250 reception.
RENTAL FEE $500–$2,000 depending upon number of people, time and day of event.
HOURS 9 P.M.–4 A.M.; other times by arrangement.
PARKING On the street.

Courtesy of Big Time Productions

Chicago's oldest dance club, Neo has been on the cutting edge of music and fashion since 1979. Neo is located at the end of a dramatic, colorful, abstractly painted alleyway on Clark Street. A recent design facelift by Jordan Moser keeps Neo on the edge of post-modern hipness. Concrete pillars, arches, and an irregular tiered seating area give the club the feel of a cavernous underground amphitheater. Slide projections on the walls and large old metal factory doors create the illusion of a Gothic cathedral amidst the industrial deconstruction.

This Lincoln Park legend offers a simple space for high energy entertainment. Uncomplicated and self-contained, this moderately sized venue is an excellent choice for medium-sized dance parties, charity events, and theme parties.

City Clubs and Women's Clubs

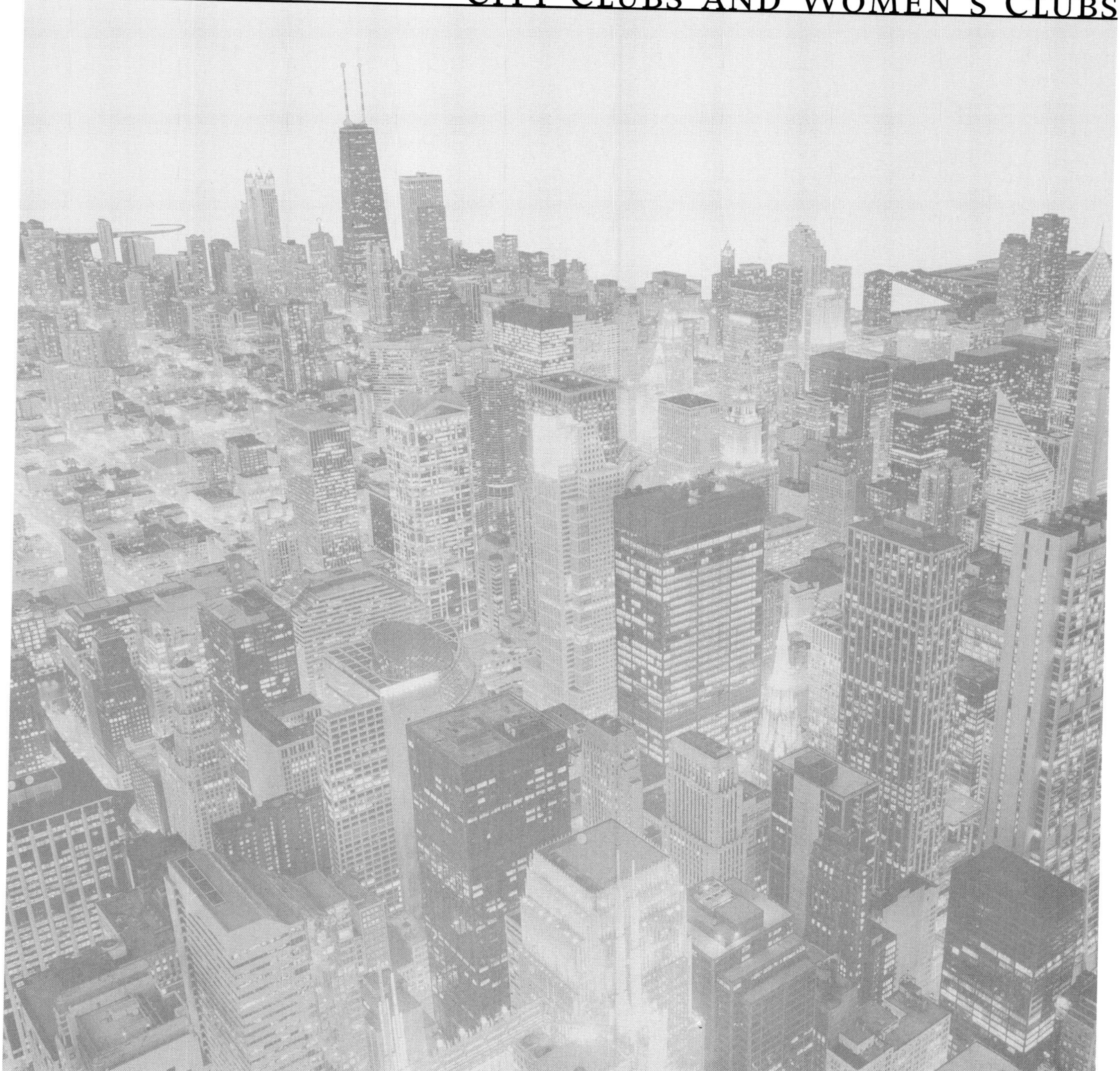

CITY CLUBS AND WOMEN'S CLUBS

410 Club and Conference Center

Chicago Bar Association

Kenilworth Club

La Strada's Top of the Plaza

Metropolitan Club, The

Mid-America Club, The

Nineteenth Century Club

Plaza Club

Rookery Building, The

Top of the Tower

Tower Club

Woman's Club of Evanston

Woman's Club of Wilmette

Woman's Library Club of Glencoe

410 Club and Conference Center

Wrigley Building
410 N. Michigan Avenue
Chicago, IL 60611
(312) 944-7600

Contact Bob Stearns, catering director
Capacity Main club, 190 banquet, 500 reception; balcony area, 60 banquet, 125 reception; conference center, 120 either banquet or classroom; smaller rooms are available.
Rental Fee Main club, a food and beverage minimum of $5,000 for a weekend event, minimum of $4,000 for a weekday evening event; conference center and private dining room have full and half–day packages with a food and beverage minimum of $175–$275. There is no room fee when food and beverage minimums are met.
Hours Weekdays, 7 A.M.–9 P.M.; weekends per client's needs.
Parking Complimentary in adjacent lot after 5 P.M. weekdays, and all day on weekends.

Photograph by Stuart Rodgers, courtesy of 410 Club

Located on the street level of the Wrigley Building, the 410 Club is perfect for a social gathering or business event. Original artwork throughout the main club quarters completes the room. On the lower level are the conference center and private dining rooms. Amenities include elegant black granite-topped bars inset into polished cherry-wood paneled walls. All audiovisual needs are state-of-the-art and are available with an on-site technician.

All food and beverage is provided by the 410 Club. Menus can be customized. Lunches include three courses and range from $20–$26 per person. Dinners are from $34–$39 per person. Wedding packages are $65–$68 per person.

Chicago Bar Association

321 S. Plymouth Court
Chicago, IL 60604
(312) 554-2124 or 554-2120,
fax (312) 554-9843
www.chicagobar.org

Contact Lisa Beissmann
Capacity Philip H. Corboy Hall, 110 banquet, 200 reception; Winston & Strawn Presidents' Room, 60 banquet, 120 reception; additional rooms, 20–150.
Rental Fee Philip H. Corboy Hall, $200–$650; Winston & Strawn Presidents' Room, $120–$400; other rooms $25–$220.
Hours Monday–Friday, 7 A.M.–midnight; weekends, by special arrangement.
Parking Street after 6 P.M.; nearby garage.

Located in the Loop, The Chicago Bar Association offers a prestigious building with affordable amenities. Philip H. Corboy Hall overlooks the Plymouth Court with its high ceilings and two-story windows, perfect for special luncheons, receptions, and dinners. The Winston & Strawn Presidents' Room has English brown oak paneling and elegant custom fixtures. This room accommodates buffet-style luncheons, formal dinners, and elegant receptions. In addition, there are 16 meeting rooms. The facility is handicapped accessible.

All food and beverage is provided by Eurest Dining Services. Customized dinner menus range from $25–$45 per person, lunches from $16–$30, and breakfasts from $7.50–$15 per person. Two-hour hors d'oeuvre receptions begin at $15. Drinks average $4. Beverage or wine packages are available. Eurest Dining Services will handle all arrangements such as flowers and entertainment. Audiovisual equipment may be rented for a nominal charge.

Courtesy of Chicago Bar Association

Kenilworth Club

410 Kenilworth Avenue
Kenilworth, IL 60043
(847) 251-1227

Contact Club manager
Capacity Entire club (ballroom, and two adjacent smaller rooms), 200 banquet, 160 with dance floor, 300 reception.
Rental Fee Saturday, $1,800; Sunday–Friday, $1,500.
Discounts For club members.
Hours Daily, 8 a.m.–midnight.
Parking On the street; nearby lot.

Photograph by Steven Breitberg, courtesy of the Kenilworth Club

This one-story clubhouse was designed in 1907 by George W. Maher. The club's design clearly exemplifies Prairie-style architecture with open space and art-glass windows. The Ballroom has 2,500 square feet of space with two adjoining smaller rooms, plus a fully-equipped kitchen. The larger of the two adjacent rooms is the intimate Neighbors' Room, which features a working fireplace.

When the weather is nice, you can also host your event on the large lawn. Note that the restrooms are not handicapped accessible.

Select your own caterer. The club will provide a list of their recommendations. Included in the rental fee are tables, chairs, flatware, china, and glassware.

The caterer is responsible for washing the dishes and cleaning the kitchen. The club is fully air-conditioned. A sound system with CD and cassette, projection screen, microphones, and two pianos are available. Decorations are permitted, but no nails or tacks may be used.

La Strada's Top of the Plaza

151 N. Michigan Avenue
Chicago, IL 60601
(312) 565-1312, fax (312) 565-2243
www.lastradaristorante.com
E-mail canderson@lastradaristorante.com

Contact Carl Anderson, director of catering
Best Feature Spectacular 40th floor penthouse with panoramic views of the city and the lake.
Capacity Entire facility, 360 banquet, 500 reception.
Rental Fee Based on food and beverage consumption.
Hours Flexible.
Parking Valet.

Courtesy of La Strada's Top of the Plaza

Located on the Magnificent Mile, 40 floors above Michigan Avenue, La Strada's Top of the Plaza offers a panoramic view of Lake Michigan, Navy Pier, and the Chicago skyline.

This penthouse in Doral Plaza can be divided into six separate areas depending on the size of your event. This flexibility allows La Strada to cater to smaller events such as business meetings, complete with audiovisual equipment, and larger events, such as retirement celebrations, birthdays, and extravagant wedding galas.

All events are catered by award-winning La Strada Ristorante, which is also located in the Doral Plaza. Wedding packages can be arranged and a variety of menu choices are available. Dinners range from $20–$48 per person, and complete lunches from $24–$30 per person. The site is wheelchair accessible.

The Metropolitan Club

Sears Tower, 66th and 67th floors
Chicago, IL 60606
(312) 993-2500

Contact Kimberly Polk, director of catering
Best Feature Spectacular views of the Chicago skyline and lakefront.
Capacity 17 private rooms, 2–1,500; Oak Room, 200 banquet, 400 reception; East Room, 130 banquet, 250 reception.
Rental Fee Based on food and beverage consumption.
Hours Daily, 7 a.m.–2 a.m.; some restrictions apply.
Parking Self-park pay garage across from building on Franklin Street.

Courtesy of The Metropolitan Club

Located in the world-famous Sears Tower, the Metropolitan Club offers panoramic views from every room. The elegant ambiance is the perfect setting for weddings, bar/bat Mitzvahs, corporate and convention entertaining, and black-tie dinners. The Oak Room, the largest private room, features a grand foyer and mahogany-beamed ceiling with large brass chandeliers.

The club's menu features continental cuisine. Breakfasts range from $15–$25 per person, lunch from $25–$40 per person, dinner starts at $45 per person. Wedding packages are available for a minimum of 125 guests. Packages include a four-hour bar package, champagne toast, four-course dinner, and wedding cake. A large variety of audiovisual equipment is available.

The Mid-America Club

200 E. Randolph Drive, 80th Floor
Chicago, IL 60601
(312) 861-1100, fax (312) 861-1780

Contact Doreen Fowler, director of catering
Best Feature Breathtaking, panoramic views.
Capacity Burnham Ballroom, 600 banquet, 1,000 reception; Grill Room, 170 banquet, 250 reception; Frank Lloyd Wright Room, 110 banquet, 150 reception.
Rental Fee None if food and beverage minimums are met.
Hours Daily, 8 a.m.–12 a.m.; some restrictions apply.
Parking Indoor garage; reasonable rates.

Celebrating their 40th anniversary, this private club is one of Chicago's best kept secrets. Located on the 80th floor of the landmark Amoco Building, the Mid-America Club offers spectacular views of Chicago. Each room at the club has a panoramic view of either Lake Michigan, the Gold Coast, Grant Park, or the distinctive skyline. In addition to the view, each room is appointed with jewel-tone colors, tapestry draping, and rich upholstered furniture.

The club's catering staff will assist in determining a menu appropriate for your event. They will coordinate rental and setup of audiovisual equipment, specialty linens, entertainment, and floral arrangements. A wedding package is available for a minimum of 75 guests. The package includes a four-hour bar, four-course dinner, wine with dinner, and an anniversary dinner for two.

Courtesy of the Mid-America Club

NINETEENTH CENTURY CLUB

178 N. Forest Avenue
Oak Park, IL 60301
(708) 386-2729, fax (708) 386-4255
E-mail NCWC1891@AOL.COM

CONTACT Clarmarie Keenan, executive director
CAPACITY First floor, 350 reception; North Dining Room, 80 banquet; South Dining Room, 180 banquet; second-floor auditorium, 300 banquet, 400 theater.
RENTAL FEE Hourly fee without food service; per person with food.
DISCOUNTS Reduced pricing for nonprofit organizations.
HOURS Receptions daily to 11:30 P.M.; viewing Monday–Friday, 9 A.M.–4 P.M., or by appointment.
PARKING Fifty-car lot adjacent to building; four-level structure adjacent to lot.

Built in 1927, this historical, two-story redbrick clubhouse has the feel of a private home. The first-floor lounge is

Photograph by Steve Matteo

comfortable and spacious with a fireplace and baby grand piano. The South Dining Room has a small stage, and the smaller North Dining Room is appropriate for cocktails and dancing. The second-floor auditorium has a stage with a baby grand piano. The Clubhouse is a nonsmoking facility, and is ADA compliant.

The club staff provides all food service with the exception of wedding cakes. Meal prices include six hours of occupancy. Alcohol is allowed but not provided by the in-house caterer. Corkage fees are assessed based on usage. Tables, chairs, meeting and audiovisual equipment, linens, china, and flatware are provided. The auditorium is not air-conditioned. There is a 20 percent service charge that includes facility security and gratuity.

PLAZA CLUB

PRUDENTIAL BUILDING
130 E. Randolph Street
Chicago, IL 60601
(312) 861-3300, fax (312) 861-9284
WWW.PLAZACHICAGO.COM

CONTACT Beth Knudson, catering director
BEST FEATURE Spectacular unobstructed view of the city.
CAPACITY Main dining room (available Sunday and Monday evening only or special request), 150 banquet, 250 reception; three additional private rooms.
RENTAL FEE Varies.
HOURS Monday–Friday, 7 A.M.–2 A.M.; Saturday and Sunday by special arrangement.
PARKING Available in the building for a discount or valet.

Located on the top floor of the Prudential Building, this city club offers sweeping views of the Loop, Lake Michigan, and Grant Park. The main dining room is open only to members or to nonmembers by special arrangement. The West End Room is most often used for private events. It has blue- and rust-colored chairs and patterned carpet. However, the view from the surrounding windows dominate the decor. There are four additional private rooms that are perfect for smaller events. The club is handicapped accessible. Audiovisual equipment is available.

The Plaza Club offers outstanding cuisine. The catering director will help you select a menu and coordinate additional services such as entertainment, flowers, and decorations. The club claims that the only thing they overlook is the city.

Courtesy of Plaza Club

THE ROOKERY BUILDING

209 S. LaSalle Street
Chicago, IL 60604
(312) 745-2295, fax (312) 747-3998

Contact Teresa Harris, event specialist
Best Feature Magnificent Light Court.
Capacity Light Court including lobbies, 250 banquet, 500 reception.
Rental Fee Monday–Thursday, $2,500; Friday-Sunday, $3,500.
Hours Daily, 3 p.m.–midnight.
Parking Nearby public garages.

Designed by Daniel H. Burnham and John Wellborn, then modernized by Frank Lloyd Wright, the historically and architecturally renowned Rookery Building is centered around the magnificent Light Court with a domed skylight. The bright court sparkles with Carrera marble walls etched in gold leaf. Using the majestic Grand Stair your guests can view this setting

Photograph by Merrick, Hedrich-Blessing, courtesy of Baldwin Development Company

from a mezzanine, with a translucent glass-block floor that encircles the area. Along with elegance and grandeur, the Light Court setting also provides an intimate atmosphere that is both festive and fun for groups of 50 to 500.

The Rookery has been the site for scenes from such films as, *The Untouchables, Home Alone 2,* and *A League of Their Own.*

A caterer must be brought in. The site is handicapped accessible.

TOP OF THE TOWER

233 S. Wacker Drive
Chicago, IL 60606
(312) 993-9801, fax (312) 906-8193

Contact Donna Egan, event planner
Best Feature Chicago's highest event site.
Capacity 99th Floor, 230 banquet with dance floor, 280 banquet, 400 reception; Grand Lobby, 500 banquet, 1,000 reception.
Rental Fee 99th Floor, $2,000 (includes basic equipment and standard linens), $500 for wedding ceremony if reception is held there; Grand Lobby, $5,200 (includes basic equipment, standard linens, security, cleaning staff, and elevator operators), $1,000 for wedding ceremony if reception is held there.
Hours Flexible; Grand Lobby available Saturday and Sunday only
Parking Garage across from the Franklin Street entrance.

The sky's the limit when you're planning an event at the Top of the Tower, the highest site in Chicago. Located on

Courtesy of Top of the Tower

the 99th floor of the Sears Tower in one of the city's most well-known buildings, the Top of the Tower is a stunning setting for any corporate or social event. This glass-enclosed showcase offers a sensational panoramic view of Chicago, while serving as the ultimate venue for business occasions, weddings, anniversary parties, and

bar/bat mitzvahs. Should an event call for larger space, the Grand Lobby can host up to 1,000 guests.

All catering is done by the Levy Restaurants. The event staff will assist in arranging decor, specific audiovisual needs, or any details that you may require.

TOWER CLUB

20 N. WACKER DRIVE
CHICAGO, IL 60606
(312) 726-2410, FAX (312) 726-2554

CONTACT Wedding catering
BEST FEATURE Exclusive use of entire club in downtown Chicago.
CAPACITY Entire club, 300 reception; main dining room, 200 banquet, 300 reception; Ambassador and Tower rooms, 60 banquet, 125 reception; Grill Room, 40 banquet; Williamsburg and Presidents Rooms, each 20 banquet.
RENTAL FEE $200.
HOURS Monday–Friday, 7 A.M.–7 P.M.; Saturday and Sunday, as dictated by private event.
PARKING Nearby public lots.

Courtesy of the Tower Club

The Tower Club had its origin as the Electric Club in 1916. Its primary function was as a pre-theater dining club. In 1930, the Electric Club moved to the present location on the 37th to 39th floors of the Civic Opera Building. It has remained a premier dining club and in 1952 the name was changed to the Tower Club. Blending the rich tradition of the past with the needs of the present, the Tower Club offers an elegant, refined atmosphere for a special event. The site is handicapped accessible.

The Tower Club caters all events.

Dinner receptions with four courses and a four-hour bar are inclusive of taxes and gratuities starting at $75 per person. Catering will arrange a menu to your specifications. Some audiovisual equipment is available on-site, additional equipment can be ordered, and in-house engineers can be hired for $200 per event.

WOMAN'S CLUB OF EVANSTON

1702 CHICAGO AVENUE
EVANSTON, IL 60201
(847) 475-3800
WWW.WCOFE.ORG

CONTACT Office manager
CAPACITY Entire clubhouse, 400; first floor, 125–175 banquet; second floor ballroom, 250 banquet.
RENTAL FEE Call for rates and availability.
HOURS Flexible.
PARKING Public lot behind building; garage across the street.

Courtesy of the Woman's Club of Evanston

Built in 1912, the Woman's Club of Evanston offers renters two elegant atmospheres ideal for any occasion. The first floor parlor has the ambience of a well-appointed traditional home: it boasts a lovely entrance hall with a grand staircase, large tearoom, sunroom, and music room. The main room is graced with fluted columns, white woodwork, crystal chandeliers, oil paintings, and antique furnishings. The spacious grand ballroom dominates the second floor with its two-story ceiling, distinctive white molding, chandeliers, parquet dance floor, and stage. A second-floor sunroom offers additional charm.

The club provides china, glassware, flatware, 60-inch round tables, buffet tables, chairs, and baby grand and upright pianos. The full-service kitchen on the first floor and a serving kitchen on the second floor are a boon to the club's preferred caterers. There is no air conditioning, and smoking is not permitted. Handicapped-accessible elevator and ramps are available.

Woman's Club of Wilmette

**930 Greenleaf Avenue
Wilmette, IL 60091
(847) 251-0527
www.womansclubofwilmette.org
E-mail wcwreservations@ woman-
sclubofwilmette.org**

Contact Events coordinator/calendar chair-
man

Capacity Auditorium with stage, 200 banquet; dining room, 80 banquet; studio (for
exercise or art classes), 25.

Rental Fee Entire club for five hours, $1,500;
other plans with flexible rates for rooms and
hours needed are available.

Hours Flexible.

Parking Ample street parking.

Founded in 1891, this dignified club is
located in a quiet residential neighborhood among many stately and historical homes. The auditorium with its
stage and Steinway grand piano is a

Courtesy of the Woman's Club of Wilmette

favorite venue for weddings, bar/bat
mitzvahs, benefits, plays, lectures, and
other events. The clubhouse entry
and foyer boast stained glass and dark
wood paneling detail. A carpeted parlor offers comfortable seating, a fireplace, and a second Steinway grand
piano. The dining room, adjacent to
both auditorium and parlor, is perfect
for dinners, luncheons, cocktail receptions, and business seminars. A fully

equipped kitchen offers plenty of room
for caterers to work.

You may choose your own licensed,
insured caterer. The club provides
tables, banquet chairs, china, flatware,
and water glasses. Supply your own
linens and stemware. Liquor is allowed
but may not be sold. A wheelchair
ramp is available. The club is air-conditioned and has built-in speakers and a
microphone.

Woman's Library Club of Glencoe

**325 Tudor Court
Glencoe, IL 60022
(847) 835-4199**

Contact Sue Olson, reservations

Best Party Weddings are their specialty.

Capacity Auditorium, 200 banquet; dining
room, 100 banquet; sunroom, 75 reception.

Rental Fee $1,500 entire club; auditorium
only, $950; dining room only, $450 (Friday,
Saturday, Sunday).

Discounts Fifty percent off for events during
the week; negotiable for nonprofit organizations.

Hours Daily until 1 A.M.

Parking Free lot.

The Woman's Library Club of Glencoe
was built in 1938. The handsome red
brick facade features pillars and a balcony. Inside, there's a foyer and central
hall, a comfortable antique-filled living
room for wedding photos, a charming

Courtesy of Woman's Library Club of Glencoe

sunroom, and a large auditorium. The
latter has a full stage (with curtains,
theatrical lighting, dressing rooms, and
a grand piano) on one side and a small
balcony on the other. Outside the auditorium, a brick patio connects to the
sunroom. On the second floor is an
attractive dining room with colonial
chandeliers and an ornamental fireplace.

Bring your own caterer and alcohol.
There is a small kitchen on the main

floor and a larger catering kitchen
adjacent to the dining room on the
second floor. Rental includes use of the
club's tables, chairs, china (for 200),
and flatware. Linens, serving pieces,
glassware, and audiovisual equipment
must be brought in. No liquor can be
served after midnight. The facility is
air-conditioned. The restrooms are not
handicapped accessible.

CONFERENCE CENTERS, INNS, AND RESORTS

American Club, The

Best Western Clock Tower Resort & Conference Center

Camp Shaw-waw-nas-see

Deer Path Inn

Eagle Ridge Inn & Resort: Conference Center

Heidel House Resort

Herrington Inn: Atwater's Restaurant

Indian Lakes Resort

Inland Meeting and Exposition Center

International Conference Center, The

Katherine Legge Memorial Lodge

Lake Lawn Resort

Loyola at the Cenacle

Manor House at Harrison Conference Center, The

Margarita European Inn

Marriott Hickory Ridge Conference Center

Navy Pier

NIU Hoffman Estates Education Center

Oscar Swan Country Inn

Pheasant Run Resort and Conference Center

Summit Executives Centre

Telcordia Conference and Learning Center

University of Chicago Graduate School of Business: Gleacher Center

University of Illinois at Chicago Pavilion

THE AMERICAN CLUB

HIGHLAND DRIVE
KOHLER, WI 53044
(800) 344-2838, FAX (920) 457-0299
WWW.AMERICANCLUB.COM

CONTACT Tim Pierson, director of sales
BEST FEATURE AAA, five-diamond resort.
CAPACITY Great Lakes Room, theater style, 1,000, banquet, 600, reception, 880; Outdoor gazebo, 150 banquet; 19 meeting rooms, 2–1,000.
RENTAL FEE Varies according to season.
HOURS Flexible.
PARKING Free lot.

The American Club is a stately red-brick structure that was built in 1918 to house the many immigrants, "single men of modest means," who came to work at the Kohler Company. Refurbished and reopened in 1981 as a luxurious resort hotel, it continues to honor its heritage today, welcoming guests with an "old world" elegance and style. Handcrafted woodwork, sparkling chandeliers, and elegant marble create a luxurious atmosphere perfect for weddings, benefits, or corporate meetings. Summer events can be held outdoors, where the well-tended grounds and a gazebo provide a beautiful backdrop for photos. The hotel offers complete conference facilities, outstanding guest accommodations, and recreational opportunities.

The American Club's seven restaurants provide the guest with a wide array of menu options. Meeting packages and wedding packages can be arranged. Recreational opportunities include a spa, a hunting and fishing club, and a fitness and racquet club.

Courtesy of the American Club

BEST WESTERN CLOCK TOWER RESORT & CONFERENCE CENTER

7801 E. STATE STREET
ROCKFORD, IL 61125
(815) 398-6000
WWW.CLOCKTOWERRESORT.COM
E-MAIL SALES@ CLOCKTOWERRESORT.COM

CONTACT Don West, general manager
CAPACITY Wallingford Center, 1,000 banquet, 1,500 reception; Howard Center, 220 banquet, 400 reception; Eli Terry/John Harrison, 60 banquet, 175 reception; parlors, 20 banquet, 40 reception.
RENTAL FEE $120–$5,000.
FOR THE KIDS Special menus and entertainment options.
HOURS 24 hours a day, 7 days a week.
PARKING More than 1,000 spaces.

The Clock Tower Resort & Conference Center is a year-round resort hotel. Its 23 function rooms provide more than 30,000 square feet of banquet/ meeting space. The oak-paneled, Wallingford Center can be divided into six sections, the Howard Center into four, and Eli Terry/John Harrison into two. The theater contains a permanent stage with seating for 166. The Court Pavilion, surrounded by local flora and fountains provides outdoor space for banquets of up to 200 people with an adjacent gazebo. The Figgs banquet space has an indoor setting with an outdoor feel. The site is handicapped accessible.

There are 251 deluxe guestrooms surrounding the facility with two restaurants and a fitness center. Audiovisual equipment is available.

Courtesy of the Clock Tower

Camp Shaw-waw-nas-see

6641 N. 6000 West Road
Manteno, IL 60950
(815) 933-3011, fax (815) 933-3028
www.campshaw.org
E-mail campshaw@keynet.net

Contact Jeff Althoff, camp director
Best Feature Rustic dining hall, outdoor setting.
Capacity Dining Hall, 200 banquet; open pavilion, 200 banquet.
Rental Fee $4–$6 per person for day rentals. Call for overnight rates.
Hours Flexible.
Parking Ample parking in free lot.

Courtesy of Camp Shaw-waw-nas-see

Camp Shaw-waw-nas-see is located adjacent to the Kankakee River State Park, 10 miles northwest of Kankakee and approximately one hour's drive from the Chicago Loop. The camp offers a private outdoor setting for parties, picnics, and groups of all kinds. Featuring a large, rustic dining hall with seating for 200 people and an open-air pavilion, the grounds include 105 acres of rolling woodlands with a 30-foot-deep limestone canyon cutting through the center of camp. Guests may choose to walk the five miles of wooded trails, ride horses, canoe, swim in the outdoor pool, participate in a competition on the team obstacle course, or just take in the beauty of nature.

Inexpensive basic camp fare is available or you may bring a caterer. There is a full-service kitchen. Liquor may be served at adult functions. Limited audiovisual equipment is provided.

Deer Path Inn

255 E. Illinois Road
Lake Forest, IL 60045
(847) 234-2280, fax (847) 234-2903
www.dpihotel.com

Contact Michael Blanker, catering manager
Capacity Windsor Hall, 270 banquet, 300 theater; Hearth Room, 40 banquet; Hunt Room, 50 banquet; boardroom, 10 meeting.
Rental Fee Windsor Hall, $1,000; smaller rooms, $300.
Hours Afternoon functions must end by 4 P.M.; evening functions must begin after 6 P.M.
Parking Free lot.

Courtesy of Deer Path Inn

The original Deer Path Inn was built in the 1860s as a hunter's log cabin. It was eventually rebuilt as a popular weekend retreat for the city's elite. Today, the charming Tudor-style manor home can be rented for private events. Windsor Hall can accommodate large groups or be divided for smaller groups. The beautiful English Room and courtyard garden is perfect for wedding ceremonies and other special occasions. The intimate Hearth and Hunt rooms offer an inviting atmosphere with fireplaces and cozy furniture. The facility is wheelchair accessible.

The inn caters all events. A minimum of two refreshment breaks and a luncheon are required for all meetings or the room rental fee will be increased. Meeting luncheons start at $18 per person; dinners start at $32 per person. A wedding package with four-hour premium bar, hors d'oeuvres, champagne toast, and four-course dinner ranges from $78.50–$93 per person. All private social functions are subject to a room set-up charge. Audiovisual equipment is available.

EAGLE RIDGE INN & RESORT

Conference Center

444 EAGLE RIDGE DRIVE
GALENA, IL 61036
(815) 777-2444 OR (800) 988-MEET,
 FAX (815) 777-0445
OFFICE:
P.O. BOX 656
BATAVIA, IL 60510
WWW.EAGLERIDGE.COM
E-MAIL PNOONE@EAGLERIDGE.COM

CONTACT Peg Noone
CAPACITY Eagle Ballroom, 400 banquet, 600 theater; Woodlands, 72 banquet; Galena Room, 250 banquet, 378 theater; five boardrooms, 24 banquet, 30 theater. Also, there is a large selection of resort homes suitable for meeting as well as lodging.
RENTAL FEE Call for rates.
FOR THE KIDS Youth camps.
HOURS Flexible.
PARKING On-site lot.

Courtesy of Eagle Ridge Inn & Resort

Eagle Ridge Inn & Resort is a secluded and luxurious, all-season retreat in northwest Illinois. The two-story conference center has 16 function rooms, each with an outer deck or patio to enjoy the lovely views. Eagle Ridge will arrange theme parties and group recreation programs that are sure to break the ice. You can choose one of their themes—a country western party, Mardi Gras, sports party, or Carribean beach party. Group recreation ideas include picnics, scavenger hunts, craft programs, a tour of historic Galena, and more. The site is handicapped accessible.

There are two restaurants in the resort and the catering staff will work with you to determine exactly what type of menu is appropriate. Audiovisual equipment is available on a rental basis only.

HEIDEL HOUSE RESORT

ILLINOIS AVENUE
GREEN LAKE, WI 54941
(920) 294-3344 OR (800) 444-2812, FAX (920)
 294-6128

CONTACT Mary Godard
CAPACITY Dartford Ballroom, 260 banquet, 400 reception; Sandstone, 120 banquet, 150 reception; President's Room, 100 banquet, 120 reception; Sunroom, 86 banquet, 100 reception; five suites, 10–16 banquet, 25–30 reception.
RENTAL FEE Varies; call for rates.
FOR THE KIDS Camp Heidel, during the summer months for kids from 4–12, includes activities, a boxed lunch, arts and crafts, and a souvenir for $35 per day.
HOURS Flexible.
PARKING Plenty on site.

Set on the shores of Green Lake in Wisconsin, this resort encompasses more than 20 acres of woods, nature

Courtesy of Heidel House Resort

trails, and charming buildings. The center contains more than 10,000 square feet of function space with outdoor decks, a terrace, and a variety of meeting rooms that can accommodate up to 350 guests. The *Escapade*, a 60-foot catamaran-style vessel, is available for cocktail parties, dinner cruises, and Green Lake sightseeing tours.

The resort caters all events. You can choose anything from an elegant five-course sit-down dinner to a light sandwich buffet. As for entertainment, Heidel singers perform Wednesday–Saturday during the summer and House Cats for dancing and listening year-round, as well as hiking, skiing, tennis, golf, swimming, boating, balloon rides, and more.

HERRINGTON INN

Atwater's Restaurant

15 S. River Lane
Geneva, IL 60134
(630) 208-7433

Contact Catering manager
Best Feature Quaint atmosphere in Fox River Valley area.
Best Parties Bridal showers and luncheons, corporate executive retreats.
Capacity Dining room, 50 banquet, 125 reception.
Rental Fee Based on food and beverage consumption.
Hours Daily; lunch and dinner.
Parking Free on-site.

Courtesy of Herrington Inn

Whether you're planning a bridal or baby shower, meeting or awards luncheon, sit-down dinner, or cocktail reception, the Herrington Inn can accommodate your needs. The dining room boasts a spectacular view of the Fox River, a romantic fireplace, exquisite cuisine, and professional service. The room is complete with floral bud vases and votive candle holders, as well as china, glass, linen, and silverware.

Atwater's Restaurant caters all events. Luncheons start at $21.50 per person; dinners at $51.25 per person. The hors d'oeuvres are priced by the dozen, food stations per person, and carving stations by item. A four-hour open bar with premium brands is $23 per person. To confirm an event a deposit of $250 is required. If you bring in a cake, the cake-cutting fee is $4.75 per person. If you bring in your own wine, there is a $15 per bottle corking fee.

INDIAN LAKES RESORT

250 W. Schick Road
Bloomingdale, IL 60108
(630) 529-0200, fax (630) 529-0675

Contact Priscilla T. Lorenzin, director of sales and marketing
Capacity 28 multifunction rooms with 36,000 square feet of meeting space.
Rental Fee Based on guest rooms and food and beverage consumption.
Hours Flexible.
Parking 1,200 free parking spaces.

Courtesy of Indian Lakes Resort

Located just 40 minutes from Chicago and 15 minutes from O'Hare International Airport this "nearby getaway" is perfect for meetings as small as 12 and conventions as large as 1,200. Situated on 260 beautifully landscaped acres this resort is complete with newly renovated guest rooms, 28 multifunction meeting rooms, and two championship golf courses. Meeting rooms are designed for multimedia presentations. The hotel lobby has a waterfall bar, perfect for greeting guests. The Great Lakes Ballroom in the Thunderbird Meeting Center is a beautiful setting for wedding receptions and can seat up to 1,100 guests. The ballroom can be divided into four separate rooms for smaller events.

All food and beverage must be supplied by the resort. Wedding packages include a three-hour open bar, wedding cake, linens, and bridal suite. Banquet dinner prices vary. A 50 percent deposit is required. Audiovisual equipment is available for rent.

Inland Meeting and Exposition Center

400 E. Ogden Avenue
Westmont, IL 60559
(630) 575-8500

Contact Charlene Danko, director of sales
Best Feature Exhibition Hall.
Capacity Entire facility, 2,143 banquet, 3,586 reception; Illinois Exhibition Hall, 1,000 banquet, 2,000 reception; Skyline Auditorium, 360 banquet, 500 reception; DuPage Auditorium, 240 banquet, 350 reception; nine additional rooms, 12–120 banquet, 10–250 reception.
Rental Fee Based on room size and length of time used.
Hours Daily, 7 A.M.–12 A.M.
Parking Free on-site.

Inland Meeting and Exposition Center is a beautifully decorated modern structure with relatively low rental rates and

Photograph by Steve Matteo

more than 45,000 square feet of space. The Illinois Exhibition Hall has 15,000 square feet of unobstructed space for trade shows, auctions, expos, and banquets. The Skyline Auditorium is a spacious room enhanced by a relief of downtown Chicago along one wall, a recessed projector screen, a stage, and a sound system. There are an additional

11 rooms available for events of just about any size. Each of the rooms has a modern "clean" decor with few embellishments to distract from your event.

The in-house caterer will design a meal to meet your needs or you can choose from an array of set menus. Audiovisual equipment must be rented.

The International Conference Center

4750 N. Sheridan Road
Chicago, IL 60640
(773) 769-6363, fax (773) 769-1144
E-mail iccchgo@aol.com

Contact Robert Hawley or Marge Philbrook, managers
Best Feature Located in an international neighborhood.
Capacity Mathews Hall, 250 banquet; Lumumba Room and Gandhi Room, each 60 banquet; Kartini Room, 40 banquet; MLK Room, 25 banquet.
Rental Fee Mathews Halls, $350; Lumumba and Gandhi Rooms, $100; Kartini, $85; MLK, $45.
Hours 6 A.M.–midnight for nonresidential meetings.
Parking Adjacent lot, $5 per car.

Located in an old high-rise building, this not-for-profit conference and retreat center is suitable for everything from a

Photograph by Steve Matteo

short meeting to a month-long retreat. The center is also the home of the community resource center of the Institute of Cultural Affairs. The clients of the 30 agencies in the building speak around 72 languages, creating a truly global environment. Mathews Hall, the largest room, is located on the ground floor and includes a lounge area and a serving counter. In addition to meeting space, the facilities of the ICC include lodging accommodation and food service.

Two-person rooms with twin or double beds and dormitory-style rooms with bunk beds are $14–$28 per person per night. Guests share bathrooms and shower facilities. In-house catered meals are $4.50–$6.50 per person in the dining area, $1 per person more if served in the other rooms. There is a $1 per person support fee for a group who uses an outside caterer. No alcohol may be served and no smoking is allowed in lodging rooms.

KATHERINE LEGGE MEMORIAL LODGE

5901 S. COUNTY LINE ROAD
HINSDALE, IL 60521
(630) 789-7095, FAX (630)789-7093
WWW.VIL.HINSDALE.IL.US/LODGE.HTM

CONTACT Jo Allen, reservations
BEST FEATURE Beautiful woodland setting suitable for all occasions.
CAPACITY Entire building, 230 banquet, 240 reception.
RENTAL FEE Weekends, $725 for 4-hour rental; weekdays, $225 for 4-hour rental.
DISCOUNTS Available for Hinsdale residents and nonprofit groups.
HOURS Flexible.
PARKING Available on-site.

Photograph by Steve Matteo

The Katherine Legge Memorial Lodge is a Tudor-style hunting lodge, located in a beautiful wooded 52-acre park in Hinsdale. The Lodge's Old World charm is displayed with its beautiful floor-to-ceiling stone and brick fireplaces, large living room area, second floor ballroom, and window-encased dining room overlooking the patio and beautiful grounds. The KLM Lodge is an ideal setting not only for banquets, but also for business conferences, planning sessions, training courses, or meetings. The second floor ballroom can serve as a meeting area, while the first-floor living room can be used for greeting or taking a break, and the adjacent dining room for meals. Please note that there is no handicapped accessibility to the second floor.

Choose a caterer from an approved list or bring your own. The Lodge kitchen is full service, which allows for on-site preparation. The Lodge can provide dinnerware, flatware, tables, and chairs, but table linens, glasses, and audiovisual equipment need to be brought in.

LAKE LAWN RESORT

2400 E. GENEVA STREET., HWY 50
DELAVAN, WI 53115
(414) 728-7050 OR (800) 338-5253
WWW.LAKELAWNRESORT.COM
E-MAIL SALES@LAKELAWNRESORT.COM

CONTACT Robert Anderson, director of catering
BEST FEATURE The scenic shoreline of Delavan Lake.
CAPACITY Geneva Room, 425 banquet, 750 reception; Great Room, 400 reception; Wisconsin Room, 200 banquet, 300 reception; Sherwood Lounge, 75 reception; Courtyard Rooms, 16–40 meeting; 21 other function rooms.
RENTAL FEE Call for rates.
FOR THE KIDS The Clown Town Fun Club, a fully supervised, year-round program that is a three-ring circus of nonstop games and activities including ice skating, hay rides, miniature golf, and more.
HOURS Flexible.
PARKING Large free lot.

Lake Lawn Resort, nestled among 275 wooded acres along the shoreline of scenic Delavan Lake, provides a casual setting for both business and pleasure. There are 21 function rooms to suit almost any occasion. The Great Room has a stone fireplace, a cathedral ceiling, and burgundy and forest green decor. Sherwood Room has an intimate, ski lodge ambience for smaller private parties. Other rooms provide views of the lake and lawns. The site is handicapped accessible.

Lake Lawn provides all food and beverages. You must bring in your own cake; there is no cutting fee. Audiovisual equipment must be rented.

Courtesy of Lake Lawn Resort

LOYOLA AT THE CENACLE

513 W. FULLERTON PARKWAY
CHICAGO, IL 60614
(773) 529-7700, FAX (773) 528-2456

CONTACT Tim McGuriman, director
BEST FEATURE Affordable retreat house and conference center located in the heart of Lincoln Park.
CAPACITY A number of flexible meeting rooms are available, largest room accomodates 70 people.
RENTAL FEE $80 per person per night for a single room; $60 per person per night for a double room. Rates include three meals a day.
HOURS Flexible.
PARKING Free lot for 25 cars.

Courtesy of Loyola at the Cenacle

Loyola at the Cenacle is a 70-bed retreat and conference facility with spacious meeting rooms, a library, and a chapel. Located in Lincoln Park just two blocks from the Lincoln Park Zoo and Lake Michigan, the Cenacle offers groups the opportunity to find a quiet, reflective place with easy access to some of Chicago's greatest attractions. This center is perfect for nonprofit groups and is an excellent choice for retreats, staff meetings, and planning sessions.

Loyola at the Cenacle provides all meals. Full catering services are available.

THE MANOR HOUSE AT HARRISON CONFERENCE CENTER

GREEN BAY ROAD
LAKE BLUFF, IL 60044
(847) 295-9307, FAX (847) 295-8792
WWW.HARRISONCONFERENCE.COM

CONTACT Nancy Lindemer, director of sales, or Faye Kelly, special events manager
BEST FEATURE Secluded 45-acre estate.
CAPACITY Great Hall, 200 banquet/theater; Dining Room, 250 banquet; Chestnut Room, 80 banquet; Hunt Room, 110 theater, 65 classroom; Blue Room, 75 theater, 55 classroom; eight additional rooms, 25–60 theater, 15–50 classroom.
RENTAL FEE Call for rates.
HOURS Flexible.
PARKING On-site lot, valet available for additional fee.

Photograph by Liz Chilsen, courtesy of Harrison Conference Center

This elegant country estate provides an ideal setting for management development, training sessions, sales meetings, and special events. The readers of *Corporate Meetings and Incentives* magazine have rated it one of the "Ten Best Conference Centers" in the nation. The Italian villa-style Manor house was designed by famous architect Howard Van Doren Shaw. The property has been restored rather than renovated in order to preserve the dignity of the original estate. The striking Gothic arches at the front portico and the Byzantine towers which overlook the rear terraced garden are just some of the features that have been maintained. The Conference Center is handicapped accessible.

Harrison offers complete meeting package that include guest room accommodations. Harrison's on-site catering department is available to handle holiday parties, picnics, wedding ceremonies, and receptions. Audiovisual equipment is available on site.

MARGARITA EUROPEAN INN

1566 OAK AVENUE
EVANSTON, IL 60201
(847) 475-7902, FAX (847) 475-7825
WWW.MARGARITAINN.COM

CONTACT Patrick Igo, director of catering

CAPACITY Garden Rooftop, 40; Grand Parlour, 52; Verdi Room, 90; Solera Room, 72; Ivory Room, 60; five additional rooms, 10–20.

RENTAL FEE Varies based on space required, $100–$650.

HOURS Flexible.

PARKING Valet available, limited street.

Courtesy of Margarita European Inn

The Margarita Inn is a quaint bed and breakfast filled with antiques and vintage furnishings. The gracious Grand Parlour features a fireplace, French doors leading to a small balcony, and a grand piano, and is a charming location for wedding ceremonies, receptions, and intimate dinner parties. The Rooftop Garden is available for cocktails and hors d'oeuvres. Smaller rooms are available for board or retreat-style meetings and conferences. The Inn has 42 guest rooms decorated with vintage pieces, and most are handicapped accessible.

Va Pensiero, a restaurant located within the inn, provides all food and beverages.

Outside caterers are not allowed. The restaurant offers an extensive menu which can be easily adapted to your event. Lunches range from $30–$65 per person, including tax and service charge. Dinners range from $65–$125. Audiovisual equipment is available for rental.

MARRIOTT HICKORY RIDGE CONFERENCE CENTER

1195 SUMMERHILL DRIVE
LISLE, IL 60532
(630) 971-5023, FAX (630) 971-6939
WWW.CONFERENCECENTERS.COM/CHIHR/

CONTACT Sales and catering sales department

CAPACITY 47 meeting rooms and 75 break-out rooms; flexible banquet space for social events, too. Chicago Room, 130 banquet, 180 reception, 198 classroom; theater, 90.

RENTAL FEE Complete meeting packages includes guest room, meals, breaks, audiovisual equipment, and meeting room, $165–$235 single complete.

HOURS Flexible.

PARKING Free lot for 500.

Courtesy of Marriott Hickory Ridge Conference Center

Situated on a 26-acre campus, surrounded by an arboretum, this Marriott conference center is less than an hour from Chicago. The center boasts a distraction-free environment for successful, productive meetings. Each meeting room is equipped with a guest services hotline, separate lighting and temperature controls, ergonomically designed chairs, and wiring for the latest technology. Handicapped accessible. Audiovisual equipment is available.

At Marriott Hickory Ridge, breakfast and lunch are served buffet-style; themed setting is offered for dinner. Morning and afternoon refreshment breaks and complimentary beverages are provided daily, with a choice of coffee, tea, sodas, and juices. Special events are also on the menu—from a picnic in the wooded setting to a banquet in one of the banquet rooms. Rates vary depending upon space and service desired.

NAVY PIER

600 E. GRAND AVENUE
CHICAGO, IL 60611
(312) 595-5100
WWW.NAVYPIER.COM

CONTACT Trade show and conventions (312) 595-5107; Public shows or consumer shows (312) 595-5080; meetings or banquets (312) 595-5300.
CAPACITY Grand Ballroom, 1,100 banquet, 2,000 theater; Shelter Building, 600 banquet, 1,500 reception; 36 function rooms, 80–665 banquet, 60–550 reception.
RENTAL FEE Grand Ballroom, $7,000; meeting rooms, $1,500 and up.
FOR THE KIDS Site of Chicago Children's Museum (see separate listing).
HOURS Daily, 8 A.M.–midnight.
PARKING Enclosed garage for 1,750 cars.

Navy Pier is an exciting year-round tourist attraction and convention center located on Chicago's lakefront. The site has more than 170,000 square feet of

Photograph by Doug Snower, courtesy of Navy Pier

exhibit space and a 65,000-square-foot multipurpose Festival Hall with adjacent meeting room space. Festival Hall is perfect for small- to medium-sized trade, public, and private shows. The facility is divisible into two areas of 56,700 and 113,400 square feet. It features ceiling heights of up to 60 feet. The Grand Ballroom, with its 80-foot domed ceiling, serves banquet, performance, and

special exhibit needs as it has since the Pier first opened in 1916. The Grand Ballroom also offers panoramic views of the lake.

All food and beverage is provided by Navy Pier. A full range of electrical, telecommunications, and audiovisual equipment is available. Navy Pier is handicapped accessible.

NIU HOFFMAN ESTATES EDUCATION CENTER

5555 TRILLIUM BOULEVARD
HOFFMAN ESTATES, IL 60192
(847) 645-3000 EXT. 36, FAX (815) 753-8865
WWW.NIU.EDU/HEEC/
E-MAIL MKEYES@NIU.EDU

CONTACT Martha Keyes, conference services
CAPACITY Auditorium, 250 theater; computer labs, each 16–20 classroom; 20 additional meeting rooms including tiered classrooms and breakout rooms, 6–50 classroom.
RENTAL FEE Call for rates.
HOURS Flexible.
PARKING Free parking on site.

The Education Center at Hoffman Estates was designed for evening graduate programs as well as for professional training sessions and meetings. A two-story atrium welcomes visitors and is ideal for morning and afternoon break service.

The 250-seat auditorium has a user-friendly audiovisual system and a raised stage. The computer labs have Novell networked PC's with Internet access. Meeting rooms have a variety of configurations: tiered and traditional classrooms, U-shape, hollow square, or team setting. NIU's sunlit rooms feature soundproof walls, padded swivel chairs, tack strips, adjustable lighting, and individual climate controls. Standard audiovisual equipment is included with all room rentals. Additional equipment is available for rental.

The Education Center caters all in-house meetings with comprehensive packages. The site is handicapped accessible.

Courtesy of NIU Hoffman Estates Education Center

OSCAR SWAN COUNTRY INN

1800 W. STATE STREET
GENEVA, IL 60134
(630) 232-0173, FAX (630) 232-2706
WWW.OSCARSWAN.COM

CONTACT Nina and Hans Heymann
CAPACITY Entire first floor of mansion, 80 people; the Gathering, 150 people; outdoor events, 200–400.
RENTAL FEE Varies depending upon event, $750–$2,000.
HOURS Flexible.
PARKING Space for 120 cars.

Courtesy of Oscar Swan Country Inn

This colonial estate nestled amid tall trees on eight wooded acres began as a gentleman's farm in 1902. Today, this renovated bed and breakfast is available for parties, receptions, and other special events. The inn is filled with mahogany antiques, floral upholstery, and rich floor coverings. One of the best things about this site is the impeccably maintained landscape.

The expansive front grounds welcome guests with 1,000 spring daffodils. The back garden, with a small built-in swimming pool and a formal perennial garden, is a picturesque backdrop for any event. Eight sleeping rooms are available for $98–$149 per night.

The Carriage House, a converted garage equipped with a dance floor, can accommodate bands or DJs. String quartets, harpists, and other smaller musical groups can play inside the main house. Audiovisual equipment must be brought in. The inn caters all events. Lunches range from $18–$29 per person and dinners from $37–$55. An open bar is $15–$23 per person for three hours. China is supplied, but linens are an additional charge.

PHEASANT RUN RESORT AND CONFERENCE CENTER

4051 E. MAIN STREET
ST. CHARLES, IL 60174
(630) 584-6300 OR (800) 4-PHEASANT,
   FAX (630) 584-9827
WWW.PHEASANTRUN.COM
E-MAIL GROUPSALES@PHEASANTRUN.COM

CONTACT Group sales
CAPACITY Megacenter, 3,000 banquet, 4,800 reception; St. Charles Ballroom, 1,000 banquet, 1,800 reception, 1,110 schoolroom; President's Rooms, 40–200 banquet, 60–450 theater; Gallery Hall, 45–300 theater, 32–200 schoolroom; Gem Rooms, 75–160 reception, 50–100 schoolroom; Van Gogh Room, 45 theater, 32 schoolroom, 24 conference.
RENTAL FEE Varies according to event.
HOURS Flexible.
PARKING Free.

This is one of the largest, most diverse meeting spaces of any resort in the Midwest. There is a space for every type of event from the Megacenter with 38,250 square feet of exhibition space to the Marsalis I Room for a more intimate gathering. Entertainment options abound—an 18-hole golf course, a dinner theater, Zanies Comedy Club, shopping, a spa and fitness center, three swimming pools, and tennis, volleyball, and basketball courts. The entire resort is handicapped accessible.

Pheasant Run's catering staff can help you choose the perfect menu for your event, and can organize everything from snack breaks to full meals to themed parties. State of the art audiovisual equipment is available through the resort's professional AV department.

Courtesy of Pheasant Run Resort and Conference Center

SUMMIT EXECUTIVES CENTRE

205 N. MICHIGAN AVENUE, TENTH FLOOR
CHICAGO, IL 60601
(312) 938-2000, FAX (312) 861-0324
WWW.SUMMITCHICAGO.COM
E-MAIL LSILBERMAN@SUMMITCHICAGO.COM

CONTACT Louise Silberman, managing director
BEST FEATURE Ergonomic meeting environment with the latest audiovisual equipment.
CAPACITY 9+ meeting rooms, 50–250 theater, 10–40 U-shaped, 10–125 schoolroom.
RENTAL FEE Call for details.
HOURS Flexible.
PARKING Public lot in the building.

The Summit Executives Centre is the only downtown conference center accredited by the International Association of Conference Centers. Each room at the center is specifically designed for learning, with comfortable chairs, wide tables, nonglare surfaces for presentation materials, flexible lighting,

adjustable thermostats, and triple insulated walls to eliminate outside noise. Audiovisual equipment is continuously upgraded to provide the latest in technology and the knowledgeable technical staff is available for assistance. A fully staffed business center will help with faxes, copies, incoming telephone calls, and last minute meeting requests. The center is handicapped accessible.

A continuous assortment of healthy food and beverage options are available throughout the day, so your meeting can break whenever it is convenient. The complete meeting package with room, amenities (pads of paper, pencils, hard candy, ice water), basic audiovisual equipment, continental breakfast, unlimited beverages and snacks, buffet lunch with tax and service charge included is $119 per person.

Courtesy of Summit Executives Centre

TELCORDIA CONFERENCE AND LEARNING CENTER

6200 ROUTE 53
LISLE, IL 60532
(630) 960-6053, FAX (630) 960-6190
WWW.800TEACHME.COM
E-MAIL TEACHME@TELCORDIA.COM

CONTACT Louise Bouret, conference sales
BEST FEATURE Conference and training center with 343 sleeping rooms.
CAPACITY 42 meeting rooms and 65 breakout rooms, 8–90.
RENTAL FEE Varies depending on needs.
HOURS Daily, 24 hours.
PARKING Ample free parking.

Telcordia Conference and Learning Center is ideal for small to midsize group meetings and training seminars. Amenities include 42 meeting rooms, with full audiovisual support and computer hookups, plus 65 breakout rooms.

All rooms can be configured to your specifications: U-shaped, closed square, herringbone, or classroom style. Telcordia is truly a state-of-the-art, multimedia meeting environment, with educational events being their specialty. For overnight guests, the on-site hotel complex features 343 private guestrooms. The facility is handicapped accessible.

Telcordia offers three meals a day, buffet fare, as well as mid-morning and mid-afternoon break service, evening cocktail receptions, and private or specialty dining. If you are interested in recreational activities, there are basketball, volleyball, and tennis courts, plus swimming, a horseshoe pit, and a nine-hole putting green.

Courtesy of Telcordia Conference and Learning Center

University of Chicago Graduate School of Business Gleacher Center

450 N. Cityfront Plaza, Chicago, IL 60611
(312) 464-8787, fax (312) 464-8683
www.gsb.uchicago.edu/confcntr/
E-mail gleacherctr@gsb.uchicago.edu

Contact Sales department

Capacity Dining room, 250 banquet, 350 reception or theater; glass-enclosed lounges, 60 banquet, 80 reception; 13 amphitheaters, 70–135 classroom; seminar rooms, 30 classroom; boardrooms, 18 conference.

Rental Fee $400–$2,000 per day depending on the room; hourly and half day rates available.

Hours Monday-Saturday, 7 A.M.–11 P.M.; closed Sunday and major holidays.

Parking Several lots and garages within a block; discounts available.

Courtesy of Gleacher Center

This striking stone and glass conference center is located in the heart of downtown Chicago. It's 3,000-square-foot dining room with wall-to-wall windows creates a dramatic backdrop for any event. Built to house the Continuing Studies Program, the facility is available during the day for business meetings, seminars, and other events. A full range of meeting rooms, boardrooms, and amphitheaters are available. Many of these rooms offer high-tech amenities.

Wolfgang Puck Catering, will prepare anything from pizza to a multicourse gourmet dinner on-site. Meeting packages start at $61 per person. Audiovisual equipment is available.

University of Illinois at Chicago Pavilion

525 S. Racine Avenue
Chicago, IL 60607
(312) 413-5781, fax (312) 413-5774
www.ssb.uic.edu/pavilion/

Contact Anne Inouye, public functions manager

Best Feature Large arena.

Capacity Seating for 3,000-10,500; banquet, 700; exhibit booths, 139.

Rental Fee $7,500 versus 10 percent of gross receipts (if applicable); negotiable.

Hours Flexible.

Parking $10 per car, $12 per bus.

Located downtown on the campus of the University of Illinois at Chicago, this 10,500-seat sports and entertainment arena can accommodate corporate meetings, conferences, exhibits, banquets, trade shows, and sporting events.

Courtesy of University of Illinois at Chicago Pavilion

Location, easy access, and plentiful parking are among the pavilion's best features. The pavilion is fully handicapped accessible. There is a full sound system available, and arrangements can be made for audiovisual and theatrical lighting packages.

The University caterer or an approved outside vendor can provide food service. Where applicable, stagehands and Teamsters will be used for load-in, rehearsal, day of show, and load-out. A full computerized box office is available. The facility is fully heated and air-conditioned. There are six dressing rooms, drive-in ramp to backstage, four concession stands, a press booth, and special needs seating.

COUNTRY CLUBS AND GOLF CLUBS

Brae Loch Golf Course:
  Lake County Forest Preserve

Cantigny Golf and Tennis

Carriage Greens Country Club

Chevy Chase Country Club

Cog Hill Golf and Country Club

Country Lakes Country Club

Glenview Park Golf Club

Highland Park Country Club

Mission Hills Country Club

Oak Brook Bath & Tennis Club

Oak Meadows Golf and Banquet
  Facility

Poplar Creek Country Club

Valley Lo Sports Club

Brae Loch Golf Course

Lake County Forest Preserve

33600 N. Route 45
Grayslake, IL 60030
(847) 223-5542

Contact Peggy Hoger, assistant manager of banquets

Capacity Main room, 280 banquet, 300 classroom.

Rental Fee Based on food and beverage consumption.

Hours Flexible.

Parking On-site lot.

The banquet room at Brae Loch is a great setting for everything from an elegant reception to a high-powered business meeting. The highlight of the room is its view of the well-manicured landscape that includes the 18-hole golf course. The room also features a huge oak dance floor and a pale peach decor.

Fresh flowers on every table, elegant dinner music, fine china, and linens add a special touch.

Brae Loch will cater your special event. The banquet dinner buffet is $24 per person and includes a three-course meal, china and linen service, a centerpiece for each table, and cake cutting. A wedding reception package is available for a minimum of 100 people. In addition to the regular package, the wedding package includes five hours of unlimited cocktails and a champagne toast for $34 per person. All taxes and service charges are included in the package cost. There are also several golf outing packages available. Minimal audiovisual equipment is available.

Courtesy of Brae Loch Golf Course, Lake County Forest Preserve

Cantigny Golf and Tennis

27W270 Mack Road
Wheaton, IL 60187
(630) 260-8188, fax (630) 668-8682
www.cantignygolf.com

Contact Mike Machay, restaurant supervisor

Capacity Fareways Restaurant, 174 banquet, 200 reception; Fareways Lounge, 50 banquet, 100 reception; two outside patios, 50–100 reception; Medill Room, 18 conference.

Rental Fee Fareways Restaurant, $400; Medill Room, $150, ⅓ of Fareways, $150.

Discounts 50 percent for nonprofit groups.

Hours During golf season, restaurant open 7 A.M.–3 P.M., lounge open until dusk. During winter months, restaurant open 11 A.M.–3 P.M., lounge open until dusk. Closed Mondays, except for special golf outings. Sundays, open year-round for brunch 10 A.M.–2 P.M. Banquet hours are flexible.

Parking Available on grounds.

Courtesy of Cantigny Golf and Tennis

Cantigny Golf and Tennis is located on the former country estate of *Chicago Tribune* publisher and owner Joseph Medill, and his grandson Colonel Robert McCormick. In addition to the modern clubhouse, golf course, and tennis facility, the grounds offer 10 acres of beautiful gardens, a mansion museum, a military museum, nature trails, and a visitors center. The Fareways Restaurant and Lounge offer a spectacular view of the golf course. The Fareways Lounge also includes a brick fireplace and oak paneled bar. The Medill Room offers a complete view of the McCormick property.

Dinners start at $21 per person, plus liquor, tax, and a 20 percent gratuity. Lunches start at $12. An open bar is available starting at $9 per person. Audiovisual and other meeting equipment is available. The facility is handicapped accessible.

CARRIAGE GREENS COUNTRY CLUB

8700 CARRIAGE GREENS DRIVE
DARIEN, IL 60561
(630) 985-3400

CONTACT Banquet manager
BEST FEATURE Scenic location.
CAPACITY Main ballroom, 500 banquet; 35–500 various function rooms.
RENTAL FEE Based on food and beverage consumption.
DISCOUNTS Dinner packages are less expensive for Sunday–Friday events.
HOURS Flexible.
PARKING Ample parking in lot.

Photograph by J & J Photography and Printing Services, courtesy of Carriage Greens Country Club

Located in a lovely wooded area with rolling hills, this scenic location has a championship 18-hole golf course and is an ideal site for banquet dining. Carriage Greens Country Club is just 35 minutes from downtown Chicago and 20 minutes from Midway Airport. They are able to accommodate intimate gatherings of 35 and grand celebrations of 500 at a surprisingly reasonable price.

The country club will cater your event. Saturday dinner packages for a minimum of 100 guests range from $27.50–$32.50 per person. Sunday through Friday dinner packages are $21.75–$28.50 per person. Liquor packages are $13 per person for a four-hour open bar. Unlimited wine with dinner is an additional $3 per person. A guarantee of the exact number of guests is required 72 hours prior to the event.

CHEVY CHASE COUNTRY CLUB

1000 N. MILWAUKEE AVENUE
WHEELING, IL 60090
(847) 537-0362

CONTACT Catering Sales Office
CAPACITY Main Ballroom, 600 banquet and reception; Devonshire Room, 120 banquet, 150 theater; Wayside Room, 80 banquet, 100 theater.
RENTAL FEE None if full catering service is used.
HOURS Friday and Saturday, until 1 A.M.; Sunday–Thursday, until midnight.
PARKING Free lot on grounds.

Courtesy of Chevy Chase Country Club

Owned by the Wheeling Park District, this site was once a favorite nightclub and gambling spot for Chicago's socialites and gangsters. Al Capone himself was reported to be one of the patrons. The escape tunnels and secret rooms built during Prohibition have been sealed off, but the overall decor is reminiscent of the 1920s. Spacious grandeur and a large hardwood dance floor in the Main Ballroom makes this an ideal setting for a wedding reception or fundraiser. Adjoining the ballroom is a large room with a cathedral ceiling and stained-glass windows that can be used for greeting guests and socializing. The Devonshire Room has large windows that overlook the golf course and a warm, neutral decor.

The club caters all events. A deli sandwich buffet is $10.35 per person. Dinner packages that include a four-course meal, private room, four-hour open bar, and taxes and gratuities, start at $35.15 per person. Golf packages are an option with the booking of an event only. A variety of audiovisual equipment is available. You must book early to get this site.

Cog Hill Golf and Country Club

12294 Archer Avenue
Lemont, IL 60439
(630) 257-5872 ext. 301, fax (630) 257-3665
www.coghillgolf.com
coghillgolfclub@worldnet.att.net

Contact Jim Mattas, special events manager
Capacity Three dining rooms and patio, 300 banquet.
Rental Fee None if full catering service is used.
Hours 6 a.m.–midnight.
Parking Two lots.

Courtesy of Cog Hill Golf and Country Club

Cog Hill is a privately owned, open to the public, golf complex located 30 miles southwest of Chicago. The club house has three dining rooms available for private events. Each room can function separately or they can be connected to form one large room for 300. The main dining room has a 30-foot ceiling with massive wood beams and leaded-glass windows. All of the dining rooms offer dramatic views of both the golf course and the flower gardens. The adjacent patio is available for wedding receptions and other outdoor events.

The club caters all events. Wedding packages are available for $37–$51 per person, including a four-hour open bar, wine with dinner, tax, and tip. A podium, microphone/sound system, and video monitor are available, but additional audiovisual equipment must be rented. Handicapped accessible.

Country Lakes Country Club

1601 Fairway Drive
Naperville, IL 60563
(630) 420-1068, fax (630) 420-7111

Contact Michael Angelakos
Capacity Lakeside Banquet Room, 250 banquet; Village Banquet Room, 100 banquet; Golfer's Room, 50 banquet; Emerald Room and Executive Banquet Room, each 40 banquet.
Rental Fee None if in-house caterer is used.
Hours Sunday–Thursday, 11 a.m.–12:30 a.m.; Friday and Saturday, 11 a.m.–2 a.m.
Parking Lot on premises

Courtesy of Country Lakes Country Club

Cathedral ceiling, carved ice sculptures, sterling silver candelabras, tuxedo-attired serving assistants, and fresh floral arrangements all give the Lakeside Banquet Room an elegant ambiance. Large windows on three sides of the room offer excellent views of the golf course. This room is ideal for weddings, rehearsal dinners, corporate affairs, and other formal events. For more casual parties, you can choose the lower-level Golfers Room that also overlooks the golf course.

The club will provide all food and beverage. Luncheon buffets range from $13.50–$17.95 per person. A "Grand Wedding" package with a three-course dinner, five-hour open bar, fresh-cut flowers, a wood parquet dance floor, free parking, and a wedding cake starts at $30 per person. For Saturday functions this package starts at $36 per person. There are several theme dinners available: Best of the West Cookout, Cajun Buffet, and Italian Fiesta. Audiovisual equipment must be brought in, or the club will arrange for rental. The facility is wheelchair accessible.

GLENVIEW PARK GOLF CLUB

800 SHERMER ROAD
GLENVIEW, IL 60025
(847) 657-3200

CONTACT Anita Hahn, restaurant manager
BEST FEATURE Beautiful views.
CAPACITY Dining room, 110 banquet, 125 reception.
RENTAL FEE No fee with food and beverage package.
HOURS Lunch, 12 P.M.–4 P.M.; private dinners, 6:30 P.M.–12:30 A.M.
PARKING On grounds.

Courtesy of Glenview Park Golf Club

The casual, club-like setting of the dining room at the Glenview Park Golf Club is ideal for intimate affairs. The L-shaped dining room has floor-to-ceiling windows that overlook beautifully maintained grounds. The room is decorated in woodsy forest green, brown, and off-white, which successfully blends the inside and outside space. Brass chandeliers hang from the vaulted, wood-beamed ceiling and floral cornices grace the windows. A veranda makes a perfect setting for cocktails before dinner.

With the exception of cakes, the club provides all food and drink. Dinners are $16.50–$27.00 per person and lunches are $9.95–$19.50 per person. A three-and-a-half-hour open bar is $19 per person. Wedding packages are available, however there is no space for ceremonies. Tables, chairs, and some audio-visual equipment is provided. There is no smoking and no tents or catering on the golf course. The club is handicapped accessible.

HIGHLAND PARK COUNTRY CLUB

1201 PARK AVENUE WEST
HIGHLAND PARK, IL 60035
(847) 433-4000 EXT. 122, FAX (847) 433-8720

CONTACT Keith Covelle, director of catering
BEST FEATURE View of the golf course.
CAPACITY Main dining room, 300 banquet, 500 reception; West Room, 80 banquet, 250 reception; East Room, 75 banquet, 200 reception.
RENTAL FEE Based on food and beverage consumption.
HOURS Flexible. Afternoon events must end by 4 P.M. Evening events begin at 6 P.M.
PARKING Free lot on premises.

Photograph by Steve Matteo

This 1960s-vintage North Shore country club is open to the public, after operating for years as a members-only club. The main banquet room is decorated in neutral tones, and floor-to-ceiling windows overlook the manicured golf course. A permanent parquet dance floor and a baby grand piano are available for the footloose. Wedding receptions, galas, and meetings with up to 500 guests can be hosted in the main banquet room while the East and West Rooms are used for more intimate events. The facility is handicapped accessible.

All food and beverage is provided by the club's culinary staff. The catering staff will assist you in planning the perfect menu for your event; corporate breakfast, lunch, and dinner menus are available. Catering staff will also help you in selecting florists, musicians, photographers, and videographers. Wedding packages, which include a four-hour bar, start at $55 per person. Outdoor facilities are available for guests' use.

Mission Hills Country Club

1677 W. Mission Hills Road
Northbrook, IL 60062
(847) 498-3200, fax (847) 498-9107

Contact Lynne Kay, food and beverage
director

Best Feature Spectacular view of bridge,
fountains, ponds, and gazebo.

Capacity Entire facility, 350 reception.

Rental Fee Based on food and beverage
consumption.

Discounts Friday and Sunday discounts.

Hours Afternoon events must end by 4 P.M.;
evening events begin at 6 P.M.

Parking Valet or self-park in private lot.

Mission Hills Country Club is an ideal
location for business dinners, weddings,
golf outings, and many other special
events. Located just off I-294, the club
is easily accessible for your guests from
the city as well as those from the suburbs. The facility can accommodate
events from five to 300. The main banquet room has an elegant decor and a
beautiful view of the championship golf
course.

The club supplies all food and beverage. Lunches are from $18.95–$29.95 per
person, dinners from $20 per person.
Wedding packages start at $18.95 per
person. In addition to food service, the
package includes valet parking, one-
hour cocktail reception prior to dinner
and three hours following, a champagne
toast for the bridal table, unlimited
house wine with dinner, wedding cake,
and white table linens. The catering staff
will assist you with florists, bakeries,
musicians, photographers, and videographers. Audiovisual equipment must
be brought in. Wheelchair accessible.

Oak Brook Bath & Tennis Club

800 Oak Brook Road
Oak Brook, IL 60523
(630) 990-3025, fax (630) 990-3031
www.oak-brook.org

Contact Connie Craig or Julie Gies, catering
consultants

Capacity Clubhouse, 220 banquet, 350
reception

Rental Fee None if food and beverage consumption meets minimum.

Hours Daily, flexible to suit each event.

Parking Large adjacent lot; valet available.

Two hundred and sixty-nine acres of
wooded and recreational property surround the Clubhouse of the Oak Brook
Bath & Tennis Club. The glass-enclosed
Clubhouse faces a small lake—complete
with a fountain. From May through
October an outdoor ceremony site is
available, as is an adjoining covered
patio. The site is handicapped accessible.

All food is prepared on premises.
There is a sound system that will play
CDs from your collection or from theirs.
Privately hired DJs or musicians must
provide their own sound systems. The
catering consultants can arrange for
rental of specialty linens, outdoor gaze-
bos, and tents. A piano, microphone,
lectern, and portable screen are available
at no charge; additional equipment can
be rented. A 40-person minimum is
required for all events.

Oak Meadows Golf and Banquet Facility

900 N. Wood Dale Road
Addison, IL 60101
(630) 595-1800, fax (630) 595-2234

Contact Susan Daniels, banquet facilities manager

Capacity Grand Ballroom, 270 banquet; Garden Room, 150 banquet; Elm and Oak Room, each 65 banquet.

Rental Fee Based on food and beverage consumption.

Hours Flexible.

Parking Free adjacent lot.

Courtesy of Oak Meadows Golf and Banquet Facility

Owned and operated by the Forest Preserve District of DuPage County, Oak Meadows Golf and Banquet Facility is surrounded by old oak trees and many flowers. The Grand Ballroom has an Old World atmosphere with vaulted ceilings and wrought-iron chandeliers. Both the Garden Room and the Elm Room have a brighter, airy feel with large windows that overlook the golf course. For smaller events, the Oak Room with its library-like decor is comfortable and intimate.

Lunches are $12.95 per person and dinners $18.50–$27.75. A complete wedding package that includes the meal, four-hour premium liquor open bar, champagne toast, and wedding cake starts at $36.75 per person. For parties of 150 or more, the wedding package also includes a cheese and vegetable buffet with fruit garnish served with cocktails before dinner. Candle centerpieces are provided. On-site wedding ceremonies can be arranged for a minimal fee. Rooms can be equipped with state-of-the-art audiovisual equipment and lighting for meetings.

Poplar Creek Country Club

1400 Poplar Creek Drive
Hoffman Estates, IL 60194
(847) 884-0219, fax (847) 310-3621
heparks.org

Contact Jill Rance-LaLiberty, sales and catering manager; or Darin Malone, food and beverage manager

Capacity Poplar North and South, 250 combined or each 130 banquet; entire Fairway, 100 banquet; Fairway North, 60 banquet; Fairway South, 40 banquet.

Rental Fee $150–$500 per hour.

Hours Daily, seasonal hours.

Parking Valet available upon request.

Photograph by Steve Matteo

Poplar Creek Country Club, open to the public, has an 18-hole championship golf course, 55-station lighted driving range, indoor winter driving range, clubhouse with grill and bar, and banquet facilities. There are two rooms available for private events. The Fairway Room can accommodate up to 100 guests for a sit-down dinner, or it can be divided in half for smaller groups. The Poplar Room seats 250 guests and may also be divided. Both rooms provide golf course views. Poplar Creek is handicapped accessible.

The country club will provide all food and beverages. Wedding packages begin at $35 per person and include a four-hour open bar, champagne toast, four-course meal, customized wedding cake, ornate candelabra for the head table, and white table linens. Ice sculptures are available for an additional fee. On-site wedding ceremonies are available for a minimal set-up fee. Audiovisual equipment is available for a fee.

Valley Lo Sports Club

2200 Tanglewood Drive
Glenview, IL 60025
(847) 729-5550

Contact Gail Thomssen, catering director
Best Feature View of 30-acre lake and gardens.
Capacity Entire club and grounds, 400; main dining room, 240 banquet, 275 reception; three additional dining rooms, 40–100 banquet, 120 reception; two terraces, 40–60 banquet, 60–80 reception.
Rental Fee Based on food and beverage consumption; there is a rental fee for meeting rooms.
Hours Daily, Tuesday–Sunday.
Parking Large lot.

With the tranquil lake and surrounding trees, this club is perfect for outdoor ceremonies and tent parties. If the weather does not cooperate, there are beautiful rooms in the club that can

Courtesy of Valley Lo Sports Club

accommodate up to 400 guests. Each room has floor-to-ceiling windows with a fantastic view of the lake. The best view of all is from the terrace on the roof. The main dining room is located upstairs and is connected to a large bar and lounge. The other three dining rooms all have their own kitchen and bar. If the entire club is rented, guests are invited to golf, play tennis, swim, and sail.

All food and beverage is provided by the club. Lunch is from $18–$24 per person, dinners from $19–$30 per person. Wedding packages range from $35–$75 per person and include a three-to four-and-a-half-hour premium bar. Other alcohol is served on a per drink basis. Some audiovisual equipment is available (a podium, projection screen, and VCR). Additional equipment can be rented.

GALLERIES AND ART CENTERS

Bella Vista Fine Art Gallery

Chicago Fine Art Exchange

Galleria Marchetti

Kass/Meridian

Klein Art Works

Mars Gallery

Peter Miller Gallery

Studio 501

Three Arts Club of Chicago

BELLA VISTA FINE ART GALLERY

746 N. LA SALLE STREET
CHICAGO, IL 60610
(312) 274-1490, FAX (312) 274-1491
WWW.BELLAVISTAGALLERY.COM
E-MAIL ART@BELLAVISTAGALLERY.COM

CONTACT Patrick McCoy
CAPACITY 25–125.
RENTAL FEE Variable.
HOURS Flexible.
PARKING Public lot nearby.

Located in Chicago's River North gallery district, Bella Vista, which means "beautiful view," is an elegant and distinctive fine art gallery from the owners of Blue Chicago. Bella Vista Gallery features the original oil paintings of nationally renowned artist John Carroll Doyle. The gallery's classic jazz atmosphere with live music provides the perfect setting for your private cocktail reception.

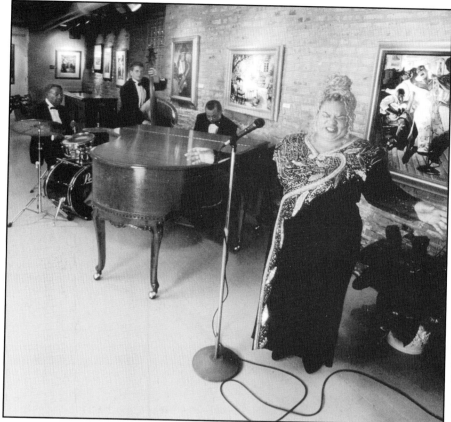

Courtesy of Bella Vista Fine Art Gallery

CHICAGO FINE ART EXCHANGE

815 N. CHICAGO AVENUE
CHICAGO, IL 60622
(312) 850-2787, FAX (312) 850-0074
WWW.CFAE.COM
E-MAIL SWAXMAN@CFAE.COM

CONTACT Steven Waxman, executive director
BEST FEATURE 20 x 60 cathedral skylight.
CAPACITY Skylight Room, 300 banquet, 500 reception; Jazz Lounge Room, 200–300 banquet and reception.
RENTAL FEE $2,500+ for both rooms.
DISCOUNTS Nonprofit organizations.
HOURS Flexible.
PARKING Complimentary valet parking.

The Exchange is both an art gallery exhibiting more than 100 pieces of artwork, as well as a beautiful and unusual event venue. By day, the 60-foot-long by 20-foot-high vaulted cathedral skylight creates a sun-filled room of beauty and color. By night, your guests can dine and dance under the stars. The fully automated lighting and sound systems create the mood of your choice as you literally see day turn into night. The dramatic skylight room and eclectic Jazz Lounge can be combined to accommodate large parties of 700.

Select a caterer of your choice. The Exchange provides many amenities not allowed, or extremely costly, at most other party sites. For example, there is no corkage or liquor fee when you bring in your own liquor. Tables, chairs, dance floor, stage, podiums, and professional sound systems are available at no extra charge. Additional audiovisual equipment must be brought in. The site is not wheelchair accessible.

Courtesy of Chicago Fine Art Exchange

GALLERIA MARCHETTI

825 W. ERIE STREET
CHICAGO, IL 60622
(312) 563-0495, FAX (312) 563-0499
WWW.GALLERIAMARCHETTI.COM

CONTACT Joe Marchetti, owner, or Mary Ellen Powers, special events coordinator

CAPACITY Banquet room, adjacent garage space, and adjoining outdoor courtyard, 160 banquet, 250 reception; outdoor tented pavilion, 500 banquet.

RENTAL FEE Depends on the number of guests.

DISCOUNTS For nonprofit organizations.

HOURS Flexible.

PARKING Valet.

Courtesy of Galleria Marchetti

Entertaining at the Galleria is like entertaining in your own home with your own private chef and serving staff. Located in the River West area, this site is 3,500 square feet, with an adjacent open-air kitchen. From March to December most people do their entertaining in the courtyard and under the white pavilion. Whether inside the contemporary gallery space or outside in the courtyard, Galleria Marchetti offers a unique option for special events. The site is handicapped accessible.

The Galleria caters all events. Italian and continental fare are prepared on-site. Menus can be custom-designed. Wedding packages are available and include appetizers, dinner, a four-hour open bar, and service. The Galleria can assist you in selecting a florist, photographer, and entertainment. Audiovisual equipment is available for an additional fee.

KASS/MERIDIAN

215 W. SUPERIOR STREET
CHICAGO, IL 60610
(312) 266-5999, FAX (312) 266-5931
WWW.KASSMERIDIAN.COM

CONTACT Grace Kass, owner

BEST FEATURES Trendy area; light, cheerful ambiance.

CAPACITY One large space divided into two galleries, 150–250 depending on type of event.

RENTAL FEE Rates vary.

HOURS Flexible.

PARKING Metered street parking; numerous lots.

Photograph by Steve Matteo

This spacious second-floor loft space is open, bright, and chic with high, exposed beam ceilings, white walls, track lighting, and bare wood floors. Located in the trendy River North area, the gallery's walls are usually hung with brightly colored artwork by well-known contemporary artists. The gallery has an interesting atmosphere that is suitable for formal dinners, cocktail receptions, luncheons, or meetings.

You may bring in your own food or choose from the gallery's list of approved caterers. Liquor may be served only by an insured caterer and liability insurance is required. A sound system is available, along with two restrooms, a work sink, and back set-up area for caterers. All tables, chairs, heating and cooling elements must be brought in. There is no smoking or candles. A speaker system and CD player are available; other audiovisual equipment must be brought in. Wheelchair accessible.

KLEIN ART WORKS

400 N. MORGAN STREET
CHICAGO, IL 60622
(312) 243-0400, FAX (312) 243-6782
E-MAIL INFO@KLEINART.COM

CONTACT Paul Klein or Monique Martin, directors
BEST FEATURE Sophisticated gallery off the beaten path.
CAPACITY Gallery with outdoor sculpture garden, 125 banquet/reception.
RENTAL FEE Average $800–$1,000 plus refundable damage deposit.
HOURS Tuesday–Saturday, after 5:30 P.M.; Sunday and Monday, all day.
PARKING On-site lot and street parking, neighboring lot available for nominal fee.

Courtesy of Klein Art Works

For entertaining with an artful flare, this gallery with its steel floor and wooden vaulted ceiling is perfect. Rotating exhibits of contemporary abstract art by internationally known and emerging artists decorate the otherwise pristine white walls. At 4,000 square feet, this facility can easily accommodate weddings, recitals, corporate events, wine tastings, and other events. Recognized as one of the best in Chicago, the half-acre sculpture garden boasts dramatic views of the city skyline.

A list of suggested caterers and a small kitchen are available. Liquor may be served, but only with the appropriate permits and insurance. A small number of tables and chairs are included in the rental. Extra equipment will need to be rented. An audio system is available. There is no dancing indoors. The gallery and sculpture garden are wheelchair accessible.

MARS GALLERY

1139 W. FULTON MARKET
CHICAGO, IL 60607
(312) 226-7808
WWW.MARSGALLERY.COM

CONTACT Barbara Gazdik, owner
CAPACITY Main gallery, 75 banquet, 150 reception.
RENTAL FEE Sunday–Friday, $75 per hour; Saturday, $100 per hour.
HOURS Flexible.
PARKING Ample parking at night.

Courtesy of Mars Gallery

Mars Gallery is a beautiful, fully renovated, turn-of-the-century loft located on historic Fulton Market Street in downtown Chicago. The district is unusual and may seem a bit funky to first-timers, but it offers an opportunity to discover a new neighborhood, one that is very similar to New York's SoHo district. The gallery specializes in outsider and pop art. Solid maple hardwood floors and beautiful wood-beamed ceilings combine with the art to create an enchanting environment. The front of the gallery overlooks Fulton Street, and a hallway leads to a large room suitable for a DJ or live band. Off to one side of this room is a built-in bar housed in an antique elevator shaft.

You are free to select your own caterer, or the gallery can provide a list of recommendations. A full kitchen is available for cooking on the premises. The gallery has its own loading dock and is wheelchair accessible. There is a high quality sound system, complete with automatic CD and cassette changers.

PETER MILLER GALLERY

118 N. PEORIA DRIVE
CHICAGO, IL 60607
(312) 226-5391, FAX (312) 226-5441

CONTACT Natalie Domchenko, director
BEST FEATURE Contemporary art.
CAPACITY Entire gallery, 50 banquet, 80
reception.
RENTAL FEE $150 per hour including setup
and breakdown.
HOURS Flexible.
PARKING On the street.

A sophisticated setting in the West
Loop, this gallery exhibits contemporary art in a wide range of media. The
gallery is spacious and has high ceilings, hardwood floors, columns, and tall
windows that let in plenty of light.

You must bring in your own caterer as
well as all equipment, including tables
and chairs. To serve liquor, the caterer
must be licensed and insured. Storage
space is available, but you will need
to schedule deliveries in advance.
The gallery is not air-conditioned. It
is not handicapped accessible. A
VCR and monitor are available, but
additional audiovisual equipment
must be brought in.

Courtesy of Peter Miller Gallery

STUDIO 501

501 W. HURON STREET
CHICAGO, IL 60610
(312) 649-0777, FAX (312) 440-1634
WWW.RONSLEY.COM/STUDIO501.HTML

CONTACT David Epstein, event director
BEST FEATURE Large, versatile loft.
CAPACITY Entire loft, 350 banquet, 500
reception.
RENTAL FEE $5,500.
HOURS 3 P.M.–1 A.M.; other hours by special
arrangement for an additional fee.
PARKING Ample street; public lots; valet.

Having a party in this wonderfully
large loft space is like entertaining on
top of the clouds. The dance floor is in
high gloss white patent vinyl; white
confetti covers the hardwood floors;
miles of white fabric is gracefully
draped over each beam and pipe; and
every wall, beam, and statue is white-
washed. Theatrical lighting and large
windows with dramatic panoramic
views complete the effect.

You may bring your own licensed and
insured caterer or select from their list
of recommendations. There is a small
kitchen with running water. Sound
equipment and a lighting system are
available, but keep in mind that all
entertainment must be approved by
Studio 501. Linens, chairs, tables, and
audiovisual equipment need to be rented. The Ronsley Center will provide all
flowers.

Courtesy of Studio 501

THREE ARTS CLUB OF CHICAGO

1300 N. Dearborn Parkway
Chicago, IL 60610
(312) 944-6250, fax (312) 944-6284

Contact Events marketing director
Best Feature Byzantine courtyard.
Capacity Entire building (ballroom, drawing room, tea room, sitting room, library, and courtyard) 150–200 banquet, 350 reception.
Rental Fee $2,100–$2,500; recitals $200.
Discounts Nonprofit and art groups.
Hours Sunday–Thursday, 8 a.m.–10 p.m.; Friday and Saturday to 11 p.m.
Parking Public lots.

Courtesy of Three Arts Club of Chicago

This landmark building was designed in 1914 and is one of the only remaining residences for young women studying the arts. The ballroom is detailed with gold stenciling and accented by turn-of-the-century chandeliers. It can accommodate 175 guests for a cocktail party and 150 for a sit-down dinner. The highlight of this site is the open-air courtyard accented by a fountain.

Three Arts Club offers in-house catering, but they will also supply referrals for other caterers. Outside caterers are not allowed Monday–Thursday. Tables and chairs are available, as is audiovisual equipment. There is a canopy to enclose the courtyard. Heat for the courtyard is an option in cooler weather. Basic, yet comfortable, overnight accommodations are available during the summer months.

HOTELS

AmeriSuites

Carleton Hotel, The: Philander's Oak Park

Chicago Marriott Downtown

Claridge Hotel, The

Congress Plaza Hotel, The

Doubletree Guest Suites

Doubletree Guest Suites Chicago

Drake Hotel, The

Embassy Suites

Evanston Holiday Inn and Conference Center

Executive Plaza Hotel

Fairmont Chicago

Four Seasons Hotel Chicago

Georgios Hotel and Conference Center

Hilton Chicago

Hilton Oak Lawn Hotel and Conference Center

Holiday Inn Chicago City Center

Holiday Inn Chicago Mart Plaza

Holiday Inn Elk Grove Village

Holiday Inn Elmhurst

Hotel Inter-Continental

Hyatt on Printers Row

Hyatt Regency Chicago

Hyatt Regency O'Hare

Omni Orrington Hotel

Palmer House Hilton

Raphael Hotel, The

Regal Knickerbocker Hotel

Ritz-Carlton, The

Sofitel Chicago O'Hare

Sutton Place Hotel

Westin Michigan Avenue, Chicago, The

Westin River North

AmeriSuites

**1150 Arlington Heights Road
Itasca, IL 60143
(630) 875-1400, fax (630) 875-9756
WWW.AMERISUITES.COM**

Contact Latonya Casas, director of sales
Capacity Elk Grove Room, 50 classroom, 90 theater; Elk Room, 30 classroom, 60 theater; Grove Room, 14 classroom, 25 theater.
Rental Fee $200–$350
Hours Daily, 7 A.M.–10 P.M.
Parking Free lot.

Located near the O'Hare Expo Center, the Odeum Expo Center, and the Rosemont Horizon, this no frills, value hotel has two meeting rooms that can be combined to accommodate up to 90 attendants. AmeriSuites boasts a Meeting Program Guarantee (MPG) that every detail of your meeting will be handled exactly as planned or they will deduct a portion from your bill. The program also offers a discount on a

Photograph by Steve Matteo

business suite for overnight accommodations. The facility is handicapped accessible.

A deluxe continental breakfast is $4.95 per person. Refreshment breaks are $2.50 per person; $3.45 per person with cookies or brownies. There are several menu options available to suit your needs. A white board, flip charts, overhead projector, and screen are available for meetings.

The Carleton Hotel

Philander's Oak Park

**1120 Pleasant Street
Oak Park, IL 60302
(708) 848-4250, fax (708) 848-0537**

Contact Trish Stewart or Joe Hayes
Best Feature Turn-of-the-century decor.
Capacity Grand Ballroom, 175 banquet; main dining room, 100 banquet; Foxboro Room, 70 banquet; Columbian Room, 50 banquet; Barclay Room, 35 banquet.
Rental Fee Based on food and beverage consumption; $50–$300 set-up fee.
Hours Dinners Monday through Saturday; private functions, flexible.
Parking Street, valet, some private lot space.

You would never guess this quaint, historic hotel located on a quiet, tree-lined street in the heart of Oak Park is just six blocks from I-290. The Carleton Hotel

Courtesy of The Carleton Hotel

and its restaurant, Philander's, each have a private party room. The Foxboro Room is located off the hotel's lobby and is decorated in blues and creams with floral wallpaper. The Barclay Room, located in Philander's, looks more like a men's club with historical photos and lots of oak. Jazz music is featured nightly in the comfortable bar. The Carleton Hotel offers 154 unique rooms. The site is wheelchair accessible.

Renowned for seafood, Philander's also offers a select choice of prime steak and chops. Outside caterers are not allowed. You may bring in flowers and wedding cakes or they can be arranged through Philander's. A selection of audiovisual equipment is available and other business services such as photocopying and faxing can be provided.

CHICAGO MARRIOTT DOWNTOWN

540 N. MICHIGAN AVENUE
CHICAGO, IL 60611
(312) 836-0100, FAX (312) 836-6124

CONTACT Bill McCluskey, director of catering sales

CAPACITY Grand Ballroom, 1,800 banquet, 3,000 reception; Chicago Ballroom, 1,000 banquet, 1,800 reception; Avenue Ballroom, 180 banquet, 250 reception; 50 additional rooms available, 10–100; Outdoor ninth-floor patio, 600.

RENTAL FEE Varies.

PARKING Valet.

Courtesy of Chicago Marriott Downtown

Located in the heart of the city on the Magnificent Mile, the Chicago Marriott Downtown offers top-notch service and amenities at an ideal location. A marble and cherry wood lobby welcome guests. The Grand Ballroom, with its 20-foot chandeliered ceilings and neutral tones, is a warm and inviting atmosphere for any social event. The Chicago Ballroom offers an intimate setting, unique and striking décor options, and easily divisible space. Both ballrooms offer exceptional foyer space for prefunction events.

This hotel features excellent cuisine, professional service, and an award-winning culinary staff. Lunches start at $28.95 per person; dinners at $38.95 per person, and hors d'oeuvre receptions at $30 per person. Liquor, tax, and gratuities are additional. Complete wedding packages including hors d'oeuvres, four-hour premium bar, champagne toast, wine during dinner, wedding cake, and continental coffee service start at $92 per person, inclusive of service charge and tax.

THE CLARIDGE HOTEL

1244 N. DEARBORN PARKWAY
CHICAGO, IL 60610
(312) 787-4980 EXT. 621, (800) 245-1258, FAX (312) 787-4069
WWW.CLARIDGEHOTEL.COM

CONTACT Paul Richards, director of food and beverage.

CAPACITY Orchard Room, 50 banquet, 65 reception; three boardrooms, each 8 banquet.

RENTAL FEE Orchard, $500; each boardroom, $175.

HOURS Flexible.

PARKING Next door to the hotel, call for rates.

Photograph by Steve Matteo

Quietly nestled on a tree-lined street, it is hard to believe this hotel is just steps from shopping, entertainment, and dining. Four rooms are available for meetings and banquets. The largest is the Orchard Ballroom, which can accommodate 65 guests for a cocktail reception and 50 for a sit-down dinner. The room has an area for prefunction activities, such as registration or greeting guests, and a raised area that is perfect for the head table. The three boardrooms (Poplar, Sycamore, and Willow) can each accommodate 8 people in conference-style seating and have a separate bathroom. Not all areas are handicapped accessible.

The hotel provides all food. Breakfast buffets are $7.95–$16.95 per person and plated breakfasts start at $12.95. Luncheon buffets run $14.95–$21.95. For hors d'oeuvre receptions you can select four cold and four hot hors d'oeuvres for $16.95 per guest. A four-hour open bar with premium brands is $25.50 per person. Audiovisual equipment is available for rent.

The Congress Plaza Hotel

520 S. Michigan Avenue
Chicago, IL 60605
(312) 427-3800
www.congressplazahotel.com
E-mail dkownacki@congressplaza-hotel.com

Contact Daniel Kownacki, director of food and beverage
Capacity Great Hall, 1,100 banquet, 1,800 reception; Gold Ballroom, 300 banquet, 800 reception; Florentine Room, 150 banquet, 400 reception; Windsor Room, 200 banquet, 300 reception; 16 additional function rooms, 25–125.
Rental Fee Prices based on food and beverage minimums.
Hours Flexible.
Parking Nearby public lots, valet.

The Congress Plaza Hotel takes pride in its rich history and its grand decor. With gold domed ceilings, gold-leafed mold-ings, and candelabra sconces, the Gold Ballroom is the most impressive. The Florentine Room features arched ceilings, inlayed mahogany panels, and ornate sconces. The Great Hall is perfect for large events. The hotel is wheelchair accessible.

All food and beverage is provided by the hotel. Wedding packages start at $89.50 per person and feature a four-hour premium bar, hors d'oeuvres passed butler style, a champagne toast, three-course dinner, wine service with your meal, and a custom designed wedding cake. The catering department offers a wide variety of lunch and dinner menu items. Select the beverage service that best fits your needs, from hosted or cash bars to a complete package. Audiovisual equipment and technical support are available on site.

Photograph by Michael Lapin, courtesy of The Congress Plaza Hotel

Doubletree Guest Suites

211 Butterfield Road
Downers Grove, IL 60515
(630) 971-2000, fax (630) 971-1168

Contact Sheri Brown, catering manager
Capacity Grand Ballroom, 350 banquet, 600 reception; atrium, 250 banquet, 325 reception; boardroom, 18 banquet, 35 reception.
Rental Fee Based on food and beverage consumption.
Discounts Available Fridays and Sundays.
Hours Flexible.
Parking Large lot available.

Courtesy of Doubletree Guest Suites

Create a spectacular atmosphere for your party or event by choosing the Grand Ballroom and six-story atrium at the Doubletree Guest Suites. The Grand Ballroom is 5,200 square feet and is perfect for large events. It can be divided into six rooms for conferences and smaller events that don't require as much space. The atrium has a tropical garden-like atmosphere with palm trees, rattan chairs, marble-style tables, and skylights that fill the room with sunlight during the day and provide a view of the stars in the evening. The boardroom and conference suites are a good option for business meetings.

The Doubletree provides all catering. Lunches start at $15 and dinners at $25 per person. A wedding package is available on Saturday nights for 200 or more starting at $41.50 per person. It includes four-hour hosted bar, dinner, wedding cake, flowers, champagne toast, and a bridal suite. You may bring in a cake, but there is a cutting fee of $1 per person. Extensive audiovisual equipment is available for a fee.

DOUBLETREE GUEST SUITES CHICAGO

198 E. DELWARE PLACE
CHICAGO, IL 60611
(312) 664-1100, FAX (312) 664-8627

CONTACT Janine Silzer, senior catering manager

CAPACITY Lakeshore Ballroom, 180 banquet, 300 reception; Lincoln Park and Wheaton rooms, each 90 banquet, 200 reception; several smaller function rooms.

RENTAL FEE Based on food and beverage consumption.

HOURS Flexible.

PARKING Valet for $22.50 per day.

Courtesy of Doubletree Guest Suites Chicago

Located in the city's beautiful Gold Coast neighborhood—just off the legendary Magnificent Mile and steps from the John Hancock Center, Water Tower Place, and the Oak Street boutiques—the Doubletree Guest Suites is an excellent location for events of all kinds. The elegant, sophisticated Lakeshore Ballroom features stunning chandeliers and is perfect for elegant banquets of up to 300 people. The stately Lincoln Park and Wheaton rooms—each with high ceilings and panoramic windows that provide natural light and beautiful neighborhood views—are suitable for sit-down dinners or luncheons of up to 90 people. The hotel also offers several smaller, more intimate rooms that are ideal for meetings. The Gold Coast Boardroom offers the utmost in comfort and privacy and is perfect for corporate conferences.

Catering for all events is available from the acclaimed Park Avenue Café, named one of the city's best restaurants by the *Chicago Tribune*, *Chicago Sun-Times*, and *Chicago* magazine.

THE DRAKE HOTEL

140 E. WALTON AVENUE
CHICAGO, IL 60611
(312) 787-2200, FAX (312) 787-6324

CONTACT Nicole Quaisser, catering director

CAPACITY Gold Coast Room, 610 banquet, 1,000 reception; Grand Ballroom, 450 banquet, 500 reception; French Room, 300 banquet, 400 reception; Drake Room, 150 banquet, 300 reception; Venetian and Parkside Rooms, 100 banquet, 120 reception; several additional function and meeting rooms.

RENTAL FEE Based on food and beverage consumption.

FOR THE KIDS Charles Dickens' Parade Buffet during the Christmas holidays.

HOURS Flexible.

PARKING Valet; several lots in the area.

Photograph by Garbo Productions, courtesy of The Drake Hotel

The Drake Hotel is the epitome of refinement for business and corporate functions as well as wedding receptions and galas. Its Gold Coast Room has floor-to-ceiling windows that overlook Oak Street beach and Lake Shore Drive. The Grand Ballroom has a stage, a balcony, and a stairway. Smaller function rooms, like the Parkside Room, offer a more intimate setting.

The hotel provides all food and beverage. Wedding packages are available and include a deluxe bridal suite, changing rooms, a private function room, preferred sleeping room rates, a consultation with the chef, and a tasting prior to the event. Flowers, ice carvings, entertainment, and other amenities can be arranged per request. Each room carries a minimum number that must be guaranteed.

Embassy Suites

600 N. State Street
Chicago, IL 60610
(312) 943-3800, fax (312) 642-8132

Contact Director of Sales and Catering
Capacity Atrium, 300 reception; River North Ballroom, 260 banquet, 350 reception; four conference rooms, 36–54 banquet, 50–85 reception; Papagus Restaurant, 225 banquet, 325 reception.
Rental Fee Based on food and beverage consumption; certain minimums must be met.
Hours Flexible.
Parking Valet; indoor garage.

The highlight of this site is the ten-story atrium cascading with foliage and filled with the sound of falling water. The meeting and banquet rooms open off the atrium's second floor. The River North Ballroom is intimate and can be divided up into four smaller rooms: the Old Town, DePaul, Lakeview, and Lincoln Park rooms. The Gold Coast and Printer's Row boardrooms, perfect for small meetings, have long, pale-wood conference tables. Large parties can rent Papagus, a Lettuce Entertain You Restaurant located in the hotel on the street level.

Papagus provides all catering. This Greek Taverna specializes in seafood and Mediterranean cuisine. Family style and customized menus are avialable for all parties. A wedding package with four-hour premium bar, passed hors d'oeuvres, unlimited wine with dinner, customized wedding cake, and complimentary suite is priced from $54 per person.

Evanston Holiday Inn and Conference Center

1501 Sherman Avenue
Evanston, IL 60201
(847) 491-6400, fax (847) 328-3090
www.evanstonholidayinn.com

Contact Abigail Chen, senior sales manager
Capacity Ballroom, 350 banquet, 500 reception; Ridgeville Room, 50 banquet, 60 reception; dining room, 140 banquet.
Rental Fee Based on food and beverage consumption.
For the Kids Will plan theme birthday parties.
Hours Dining room, 6:30 a.m.–10 p.m.; closed 2–5 p.m.
Parking Complimentary attached garage.

Located in downtown Evanston among a variety of shops and restaurants, the Evanston Holiday Inn is walking distance from the Northwestern University campus and Lake Michigan. Specializing in corporate meetings and parties as well as wedding receptions, bar/bat mitzvahs, and other private social functions, the hotel is affordable and has an excellent location. It is handicapped accessible.

The hotel caters all events. Breakfasts are $7.95–$14.95 per person, lunches are $13.95–$19.95 per person, and dinners are $19.95–$27.95 per person. A wedding package is from $38–$45 per person and includes a three-hour open bar, wedding cake, champagne toast, special room rates, and a tasting prior to the event. All audiovisual equipment must be rented through the hotel.

EXECUTIVE PLAZA HOTEL

71 E. WACKER DRIVE
CHICAGO, IL 60601
(312) 346-7100, (800) 621-4005,
    FAX (312) 346-1721
WWW.EXECUTIVE-PLAZA.COM

CONTACT Catering manager
CAPACITY Cloud 39 Penthouse, 170 banquet, 350 reception; Picasso Room, 90 banquet, 125 reception; Chicago Room, 70 banquet, 100 reception; Illinois Room, 80 banquet, 125 reception; nine additional rooms, 40 banquet, 50 reception.
RENTAL FEE Varies based on room reserved and food and beverage consumption.
DISCOUNTS Special weekend and corporate rates available.
HOURS Daily, 24 hours.
PARKING Valet for a fee.

Courtesy of Executive Plaza Hotel

The Executive Plaza Hotel has a quiet, dignified presence. You can choose from fifteen different meeting rooms, accommodating groups from 10 to 300. Located 39 floors above the city, the Cloud 39 Penthouse offers a magnificent view and can make your wedding reception or banquet a memorable affair. The additional function rooms located on the fourth and seventh floors do not offer as dramatic views, but they are ideal locations for meetings.

The hotel will provide food and beverages. Specialty refreshment breaks are approximately $10.50 per guest. Lunches are $11.50–$22.50 per person and dinners are $24.50–$37.50 per person. Several dinner buffets start at $13.50 per person. There are also several bar options, but there is a charge of $75 per bartender and $60 per cashier is required for a cash bar.

FAIRMONT CHICAGO

200 N. COLUMBUS DRIVE
CHICAGO, IL 60601
(312) 565-8000, FAX (312) 856-1011
WWW.FAIRMONT.COM

CONTACT Director of catering and convention services
CAPACITY Imperial Ballroom, 1,500 banquet, 2,000 reception; International Ballroom, 900 banquet, 1,200 reception; Moulin Rouge, 380 banquet, 550 reception; Gold Room, 350 banquet, 500 reception; Crystal Room, 300 banquet, 350 reception; State Room, 140 banquet, 150 reception; Ambassador Room, 90 banquet, 125 reception; three additional rooms, 30–80.
RENTAL FEE Based on food and beverage consumption.
HOURS Flexible.
PARKING Indoor valet parking.

Courtesy of Fairmont Chicago

The Fairmont's towering 45 stories offer sweeping views of Lake Michigan, Grant Park, the Chicago Yacht Club, and the Illinois Center Golf Course. The 62,000 square foot banquet space, can accommodate almost any type of event. The Imperial Ballroom and the International Ballroom are ideal for gala affairs or large corporate meetings. The Imperial Ballroom has 20-foot ceilings, perfect acoustics, and closed-circuit TV. For smaller gatherings, you can choose one of 10 function rooms, such as the Moulin Rouge, located off the hotel's main lobby. This hexagon-shaped room is decorated as a tribute to Toulouse Latrec's favorite nightclub in 19th-century Paris.

The hotel caters all events. A kosher kitchen is available. Convention space is available for more than a hundred 8 x 10-foot booths. Every meeting room has built-in audiovisual and closed-circuit TV capabilities, and sound and light equipment. For bridal parties there are changing rooms available. The site is wheelchair accessible.

FOUR SEASONS HOTEL CHICAGO

120 E. DELAWARE PLACE
CHICAGO, IL 60611
(312) 280-8800, FAX (312) 280-9184
WWW.FOURSEASONS.COM

CONTACT Jamie Breslin, director of catering

CAPACITY Grand Ballroom, 730 banquet, 1,200 reception; State Room, 150 banquet, 150 reception; Delaware Room, 90 banquet, 110 reception; LaSalle Room, 80 banquet, 110 reception; Walton Room, 50 banquet, 70 reception; Oak Room, 18 banquet; five additional boardrooms, each 12 banquet, 20 reception.

RENTAL FEE Varies according to day, time, and space.

HOURS Daily, 24 hours.

PARKING Valet; self-park.

Located in the heart of the Magnificent Mile, Four Seasons Hotel Chicago exudes elegance, from its grand staircase to the attention paid to guests. Four Seasons has a total of 22,000 square feet of dedicated conference and banquet space. The stylish Grand Ballroom is perfect for an upscale reception or benefit. On floors 32 to 46, five fully equipped, soundproof boardroom suites provide exceptional views.

The hotel's catering department will take care of all your food and beverage needs. Wedding and meeting packages are available. Lunches are priced from $36, dinners from $48. Catering staff can assist you in selecting photographers, florists, or entertainment. A wide array of audiovisual equipment is available on-site for rental. A minimum of 30 persons is required for all food functions. For smaller groups, private dining rooms are available in the Season's restaurant.

Courtesy of Four Seasons Hotel Chicago

GEORGIOS HOTEL AND CONFERENCE CENTER

8800 W. 159TH STREET
ORLAND PARK, IL 60462
(708) 403-1100, FAX (708) 403-1105

CONTACT Banquet coordinator

BEST FEATURE Two-story skylight over the large dance floor.

CAPACITY Grand Ballroom, 1,200 banquet; smaller meeting rooms.

RENTAL FEE Based on food and beverage consumption.

HOURS Flexible.

PARKING Free lot.

Courtesy of Georgios Hotel and Conference Center

Georgios D La Parco is an elegant banquet facility located in the southern suburbs. The Grand Ballroom features an oversized parquet dance floor that is situated underneath a two-story-high skylight. The room is adorned with crystal chandeliers and decorated in silver and mauve. Additional rooms are available to accommodate board meetings or other small events. For overnight accommodations Georgios Comfort Inn offers lavish suites.

Georgios will cater all events. Dinner packages are $36–$47 per person and include gratuity and service charges, four-hour open bar, four-course meal, wine with dinner, wedding cake, and floral centerpieces. This package is for Saturday evenings only. For Friday, Sunday, and afternoon events subtract $8 from the package price.

HILTON CHICAGO

720 S. MICHIGAN AVENUE
CHICAGO, IL 60605
(312) 922-4400, FAX (312) 663-6538
WWW.HILTON.COM

CONTACT Sales Manager
CAPACITY International Ballroom, 1,880 banquet, 2,528 reception; Grand Ballroom, 1,100 banquet, 1,400 reception; Continental Ballroom, 900 banquet, 1,159 reception; seven private dining rooms, 20–80 banquet; additional meeting/function rooms.
RENTAL FEE No charge for party rooms when food and liquor are served; fees for meeting rooms vary according to size and event.
HOURS Flexible.
PARKING Hotel garage for 500 cars at $22 per day or valet for $24 per day.

With more than 234,000 square feet of meeting, banquet, and exhibition facilities, the Hilton Chicago is one of the biggest meeting and convention hotels in the area. The International Ballroom is

Courtesy of Hilton Chicago

the largest room. The beautiful two-tiered Grand Ballroom is quite elegant with mirrored accents, 34-foot ceilings, and crystal chandeliers. State-of-the-art sound and lighting systems are in all of the ballrooms. Each ballroom can be divided into smaller rooms for break-out sessions. Other rooms can accommodate

smaller functions. The hotel is handicapped accessible.

The hotel caters all events. There are several menu options that can be tailored to suit your event. A wide selection of audiovisual equipment is available. There is a 500-person minimum to reserve the ballrooms on Friday and Saturday nights.

HILTON OAK LAWN HOTEL AND CONFERENCE CENTER

CICERO AVENUE AT 94TH STREET
OAK LAWN, IL 60453
(708) 425-7800, FAX (708) 425-8111
WWW.OAKLAWNHILTON.COM

CONTACT Brian Anderson, director of catering
CAPACITY Grand Ballroom, 550 banquet, 1,000 reception; Astoria Ballroom, 350 banquet, 750 reception; Windsor, 120 banquet, 300 reception; North, 250 banquet, 500 reception; Center and South each, 100 banquet, 250 reception; additional function rooms, 40 banquet, 75 reception.
RENTAL FEE Varies by room and menu.
HOURS Flexible.
PARKING Free lot.

The Hilton Oak Lawn is an excellent site for business meetings and social affairs of all sizes. The 20,000 square feet of flexible meeting space includes 15 beau-

Courtesy of Hilton Oak Lawn Hotel and Conference Center

tifully appointed multipurpose rooms. Host your event in one of the two ballrooms, the large reception foyer, or the breathtaking Tower Room with its spectacular view of the Chicago skyline.

The hotel will provide all food and beverages. A breakfast buffet starts at $13.95 per person. A hot lunch buffet starts at $20.50 per person and a cold buffet starts at $15.95 per person.

Dinner packages include a four-hour open bar and start at $34.50 per person. On Saturday evenings, the Grand Ballroom requires a minimum of 275 guests and the Astoria Ballroom requires a minimum of 175 guests. Other functions may also require a minimum. Audiovisual equipment is available. The hotel is handicapped accessible.

Holiday Inn Chicago City Center

300 E. Ohio Street
Chicago, IL 60611
(312) 787-6100, fax (312) 787-6259

Contact Sales manager
Best Feature Convenient location.
Capacity LaSalle Ballroom, 550 banquet, 700 theater; Ontario Room, 100 banquet, 120 theater; State Rooms combined, 90 banquet, 120 theater; Superior Rooms combined, 100 banquet, 150 theater; Michigan Room, 40 banquet, 50 theater.
Rental Fee Varies depending on room and function.
Hours Flexible.
Parking Pay garage.

This award-winning hotel offers a convenient location just two blocks east of Michigan Avenue, 500 guest rooms, sports center, and 16,000 square feet of

Photograph by Steve Matteo

meeting space. The spacious LaSalle Ballroom can accommodate up to 700 guests and is equipped with state-of-the-art audiovisual equipment. The room is decorated in moss green and dusty rose, with numerous chandeliers that add a touch of elegance. There are 11 meeting rooms with ample prefunction space for registration, receptions, and refreshment breaks. During the warmer months, the fifth floor pool and sun desk is a popular choice for outdoor events with up to 100 guests.

The hotel will prepare a variety of menu options. Special meeting packages with snacks and drinks start at $9 per person. Luncheons average $15.50 per person and dinners average $24 per person. A deluxe dinner buffet is $28 per person, not including liquor. A two-hour bar package is $16 per person for house brands. An 18 percent gratuity and tax will be added.

Holiday Inn Chicago Mart Plaza

350 N. Orleans Street
Chicago, IL 60654
(312) 836-5000, fax (312) 836-0341
www.holidayinnchicago.com
E-mail sales@martplaza.com

Contact Lisa Albin, director of catering
Best Feature Views of downtown Chicago and convenient to the Merchandise Mart.
Capacity Wolf Point Ballroom, 300 banquet, 600 reception; Sauganash Ballroom, 700 banquet, 1,000 reception; Marquette Room, 150 banquet, 200 reception; additional rooms, 30–100 banquet, 60–165 reception.
Rental Fee Based on food and beverage consumption.
Discounts Available during January and February.
Hours Flexible.
Parking On-site at the Apparel Center for 1,200 cars, $18 per car with in/out privileges.

Courtesy of Holiday Inn Chicago Mart Plaza

Adjacent to the Chicago Merchandise Mart along the Chicago River, this hotel has 16 meeting/function rooms (more than 20,000 square feet), including a 7,600 square-foot ballroom and a 4,320 square foot ballroom. The Wolf Point Ballroom has breathtaking views of the city and the river. The Sauganash Ballroom can be divided into two rooms. All functions rooms have state-of-the-art audiovisual capabilities and are equipped with high-speed Internet access. The facility is wheelchair accessible.

The hotel caters all events. Luncheons start at $18.95 per person. Dinners start at $23.95 per person. Wedding package and social packages include a four-hour bar, four-course meal, and bud vases on the tables. Package prices are determined according to your budget and party needs. The catering staff will assist you with entertainers, photographers, florists, and additional suppliers. A full range of audiovisual equipment is available for rent.

HOLIDAY INN ELK GROVE VILLAGE

1000 BUSSE ROAD
ELK GROVE VILLAGE, IL 60007
(847) 437-6010, FAX (847) 806-9369

CONTACT Director of sales
BEST FEATURE Proximity to O'Hare Airport.
CAPACITY Woodfield Ballroom, 250 banquet, 550 theater; Elk Room, 40 banquet, 100 theater; Grove Room, 35 banquet, 50 theater; Village Room, 64 banquet, 65 theater.
RENTAL FEE Based on food and beverage consumption.
HOURS Flexible.
PARKING On-site lot.

Photograph by Steve Matteo

Just six miles from O'Hare Airport, this hotel and conference center is convenient for out-of-town guests. Hosting business functions is the hotel's specialty. There are six function rooms that are perfect for almost every type of meeting and comfortably seat five to 600 guests. With 4,559 square feet of space and a festival ambiance, the Woodfield Ballroom is also well-suited for receptions and private parties. For overnight stays, there are 159 guest rooms that have been recently renovated.

The Holiday Inn has a full service catering staff who will work to customize your event. For a minimum of 20 guests you can have a buffet breakfast starting at $7.95 per person. Lunch buffets are approximately $11.95 per person or you can select plated lunches beginning at $8.95 per person. Dinners range from $15.95–$24.95 per person. Three bar options are available—cash, hosted, and open. A four-hour open bar with house liquor is $17 per person. Extensive audiovisual equipment is available on a rental basis.

HOLIDAY INN ELMHURST

624 N. YORK ROAD
ELMHURST, IL 60126
(630) 279-1100, FAX (630) 279-4038
WWW.BRICTON.COM/HOLIDAY

CONTACT Judith Kelly, catering sales manager
BEST FEATURE Proximity to O'Hare airport.
CAPACITY Oak Ballroom, 150 banquet, 300 reception; Gazebo, 40 banquet, 80 reception.
RENTAL FEE Based on food and beverage consumption.
HOURS Flexible.
PARKING Lot on-site valet.

Courtesy of Holiday Inn Elmhurst

If you are looking for a location that is convenient to the airport and has more than 2,200 square feet of space, the Holiday Inn at Elmhurst is a good bet. The Oak Ballroom when used in its entirety will accommodate up to 150 banquet, 300 reception. The ballroom can be divided into three smaller rooms—Chestnut Room, Maple Room, and Walnut Room—each with a maximum capacity of 40 banquet, 80 reception, and 35 classroom/meeting. Adjacent to the Oak Ballroom is the Gazebo, which is ideal for small weddings, cocktails, or meetings. The hotel is handicapped accessible.

The hotel will prepare all meals. A premeeting coffee break with an assortment of pastries is $3.95 per person; the Health Break includes veggies, fruit, granola bars, and juices for $5.95 per person. Lunch options range from $8.95–$13.95 per person. A dinner buffet for a minimum of 30 people is $19.95 per person. Wedding packages start at $27.95 per person. A four-hour open bar with house brands is $13.95. Audiovisual equipment is available. Complimentary shuttle to and from O'Hare.

HOTEL INTER-CONTINENTAL

505 N. MICHIGAN AVE.
CHICAGO, IL 60611
(312) 944-4100, FAX (312) 944-2024

CONTACT Melissa Dorin, Elinor Tweed, Lisa Zimbler, or Steve Thompson
CAPACITY Grand Ballroom, 600 banquet, 1,000 reception; Ballroom of the Americas, 300 banquet, 500 reception; Renaissance Ballroom, 330 banquet, 500 reception; King Arthur's Court, 250 banquet, 400 reception.
RENTAL FEE $100 plus, depending on square footage needed.
HOURS Flexible.
PARKING Valet; six public lots.

This lavish hotel, renovated in 1986, was originally opened in 1929 as the Medinah Men's Athletic Club. Each ballroom is decorated in a different style. The modern Ballroom of the Americas, with 4,000 square feet, is decorated in rich jewel tones. The Renaissance Room

Courtesy of Hotel Inter-Continental

is a re-creation of a massive opulent French Ballroom with floor-to-ceiling burled elm wall paneling and five crystal and gold leaf chandeliers. The two-story elliptical Grand Ballroom has a 12,000-pound Baccarat crystal chandelier that hangs from the 21-foot ceiling.

The hotel caters all events with an extensive menu of nouveau American cuisine. Everything is a la carte. A four-course dinner ranges from $50–$70 per person, lunches from $25–$35 per person, and breakfast from $13–$30 per person. A four-hour deluxe open bar is $28 per person, with premium liquor $24 per person. A wide selection of audiovisual equipment is available.

HYATT ON PRINTERS ROW

500 S. DEARBORN STREET
CHICAGO, IL 60605
(312) 986-1234
WWW.HYATT.COM

CONTACT Fred Schroeffel, director of sales
BEST FEATURE National Historic Landmark building.
CAPACITY Burnham Room, 72 banquet, 75 reception; LeBaron Foyer, 36 banquet, 50 reception; Shedd Room, 45 banquet, 65 reception; Suite 722, 72 banquet, 75 reception.
RENTAL FEE Based on food and beverage consumption.
HOURS Flexible.
PARKING Event parking $8.

The Hyatt on Printers Row is an intimate, European boutique-style hotel with historic landmark status. By joining and rehabilitating two century-old buildings the hotel captures a spirit of a

Photograph by Mitchell Canoff courtesy of Hyatt on Printers Row

bygone age. The lobby is decorated in mahogany paneling, and veined marble, and can be used as a reception area for events in adjacent function rooms. The Burnham Room is the largest space at 1,107 square feet. Smaller events are held on the second floor in the Shedd Room, which has windows overlooking Federal Street, and in Suite 722, which offers sweeping views of the Harold Washington Library and the Auditorium Theatre.

All catering is done by the award-winning Prairie restaurant, which is designed in the style of Frank Lloyd Wright. The restaurant features cuisine from the heartland with a contemporary flair. Buffets start at $12 per person for breakfast, lunches at $24 per person, and dinners at $29. Alcohol is charged on a consumption basis. A large selection of meeting equipment is available for rent.

HYATT REGENCY CHICAGO

151 E. WACKER DRIVE
CHICAGO, IL 60601
(312) 616-6840, FAX (312) 616-6928

CONTACT Gary Marr, director of catering at (312) 616-6807 or Lynn Byard, wedding coordinator at (312) 616-6843

CAPACITY Grand Ballroom, 2,775 banquet, 3,000 reception; Regency Ballroom, 1,200 banquet, 1,800 reception; Columbus Hall, 1,200 banquet, 1,800 reception; Wacker Hall, 6,000 reception; several additional rooms.

RENTAL FEE Varies.

HOURS 24 hours.

PARKING Valet; covered parking in hotel garage.

Courtesy of Hyatt Regency Chicago

The Hyatt Regency Chicago has just completed a renovation of its 2,019 guest rooms as well as its meeting, reception, and ballroom space. The Grand Ballroom can be divided into six or eight rooms or used as a single room. A large foyer connects the Grand Ballroom to the Columbus Hall. Wacker Hall is a 70,000-square-foot exhibit hall that can accommodate booths up to 17 feet high. Fifty smaller meeting rooms are also available.

The hotel caters all events. You may bring in a wedding cake, but there is a cake cutting fee. Audiovisual equipment can be rented through the hotel.

HYATT REGENCY O'HARE

9300 W. BRYN MAWR AVENUE
ROSEMONT, IL 60018
(847) 696-1234, FAX (773) 380-1438

CONTACT Pam Davidheiser, associate director of catering

BEST FEATURE Just minutes from the airport.

CAPACITY Grand Ballroom, 5,300 reception; 61 individual meeting rooms.

RENTAL FEE Prices based on food and beverage consumption.

DISCOUNTS 10 percent off for Friday and Sunday evening weddings.

HOURS Flexible.

PARKING Pay garage and lot.

Courtesy of Hyatt Regency O'Hare

Adjacent to the Rosemont/O'Hare Exposition Center and minutes from O'Hare International Airport, this hotel features 61 individual function rooms with more than 100,000 square feet of meeting space. A spectacular atrium lobby welcomes guests into the hotel.

The Grand Ballroom is an elegant setting that is perfect for receptions up to 5,300 and banquets up to 3,000. Of importance to meeting planners is the enclosed skywalk which provides access to Rosemont/O'Hare Exposition Center.

The hotel caters all events. Their wedding package includes a five-hour open bar, hors d'oeuvres, ice carving, champagne toast, four-course dinner, wedding cake, bubble votive candles, and a honeymoon suite. The package ranges from $53.95–$62.95 per person. Indian and Kosher catering also available. The catering staff will assist you in additional services such as entertainment, flowers, and decorations. Complete business services are available at the Hyatt Business Center.

OMNI ORRINGTON HOTEL

1710 ORRINGTON AVENUE
EVANSTON, IL 60201
(847) 866-1218, FAX (847) 475-3957

CONTACT Director of catering
CAPACITY Grand Ballroom, 400 banquet, 800 reception, 1,000 theater; Heritage Ballroom, 120 banquet, 200 reception, 150 theater; Evans Room, 80 banquet; Mulford Room, 50 banquet.
RENTAL FEE None with full catering service.
HOURS Flexible.
PARKING Public lots or valet.

Courtesy of Omni Orrington Hotel

The Omni Orrington Hotel has been an Evanston tradition for more than 60 years. The guest rooms, conference rooms, ballrooms, and lobby areas are all newly redecorated. For gala events the Grand Ballroom accommodates up to 1,000 people. Its majestic sweeping staircase accentuates any wedding, dinner dance, or special occasion. For business meetings and private parties, the Omni Orrington Hotel offers a choice of function rooms. There is more than 12,000 square feet of conference and meeting space.

The hotel provides food and beverage. Their Storybook Wedding package includes overnight accommodations, four-hour open bar with wine and champagne, six different hors d'oeuvres, salad, entree, dessert, and wedding cake for $69–$79 per person, lunches from $9.50–$19.50, and dinners from $19.95–$28.95. Service charges and tax are not included. Audiovisual equipment is available for rent.

PALMER HOUSE HILTON

17 E. MONROE STREET
CHICAGO, IL 60603
(312) 422-1325
WWW.HILTON.COM

CONTACT Jane Vukovich, director of catering
CAPACITY Grand Ballroom, 1,000 banquet, 1,400 reception; State Ballroom, 360 banquet, 500 reception; Red Lacquer Room, 500 banquet, 800 reception; Crystal Room, 120 Banquet, 200 reception; Empire Room, 350 banquet, 500 reception; Adams and Monroe rooms, each 320 banquet, 400 reception; 68 additional meeting rooms for 5–1,900.
RENTAL FEE None with food service. Without meals: Grand Ballroom, $4,500 daytime, $2,500 evening; State Ballroom, $2,000 daytime, $1,500 evening. Others negotiable.
RENTAL FEE None with food service. Without meals: grand Ballroom, $6,000 daytime, $4,000 evening; State Ballroom, $3,000 daytime, $2,000 evening.
HOURS Flexible.
PARKING Nearby lots; valet.

Courtesy of Palmer House Hilton

The Palmer House's center of activity is the burgundy, rose, and honey-colored lobby which is surrounded by a balcony, perfect for private receptions. The State and Grand ballrooms can be combined to seat 1,360. The Red Lacquer Room can accommodate up to 800. For smaller events or meetings, there are the Adams and Monroe rooms. A conference center has meeting rooms and business services. The facility is handicapped accessible.

The hotel caters all events and can arrange almost any type of meeting or event. Dinner prices range from $45–$60 per person; lunches $35–$45 not including liquor. Wedding packages are $100–$130 per person and there are also packages for proms and bar/bat mitzvahs. Audiovisual equipment is available for rental.

THE RAPHAEL HOTEL

201 E. DELAWARE PLACE
CHICAGO, IL 60611
(312) 443-5000, FAX (312) 943-9483

CONTACT Director of Catering
BEST FEATURE Small elegant European-style hotel.
CAPACITY Boardroom I, 12 banquet; Boardroom II, 32 banquet, reception 50, theater 35.
RENTAL FEE $175 per day.
HOURS Flexible.
PARKING Valet $14 for up to 3 hours, $14 additional for 3–5 hours.

Courtesy of The Raphael Hotel

Surrounded by the towering glass structures of downtown Chicago, tucked away in a quiet corner of the historic Gold Coast, is this quaint hotel with Old World charm and European amenities. Different from a large hotel with its conventions and crowds, The Raphael is quiet and unobtrusive. Two stylish, modern boardrooms offer a comfortable setting for small strategy sessions or private dinners of up to 50 guests.

The Raphael Restaurant will provide food and beverages for your event. A full breakfast ranges from $7.25–$11.95; lunches and dinners range from $6.95–$17.95. Menu items include salads, sandwiches, and entrees such as Atlantic salmon, London broil, and pesto primavera. There is a wide selection of desserts to top off your event: White-chocolate Raspberry Mousse, Mochachino Pie, and Spumoni Pie. The catering staff will assist in arranging a menu to fit your needs.

REGAL KNICKERBOCKER HOTEL

163 E. WALTON PLACE
CHICAGO, IL 60611
(312) 751-8100

CONTACT Director of sales and marketing
CAPACITY Crystal Ballroom, 350 banquet, 740 reception; Continental Room, 110 banquet, 200 reception; Tower East and Tower West, each 150 banquet, 250 reception; Heritage Room, 80 banquet, 150 reception; 7 conference parlors, each 20–40 banquet, 30–70 reception; Executive boardroom, 16 banquet.
RENTAL FEE $300–$400 depending on food and beverage consumption.
DISCOUNTS Sunday discounts.
HOURS Flexible; 24 hours.
PARKING Valet; self-park $10.25–$22.

The Regal Knickerbocker Chicago opened in the mid-20s as the Davis Hotel. The hotel has since been restored and renamed. Just off the lobby is the Crystal Ballroom, which is lined with mirrors and wrapped with a balcony. The elegant Continental Room is connected to the balcony and can be used as a receiving or cocktail area.

All catering is done by the hotel; banquet dinners range from $27.95–$37 per person, and lavish buffets from $35–$50. Luncheon prices range from $18.95–$24.95. Drink package prices are $9–$27 per person. Wedding packages start at $85, and include open bar, cake, and changing rooms. A microphone and podium come with the rooms, and all other meeting equipment is available on a rental basis.

Courtesy of Regal Knickerbocker Hotel

The Ritz-Carlton

160 E. Pearson Street
Chicago, IL 60611
(312) 266-1000, fax (312) 573-5053
www.fourseasons.com

Contact Director of catering
Capacity Ballroom, 500 theater, 1,200 reception; nine additional meeting rooms, 40–130 banquet, 75–200 reception.
Rental Fee Negotiable.
Hours Flexible.
Parking Valet, $27 per day; self-park, $17.50 per day.

The Ritz-Carlton (a Four Seasons Hotel) is among the world's premier luxury hotels. It has received numerous awards including, the AAA Five Diamond Award for 18 consecutive years, Condé Nast *Traveler*'s "Third Best City Hotel in the World," and *Successful Meetings* magazine's Pinnacle Award.

Located on the Magnificent Mile atop prestigious Water Tower Place, The Ritz-Carlton is perfect for elegant, grand events. The 9,000-square-foot ballroom features a dramatic 400,000-piece lead crystal chandelier. Nine distinctive meeting salons—from the vibrant Glass Room overlooking the Spanish-tiled terrace to the Versailles Suite and recently renovated Vendome—provide intimate surroundings for mid-sized functions.

Dining room chef Sarah Stegner recently was named "Best Chef in the Midwest" in 1998 by the James Beard Foundation, and the dining room was named "Best Restaurant in Chicago" by *Gourmet* magazine in 1996. Meeting planners receive on-site assistance from the hotel's conference concierge. Audiovisual equipment must be rented.

Sofitel Chicago O'Hare

5550 N. River Road
Rosemont, IL 60018
(847) 678-9440, fax (847) 678-5710
www.sofitelchicagoohare.com
E-mail
castellano_barbara@accor-hotels.com
or stewart_kelly@accor-hotels.com

Contact Barbara Castellano or Kelly Stewart, catering managers
Capacity Le Grand Ballroom, 400 banquet; conference center with four meeting rooms, 200; additional 12 meeting/function rooms, 10–70.
Rental Fee Ceremony charge is a minimum of $350. No fee for ballroom when used for a wedding. Meeting room rental varies according to the number of guest rooms utilized by the group.
Hours Flexible.
Parking Self-parking; valet.

The Sofitel Chicago O'Hare is romantic in every sense of the word, with its traditional French decor, exquisite cuisine, and ambiance. Le Grand Ballroom is grand in every sense of the word. It can be used in its entirety for large events, or it can be divided into two rooms for smaller events. Whether you visit Sofitel Chicago O'Hare for important business, a festive affair, or an intimate celebration, you'll find the experience a perfect pleasure.

Banquets have their own personality, featuring an appetizing menu of traditional favorites and irresistible French specialties. Audiovisual equipment is available. The hotel is handicapped accessible.

SUTTON PLACE HOTEL

21 E. BELLEVUE PLACE
CHICAGO, IL 60611
(312) 266-2100, FAX (312) 266-2141
WWW.SUTTONPLACE.COM
E-MAIL INFO_CHI@SUTTONPLACE.COM

CONTACT John Paulsen, director of catering
BEST FEATURE Walls of windows provide dramatic backdrop.
CAPACITY Bellevue Room, 100 banquet, 150 reception; Bellevue Bar, 100 reception; third level, 200 banquet, 300 reception; fourth level, 100 banquet, 135 reception.
RENTAL FEE Based on food and beverage consumption.
HOURS Flexible.
PARKING Secured lot; valet.

Situated in the Gold Coast district, the Sutton Place Hotel offers striking interiors and is an elegant choice for private events. There are seven banquet or meeting rooms available for social gath-

Courtesy of The Sutton Place Hotel

erings or company meetings. The Bellevue Room is a private setting with walls of windows that overlook the posh Gold Coast neighborhood. The third floor can be reserved in its entirety for larger receptions and dinners or separated to form three smaller banquet rooms. The distinctive Board Room offers an octagonal, 18-seat mahogany table, a floor-to-ceiling arched window, and full audiovisual and online capabilities.

The hotel provides all food and beverage. Their wedding package starts at $76.95 per person and includes one-hour premium open bar before dinner, butler-passed hors d'oeuvres, champagne toast, wine with dinner, a three-course meal, three-hour open bar after dinner, and a honeymoon suite. Special room rates for out-of-town guests are provided, but they are based on availability.

THE WESTIN MICHIGAN AVENUE, CHICAGO

909 N. MICHIGAN AVENUE
CHICAGO, IL 60611
(312) 943-7200, FAX (312) 649-7456

CONTACT Ken Severin, director of catering/convention services.
CAPACITY Wellington Ballroom, 840 banquet, 1,500 reception; Cotillion Ballroom, 520 banquet, 700 reception; Consort Room, 180 banquet, 225 reception; Governor's Suite, 120 banquet, 200 reception; 17 other rooms, 10–100 banquet, 10–150 reception.
RENTAL FEE Based on food and beverage consumption.
HOURS Daily, 24 hours.
PARKING $19.75 for six hours in hotel garage; valet available.

The Westin Michigan Avenue, Chicago offers intimate rooms for social events as well as meeting facilities for groups of

Courtesy of The Westin Michigan Avenue, Chicago

all sizes. The Wellington Ballroom has two large chandeliers and a large foyer overlooking Delaware Street. The elegant Cotillion Ballroom and the Consort Room have floor-to-ceiling windows that provide excellent views of Michigan Avenue. The Governor's Suite has its own reception area, coat check, and restrooms.

The hotel caters all events. Wedding packages include a bridal suite, two changing rooms, and honeymoon promotion (subject to rules and availability). An in-house audiovisual company will take care of your meeting needs and a full-service business center is available.

WESTIN RIVER NORTH

320 N. DEARBORN STREET
CHICAGO, IL 60610
(312) 744-1900, FAX (312) 527-2664
WWW.WESTINRIVERNORTH.COM

CONTACT Ken Regnier, director of catering and conference services

BEST FEATURE Chef Jean Pierre Henry, award-winning French chef.

CAPACITY Grand Ballroom, 700 banquet, 1,200 reception; Promenade Ballroom, 240 banquet, 300 reception; Astor Ballrooms, 220 banquet, 375 reception; ten conference rooms, 5–50.

RENTAL FEE None when minimum food and beverage requirements are met.

HOURS Flexible.

PARKING Public lots; valet.

Westin River North is located on the edge of the Chicago River in the trendy River North neighborhood. There is an air of calm at this hotel that sets it apart from the hustle and bustle of other downtown venues, even though the hotel is located just blocks from State Street and the Magnificent Mile. Rich wood, Italian marble, and warm colors welcome guests. The Grand Ballroom offers access to an outdoor terrace with a fabulous view of the river and the Chicago skyline. The Astor Ballrooms also offer spectacular views. The hotel is handicapped accessible.

Lunches start at $32 per person, dinners at $45 per person, and hors d'oeuvre receptions at $55 per person. Liquor, service charges, and tax are additional. Customized wedding packages are available starting in the low $100s per person. A complete line of audiovisual equipment and services is available through the hotel's in-house audiovisual department.

Mansions and Community Houses

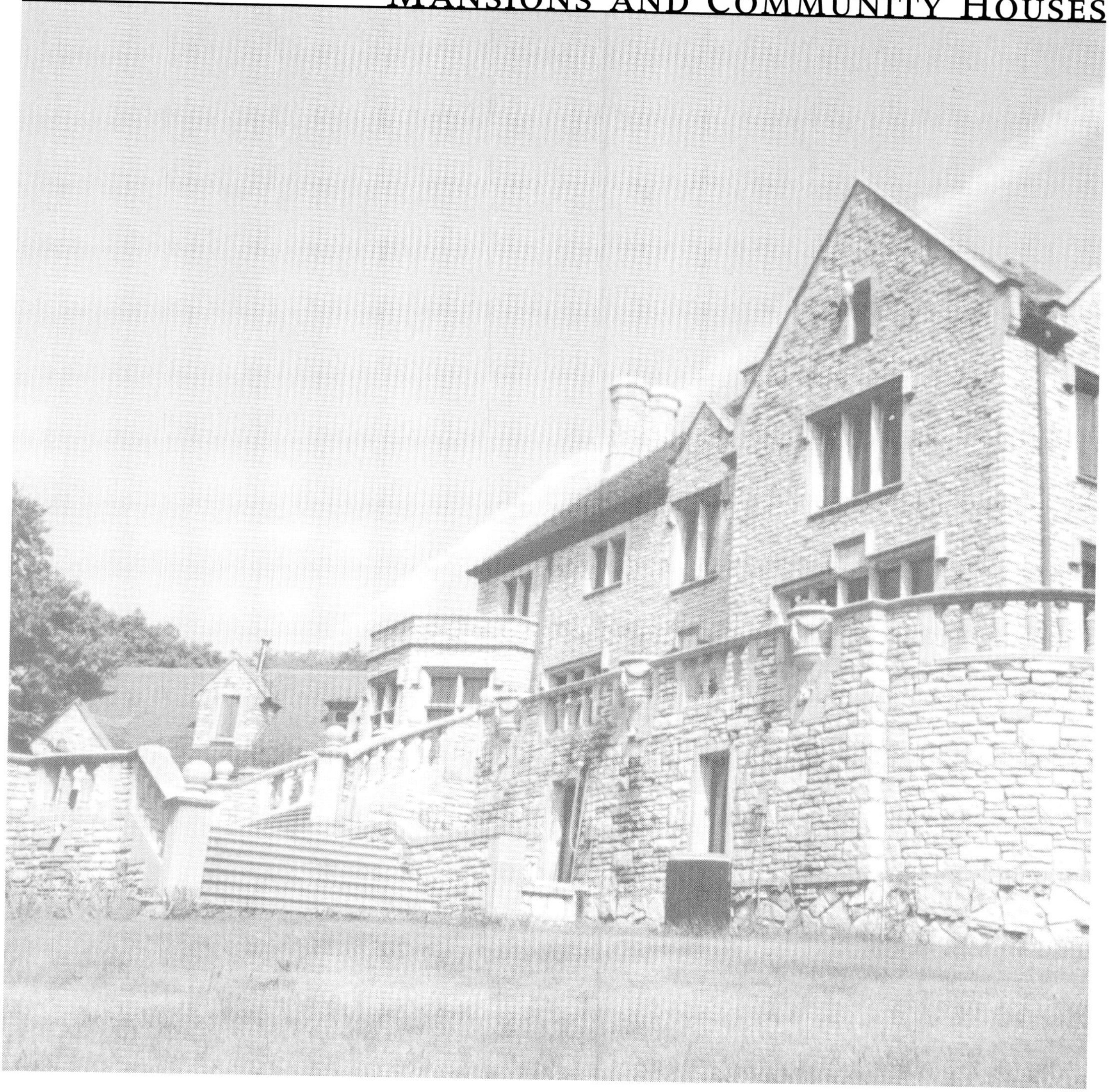

MANSIONS AND COMMUNITY HOUSES

Berger Park Cultural Center

Country Squire

Danada House

Drexel-Kenwood Mansion

Francis J. Dewes Mansion

Gorton Community Center

Highland Park Community House

Jacob Henry Mansion, The

Lexington House, The

Meyer's Castle

North Lakeside Cultural Center

Patrick C. Haley Mansion

Redfield Center at the Grove

Wheeler Mansion, The

Winnetka Community House

BERGER PARK CULTURAL CENTER

6205 N. Sheridan Road
Chicago, IL 60660
(312) 742-7871 or (312) 742-PLAY
WWW.CHICAGOPARKSDISTRICT.COM
E-MAIL PERMITS@CHICAGOPARKDISTRICT.COM

CONTACT Sue Nicotera

CAPACITY Living Room, 40 banquet, 50 reception, 45 theater; Dining Room, 20 banquet, 30 reception, 25 theater; Sun Room, 30 banquet, 40 reception, 35 theater; Ball Room, 40 banquet, 50 reception, 45 theater; Coach House, 40 banquet, 50 reception, 45 theater.

RENTAL FEE Per 2-hour period: Dining Room, $80; Sun Room $90; Living Room, Ball Room, and Coach House, $100. Corporate meetings, per 2-hour period: Living Room, Dining Room, and Sun Room, $35; Ball Room and Coach House, $50.

DISCOUNTS Nonprofit rates available.

HOURS Meetings: weekdays only, 9 A.M.–9 P.M.; weddings: Saturday–Sunday, 9 A.M.–5 P.M.

Photograph by Brook Collins, courtesy of Chicago Park District

PARKING Street.

Berger Park honors Albert E. Berger (1900–1950), a native Chicagoan and Edgewater resident. Berger lived with his family in one of the mansions that lined Sheridan Road before 1950.

He was an early proponent of developing street-end beaches on Chicago's north side.

The mansion features hardwood floors, original woodwork, and antique light fixtures. Small rooms are perfect for intimate gatherings.

COUNTRY SQUIRE

ROUTES 120 AND 45
GRAYSLAKE, IL 60030
(847) 223-0121
WWW.CSQUIRE.COM

CONTACT Gus or Karen

CAPACITY Six private rooms plus an outdoor garden accommodating 10–400.

RENTAL FEE Based on food and beverage consumption.

DISCOUNTS Seasonal and off-peak discounts available.

HOURS Flexible. Restaurant hours are Tuesday–Friday, 11 A.M.–10 P.M.; Saturday, 11 A.M.–11 P.M.; Sunday, 10 A.M.–9 P.M.; closed Monday.

PARKING Lot on grounds.

Courtesy of Country Squire

Previously the residence of Wesley Sears, this Tudor-style mansion was converted into a restaurant in the mid-50s. The banquet facility was added in 1986 and has a more modern feel. The impressive rotunda welcomes guests with its six-foot Bavarian crystal chandelier accenting a double staircase that leads to hospitality, VIP, and brides' rooms on the second floor. The banquet rooms on the main level overlook the beautifully manicured courtyard, where garden ceremonies may be held.

The restaurant handles all catering.

Seven-course dinners with a bar package range from $42.50 per person, without liquor from $24.50 per person. Wood dance floors, risers for head tables, a stage, and display tables are available. Most audiovisual equipment must be rented. Country Squire is handicapped accessible.

DANADA HOUSE

DANADA FOREST PRESERVE
3 S. 501 NAPERVILLE ROAD
WHEATON, IL 60187
(630) 668-5392, FAX (630) 668-5497

CONTACT Jill Ludvigsen, executive director
BEST FEATURE Elegant home.
CAPACITY Main floor (living room, dining room, library, solarium, porch, and terrace), 110 banquet, 150 reception.
RENTAL FEE Weekends starting Friday at 3 P.M., $700 for eight hours; weekdays, $100–$250 for four hours.
HOURS Saturday 8 A.M.–4 P.M. and 4 P.M. to midnight; Sunday–Friday, 8 A.M.–midnight.
PARKING Lot for 220 cars on grounds.

Courtesy of Danada House

The Danada Forest Preserve was formerly the estate of *Dan* and *Ada* Rice, hence the name "Danada." The Forest Preserve of DuPage County purchased the 780 acres, complete with a 19-room estate house, outbuildings, and a 23-stall Kentucky-style stable in 1980. The house is spacious and decorated in neutral tones. There are fireplaces in many of the rooms and French doors separating one room from another.

The Danada House will provide a list of nine approved caterers, and with special approval others may be used.

Linens, dishes, glassware, and flatware must be brought in. There are 130 chairs and some tables available. Liquor must be served by a licensed, insured caterer. There is no cash bar and smoking is not permitted.

DREXEL-KENWOOD MANSION

4801 S. DREXEL BOULEVARD
CHICAGO, IL 60615
(773) 373-3120, FAX (773) 373-4506

CONTACT Valerie Steel Holden, executive director
CAPACITY Ballroom, 150 banquet; first floor, 125 banquet; second floor parlor, 60 banquet.
RENTAL FEE From $1,250.
DISCOUNTS Members may be eligible for a discount.
HOURS Flexible.
PARKING Valet and street.

Photograph by Stuart-Rodgers Ltd., courtesy of Drexel-Kenwood Mansion

This beautifully restored Victorian mansion located in a historic district was built in 1901 and originally served as the private residence of Moses Born, who was a pioneer in the tailoring trade. This towering greystone is surrounded by landscaped gardens and a walkway lined with greenery. The notable features are nine wood-burning fireplaces, mosaic flooring, original woodwork with hand-carved moldings, and artistically scrolled ceilings. The breathtaking ballroom has beautiful hardwood floors and fainting alcoves. The mansion is not handicapped accessible.

You can select your own caterer or choose from the mansion's list of preferred caterers. Security is provided. Meeting equipment must be brought in. Audiovisual equipment is offered at a charge.

FRANCIS J. DEWES MANSION

503 W. WRIGHTWOOD
CHICAGO, IL 60614
(773) 477-3075, FAX (773) 477-3708
WWW.DEWESMANSION.COM
E-MAIL DEWESMANSION@JUNO.COM

CONTACT Marta Michulka, general manager
BEST FEATURE Designed to be a miniature Palace of Versailles.
CAPACITY Entire house, 350 reception, 250 banquet.
RENTAL FEE $3,500–$6,500.
DISCOUNTS For qualified nonprofit organizations.
HOURS 8:00 A.M.–midnight.
PARKING Optional valet service; public parking garage one block south of property.

You don't have to fly to Paris to host your next event at Versailles. The Francis J. Dewes Mansion, conveniently located in Chicago's Lincoln Park neighborhood, is a miniature version of the real thing. This landmark home was built in 1896 for German brewer Francis Dewes at a reported cost of $1,000,000. The mansion offers three elegant floors, and both traditional and contemporary décor. During the summer, the canopy-covered courtyard is ideal for wedding ceremonies, receptions and corporate events.

There is an approved list of caterers to choose from. A fully equipped kitchen is available and there is also a small kitchen adjacent to the ballroom. The mansion is air-conditioned. Complimentary dressing rooms are available to wedding clients.

Courtesy of Francis J. Dewes Mansion

GORTON COMMUNITY CENTER

400 E. ILLINOIS ROAD
LAKE FOREST, IL 60045
(847) 234-6060
WWW.GORTONCENTER.ORG
E-MAIL GORTON7@JUNO.COM

CONTACT Pixie Reinholz, rental coordinator
CAPACITY Community Room, 125 banquet, 175 reception; Auditorium, 350 performance; Green Room, 55 reception; seven additional meeting rooms varying in size.
RENTAL FEE Community Room, $550; Auditorium, $300; Green Room, $200; kitchen use, $50.
DISCOUNTS Reduced rates available for Lake Forest and Lake Bluff residents and nonprofit groups.
HOURS Open daily, 9 A.M.–midnight.
PARKING Adjacent and nearby lots.

The completely renovated Gorton Community Center offers a formal Community Room, with a marble fire-

Courtesy of Gorton Community Center

place, two walls of tall windows, a high ceiling, hardwood floors, and cream walls and drapes. The connecting Green Room is decorated in a living room style. The Auditorium features drive-through direct entry, new theatrical lighting and sound systems, an ample stage, a theatrical green room and staging area, and plenty of comfortable seating. An adjacent park is available for use.

The Center provides a kitchen facility, but you need to supply your own caterer, serving equipment, place settings, and linens. Liquor service requires a city license and insurance. Tables, folding chairs, and overhead and slide projectors are available. The Auditorium and Community Room have retractable screens, and several rooms have darkening shades. The entire building is air-conditioned and handicapped accessible.

HIGHLAND PARK COMMUNITY HOUSE

**1991 SHERIDAN ROAD
HIGHLAND PARK, IL 60035
(847) 432-1515, FAX (847) 432-7083**

CONTACT Debbie Smith, executive director
BEST FEATURE Private home atmosphere.
CAPACITY Main auditorium/ballroom, 200 banquet, 300 theater; living room, 40–50; lower level, 100.
RENTAL FEE $175 per hour (minimum six-hour rental required).
HOURS Monday–Friday, 9 A.M.–noon; or by appointment.
PARKING City lot; street parking.

Courtesy of Highland Park Community House

This Colonial Revival home was built in 1924 and has been completely renovated but still features charming antique furnishings. Unlike many public and private facilities that share their space with several groups at the same time, the Highland Park Community House is intimate in size, making it possible to host up to 200 guests in your own "private home" (or up to 300 in theater-style seating). Smaller groups can enjoy the comfort of our living room which seats up to 50 people. The elegant ballroom features a vaulted ceiling, vintage light fixtures, hardwood floors, and graceful arched windows overlooking our Heritage Garden. There's also a professional-level performance space.

Bring in your own caterer, linens, china, glassware, and flatware. A cash bar requires a city license, but liquor is allowed. The club has tables and white wood chairs for up to 200 guests. Audiovisual equipment must be brought in. The facility is handicapped accessible.

THE JACOB HENRY MANSION

**20 S. EASTERN AVENUE
JOLIET, IL 60433
(815) 722-2465, FAX (815) 722-3455
WWW.JACOBHENRYMANSION.COM
E-MAIL JHM1873@AOL.COM**

CONTACT Susan Pritz-Bornhofen, marketing director
CAPACITY Inside, 200–250 banquet, 400 reception; outside, 250–300.
RENTAL FEE Based on food and beverage consumption.
HOURS Office hours, 9 A.M.–5 P.M., or by appointment.
PARKING On premise.

Courtesy of The Jacob Henry Mansion

The Jacob Henry Mansion offers a delightful blend of past and present. The magnificent staircase is one of the highlights of this location. The main floor has elaborate carving and the black walnut and oak is hand-rubbed to a satin finish. Each room throughout the mansion centers around a different theme. Wedding ceremonies can be held in the room of your choice. The main Drawing Room seats 90. The Old Central Church can also be used for weddings. Listed on the Illinois State Registry, the Church seats 500 people and features its original 2200 bellow pipe organ for your use with an approved organist.

The mansion caters all events. Packages including buffet and four-hour open bar begin at $26 per person. No smoking is permitted. A full line of audiovisual equipment is available.

THE LEXINGTON HOUSE

**7717 W. 95TH STREET
HICKORY HILLS, IL 60457
(708) 598-4150, FAX (708) 598-2533**

CONTACT Marge Duda, manager
BEST FEATURE A 2,900-square-foot dance floor.
CAPACITY Entire facility, 1,000 banquet.
RENTAL FEE Varies depending on function.
HOURS Daily, 6 A.M.–1 A.M.
PARKING Ample parking.

Courtesy of The Lexington House

This elegant colonial mansion, located 25 minutes from the Loop and 35 minutes from O'Hare airport, is a 9,500-square-foot banquet facility with ample seating for 100 to 1,000. The Lexington House offers a country club atmosphere and traditional charm. Its polished hardwood dance floor is larger than many of the banquet rooms available at other locations. The Presidents Room has rubbed mahogany furniture and pictures of many U.S. presidents; it can be used in conjunction with the main room if additional space is required.

The Lexington House provides all food and beverages. Luncheons range from $7–$9.50 per person and dinners from $11–$20 per person. Liquor packages can be included. There is a stage, a large movie screen, and a complete sound system. The facility is handicapped accessible.

MEYER'S CASTLE

**1370 JOLIET STREET
DYER, IN 46311
(773) 646-5613 OR (219) 865-8452, FAX (219) 865-9169
WWW.MEYERSCASTLE.COM
E-MAIL INFO@MEYERSCASTLE.COM**

CONTACT Elizabeth Urquiza
BEST FEATURE 12-acre majestic estate.
BEST PARTY Hosted the governor of Indiana.
CAPACITY Estate with two large pavilions, 350 banquet, 500 reception.
RENTAL FEE $1,300.
HOURS Flexible, up to midnight.
PARKING Valet only.

Courtesy of Meyer's Castle

Meyer's Castle, one of seven historical castles registered in the U.S., is the private estate of Sergio and Elizabeth Urquiza. It was built in 1928 as a replica of a Scottish castle. A circular driveway leads to the castle, which sits at the top of a hill. Wedding ceremonies are held on the main patio, overlooking a breathtaking arched walkway bordered with majestic oak trees. For cocktails, dinner, and dancing there are two temperature-controlled pavilions that overlook a pond complete with swans. An aviary with exotic birds is in the center of the gardens and is open for guests to tour. Located 35 minutes from downtown Chicago, this castle only seems to be of another world. The castle is handicapped accessible.

Catering is provided by the castle's chef. Dinners start at $21.50 per person, brunches at $25 per person, and hors d'oeuvre receptions at $19.50 per person. Serving equipment, chairs, tables, and linens are provided. Audio equipment must be brought in.

NORTH LAKESIDE CULTURAL CENTER

6219 N. SHERIDAN ROAD
CHICAGO, IL 60660
(773) 743-4477

CONTACT Special events/rental coordinator
CAPACITY Two floors, 80 banquet, 200 reception; first floor only, 75 conference.
RENTAL FEE First and second floors combined $250 per hour; first floor $200 per hour (four-hour minimum required); individual room rates are flexible.
DISCOUNTS Nonprofit organizations receive half rates.
HOURS Tuesday, Wednesday, Friday, 10 A.M.–6 P.M., or call for an appointment.
PARKING Can be arranged for a fee.

This simple, but exquisite mansion is located in Berger Park on the lakefront. The rich wood-paneled foyer with its mosaic tile fireplace leads into the living and dining rooms. On the second floor there are three galleries and a sun room.

Courtesy of North Lakeside Cultural Center

A kitchen has household-size appliances and three small rooms for food preparation. The site is handicapped accessible.

Membership is required for rental: $25 for individuals, $40 for families, and $50 for nonprofits. A list of licensed caterers is provided and liquor is allowed indoors only. All serving and meeting equipment must be brought in, except tables and chairs. Ten rectangular tables and 100 folding chairs are available. An additional $20 per hour is required for security guards for groups of more than 50, if alcohol is served, or if both floors are rented. Use of the park grounds requires a park district permit. Audiovisual equipment must be brought in.

PATRICK C. HALEY MANSION

17 S. CENTER STREET
JOLIET, IL 60436
(815) 726-6800, FAX (815) 726-6891
WWW.PATRICKHALEYMANSION.COM

CONTACT Toni Reithofer
CAPACITY 350 banquet, 500 reception.
RENTAL FEE $300–$1,200 for five and a half hours, includes tented area.
HOURS Monday–Friday, 9 A.M.–5 P.M., or by appointment.
PARKING Free lot.

Built in 1891, this impressive Victorian limestone mansion, features original hardwood floors, stained-glass windows, intricate friezes, and six fireplaces. Your guests can enjoy a cocktail in one of the mansion's many rooms then enter the elegant tented facility adjacent to the mansion for dinner. The tented area has crystal chandeliers, impressive accent lighting, and a view of the lush Victor-

Courtesy of Patrick C. Haley Mansion

ian gardens. The sound of fountains, beautiful flowers, a gazebo, and white wooden chairs make this a perfect setting for a wedding reception or gala. The tent is heated so it can be rented in any season.

The mansion will cater all events.

Dinners range from $38–$48 per person. The staff will work with you to select a menu or a package that meets your needs as well as your budget. There is a private tower room and suite available for the bridal party. The facility is handicapped accessible.

Redfield Center at the Grove

1421 Milwaukee Avenue
Glenview, IL 60025
(847) 298-0095, fax (847) 299-0571

Contact Carol Di Lorenzo, rental coordinator
Best Feature National Historic landmark, located on nature preserve.
Best Party Theme weddings.
Capacity 13-room house can accommodate 125 guests.
Rental Fee Weekend rentals, $900 for four hours, $100 per additional hour.
Hours Monday–Thursday, 8 A.M.–11 P.M.; Friday–Sunday, 8 A.M.–midnight.
Parking For 65 cars.

Courtesy of Redfield Center at the Grove

This house was built in 1929 and has the picturesque look of a Northern European country villa. Its design reflects the style and tastes of an earlier age with carved wood purlins, beamed cathedral ceilings, patterned fireplace tiles, and leaded-glass windows. You will have exclusive use of the entire house and the beautiful grounds that surround it. A gazebo completes the storybook setting. The Great Room is suitable for large meetings and smaller break-out rooms are available for discussion groups.

You may bring your own caterer. A kitchen equipped with a ten-burner gas stove, double-door refrigerator, and large sink is available. The center will provide tables, folding chairs, and a podium. Audiovisual equipment is also available. A park district employee will be on the premises during your event.

The Wheeler Mansion

2020 S. Calumet Avenue
Chicago, IL 60616
(312) 945-2020, fax (312) 945-2021
www.wheelermansion.com
E-mail mail@wheelermansion.com

Contact Debra Seger, General Manager
Best Feature The only fully-restored 1870 mansion in Chicago available for rental.
Capacity Outdoor gardens, 75–100; Dining Room, 30 banquet; Great Hall, Dining, and Great Room, 55 reception.
Rental Fees $3,500 for 2–4 hours.
Hours Flexible.
Parking Included with rental; valet available.

Courtesy of The Wheeler Mansion

Winner of the Chicago Landmark Preservation Excellence Award, this boutique hotel opened in 1999 and is located two blocks from Lake Michigan, the Museum Campus, and McCormick Place Convention Center. This circa 1870 mansion contains fine antiques and precious art from around the world. The Wheeler Mansion is situated on a half-acre of beautiful outdoor gardens perfect for weddings or special events of 75–100 guests. The private dining hall features old world elegance for a sit-down dinner of 30 guests.

Elegant cocktail and hors d'oeuvres parties can be held in the Great Hall, dining, and Great Room for a maximum capacity of 55 guests. The Wheeler Mansion, "Chicago's Best Kept Secret," is perfect for a special corporate meeting, party, or event.

Winnetka Community House

620 Lincoln Avenue
Winnetka, IL 60093
(847) 446-0537
WWW.WINNETKACOMMUNITYHOUSE.ORG
E-MAIL RENTALS@WINNETKACOMMUNITY-
HOUSE.ORG

CONTACT Facility supervisor
CAPACITY Main reception room, 100 banquet,
120 reception; Auditorium, 150 banquet,
225 reception; Theatre Auditorium, 350.
RENTAL FEE Reception halls, $1,000–$1,500;
meeting and party rooms, $100–$500; the-
ater auditorium, $350 and up. Fees vary
according to time, space and type of use.
DISCOUNTS For nonprofit organizations.
FOR THE KIDS Party packages available.
HOURS 8 A.M.–11 P.M.
PARKING Street parking or parking lot.

Built in 1911, this impressive Gothic-
style building is an ideal site for a variety of receptions. For parties of 75–120,
the Tyrrell Room is an ele-
gant space. Larger parties
can use Matz Hall, an air-
conditioned auditorium
with a stage. Several smaller rooms are available.
Summer receptions are held
in the flower-filled Arches
Garden. The site is handicapped accessible.

Select your own insured
caterer. A fully-equipped
kitchen is available. Audiovisual equipment, tables,
chairs, and dinner place
settings are available for
rental at a nominal fee.
Liquor is permitted, but
insurance is required. A
nonrefundable deposit of
30 percent and security fee
is required with reserva-
tion. Not all rooms are air-
conditioned.

Courtesy of Winnetka Community House

MUSEUMS, CULTURAL CENTERS, AND ZOOS

Arabian Knights Farms: "The Barn"

Art Institute of Chicago, The

Balzekas Museum of Lithuanian Culture

Brookfield Zoo

Chicago Botanic Garden

Chicago Children's Museum

Chicago Cultural Center

Chicago Historical Society

Cuneo Museum and Gardens

DuSable Museum of African-American History

Field Museum, The

Friendship Park Conservatory

Garfield Park Conservatory

Harold Washington Library Center

International Museum of Surgical Science

Irish American Heritage Center

John G. Shedd Aquarium

Kohl Children's Museum

Lincoln Park Zoo

Museum of Broadcast Communications

Museum of Contemporary Art

Museum of Science and Industry

Newberry Library

Scholl College of Podiatric Medicine

South Shore Cultural Center

Spertus Institute of Jewish Studies

Terra Museum of American Art

ARABIAN KNIGHTS FARMS

"The Barn"

6526 CLARENDON HILLS ROAD
WILLOWBROOK, IL 60514
(630) 325-3482 OR (630) 327-7399,
FAX (630) 325-3559
WWW.AKFENTERTAINMENT.COM
E-MAIL VCI@VCICONSULTING.COM

CONTACT Michael D. Vena, vice president and
director of marketing
CAPACITY Picnic grounds, 2,500; in-door
heated show arena, 400 banquet,
800–1,000 reception; sky box and conference room, 25–75 banquet.
RENTAL FEE Varies.
FOR THE KIDS A petting zoo, pony rides, ele-
phant rides, moon bounce, nine-hole miniature golf, sand art, clowns, and more.
HOURS Varies by event; day and evening
hours available.
PARKING On-site for 200 cars, additional
1,000 via shuttle.

Courtesy of Arabian Knights Farms

"The Barn" at Arabian Knights Farms is situated on 10 beautiful acres with apple trees, cedar barns, and a variety of options for your next event. The picnic grounds, with tables for 300, include a gazebo and reviewing stand bleachers that overlook the one-eighth-mile track. A sky box overlooks the heated show area.

Arabian Knights Farms can cater a two-hour buffet for your event. Liquor is allowed with a permit. There is a small set-up fee for indoor tables and chairs. Music is allowed inside only. Meeting equipment is available. The Barn's facilities are handicapped accessible. Large groups (1,000 or more) require a first aid station and traffic control through Willowbrook police department.

THE ART INSTITUTE OF CHICAGO

111 S. MICHIGAN AVENUE
CHICAGO, IL 60603
(312) 443-3530
WWW.ARTIC.EDU

CONTACT Special events department
CAPACITY Chicago Stock Exchange Trading
Room, 350 banquet, 600 reception;
McKinlock Court Garden, 500 reception;
Chagall Windows and Gunsaulus Hall, 250
reception; Restaurant on the Park, 225 ban-
quet, 300 reception; private dining rooms,
100 banquet; Arthur Rubloff Auditorium,
949 theater.
RENTAL FEE $2,200–$10,000, plus catering.
HOURS 6 P.M.–11:30 P.M.
PARKING Garage parking nearby.

The Art Institute of Chicago has long been recognized as one of Chicago's greatest cultural assets. Appropriate for many types of parties from an elegant banquet dinner in the wood-paneled

Courtesy of The Art Institute of Chicago

Chicago Stock Exchange Trading Room to a summer cocktail party in the garden with its alfresco setting. The site is handicapped accessible.

All events are catered by the Institute. Lunches start at $22.50 per person. Complete dinner packages start at $80 per person. Weddings and wedding receptions are not allowed. The Rubloff Auditorium and other meeting rooms have full audiovisual capabilities. All types of amenities are available for an additional cost. A $2,000 nonrefundable deposit is required.

Balzekas Museum of Lithuanian Culture

6500 S. Pulaski Road
Chicago, IL 60629
(773) 582-6500, fax (773) 582-5133

Contact Stanley Balzekas, Jr., president
Capacity Amber Ballroom, 230 banquet;
Crystal Ballroom, 30 banquet.
Rental Fee Call for rates.
Discounts For cultural organizations.
For the Kids A children's museum area
available.
Hours Flexible.
Parking 75-car lot behind the building.

Give your guests an opportunity to get acquainted with Lithuanian culture and history by hosting an event at the Balzekas Museum. Lithuanian art—oil paintings, tapestries, and sculptures—provides a nice backdrop for business receptions, meetings, educational pro-

Photograph by Steve Matteo

grams, children's parties, and other special events. Rental of either the Amber Ballroom or the smaller Crystal Ballroom includes access to the main exhibit hall on the first floor. The Amber Ballroom is decorated in "Lithuanian gold" (shades of amber), with mirrored pillars, black chairs, and floral carpeting. The Crystal Ballroom is appropriate for groups of 20

to 30. The museum is handicapped accessible.

You may bring your own caterer (subject to the museum's approval) or the museum will arrange for catering. A full kitchen is available. Rental fee includes use of tables, chairs, tableware, dance floor, sound system, and concert grand piano. Audiovisual equipment is available.

Brookfield Zoo

3300 S. Golf Road
Brookfield, IL 60513
(708) 485-0263 ext. 355, fax (708) 485-3509
www.brookfieldzoo.org
E-mail catering@brookfieldzoo.org

Contact Christopher Juday, sales manager
Capacity 75–300 banquet, 100–1,000 reception; 150–10,000 for picnics.
Rental Fee $350–$2,500 depending on venue(s).
Hours Picnics during zoo hours, 9:30 a.m.–5:30 p.m.; all other events after 6 p.m.
Parking Self-park.

The Brookfield Zoo offers a wide range of events in their world-renowned habitat exhibits, where you can see giraffes move gracefully across the savannah at Habitat Africa, experience a rainforest thunderstorm in Tropic World, walk under the ocean in the Living Coast. Treat your guests to a guided Sunset Safari Tour through the 215 acres of

Photograph by Jim Schulz, courtesy of Brookfield Zoo

award-winning grounds. Following martinis with the monkeys and appetizers with the aardvarks, an elegant dinner can be served, complete with tuxedo- or safari-clad waitstaff.

Enjoy world-class cuisine prepared by the expert in-house caterer. Brookfield

Zoo has distinctive surroundings for awards and dancing. Corporate events can be arranged in secluded outdoor picnic areas under private tents. Unique meeting rooms are available with state-of-the-art audiovisual equipment. The zoo is handicapped accessible.

Chicago Botanic Garden

1000 LAKE COOK ROAD
GLENCOE, IL 60022
(847) 835-8370, FAX (847) 835-4484
WWW.CHICAGOBOTANIC.ORG
E-MAIL RENTAL@CHICAGOBOTANIC.ORG

CONTACT Megan Beasley, facility rental
CAPACITY McGinley Pavilion, 340 banquet
with dance floor, 400 reception; The Great
Hall, 250 banquet with dance floor, 500
reception, 400 theater style; Linnaeus
Room, 70 banquet and reception, 40 class-
room, 75 theater; Alsdorf Auditorium, 225
theater; cocktail reception sites include the
Rose Terrace, English Walled Garden, North
Gallery; additional rooms available.
RENTAL FEE McGinley Pavilion, $2,500–
$6,000; The Great Hall, $2,000–$3,500;
Linnaeus Room, $500–$1,500; Alsdorf Audi-
torium, $500–$1,500.
HOURS All evenings, Monday–Friday day-
time, and some weekend daytimes.
PARKING Free visitor lots; valet available.

Courtesy of Chicago Botanic Garden

The Chicago Botanic Garden is a renowned living museum—a site for all seasons. From the romance of a Rose Terrace to the drama of a lakeside tented pavilion or a skylit Great Hall, the Botanic Garden's distinctive surroundings are sure to make your event absolutely unique. From meetings for 3 to elegant dinners for 300, the staff can help you choose the perfect location. For corporate events, meetings, and conferences, the Botanic Garden offers a breath of fresh air.

The Botanic Garden has selected a full-service catering team. Custom tours, musical entertainment, speakers, and more can be arranged. Audiovisual equipment is available on site. The Botanic Garden prides itself on taking care of all the details—so you can relax and smell the roses.

Chicago Children's Museum

NAVY PIER
700 E. GRAND AVENUE
CHICAGO, IL 60611
(312) 527-1000, FAX (312) 527-9082
WWW.CHICHILDRENSMUSEUM.ORG

CONTACT Corporate events department
CAPACITY Entire museum, 1,500 reception;
Great Hall, 250 banquet; Waterfront Room
(limited basis), 150 theater; exhibit gal-
leries, 57,000 square feet.
RENTAL FEE $5,000 entire museum for
4 hours.
DISCOUNTS For nonprofit organizations.
HOURS Tuesday–Sunday, after 5 P.M.;
Monday, all day except on school holidays.
PARKING Discounts at Navy Pier garages.

Courtesy of Chicago Children's Museum

Located on historic Navy Pier, Chicago Children's Museum features exhilarating views, contemporary architecture, and three floors of hands-on exhibits. The Great Hall, featuring 40-foot ceilings and a sweeping arched glass window, is a spectacular backdrop for any event. Exploration of the exhibits is encouraged—design a flying machine in the Inventing Lab, create a 20-foot fountain in Waterways, or build a fort in Under Construction.

Caterers must be selected from the museum's preferred list. To secure a date the museum requires a certificate of insurance, a 50 percent facility rental fee deposit, and a refundable $1,000 security deposit. A film projector, overhead projector, and screen are available from the museum; additional audiovisual equipment must be brought in. No smoking is allowed inside the museum or in Navy Pier. Handicapped accessible.

CHICAGO CULTURAL CENTER

78 E. WASHINGTON STREET
CHICAGO, IL 60602
(312) 744-3094

CONTACT David Ortega, event coordinator

CAPACITY Preston Bradley Hall, 360 banquet, 700 reception; G.A.R. Memorial Hall, 220 banquet, 550 reception; G.A.R. Rotunda, 80 banquet, 300 reception; Claudia Cassidy Theater, 294; meeting rooms, 100 banquet.

RENTAL FEE Preston Bradley Hall and G.A.R. Memorial Hall, luncheon/dinner, Monday–Thursday $1,250, Friday–Sunday $2,500; G.A.R. Rotunda, luncheon/dinner, Monday–Thursday $1,000, Friday–Sunday $2,000; Claudia Cassidy Theater, Monday–Thursday $300, Friday–Sunday $500; meeting rooms $500 each. Rental fees apply to four-hour events, with a surcharge for longer events.

DISCOUNTS For nonprofit organizations.

HOURS Open daily, 9 A.M. to midnight.

PARKING Grant Park North Garage and other nearby lots.

Photograph by Chicago Photographic Co., courtesy of Chicago Cultural Center

Chicago Cultural Center is a spectacular site for parties, meetings, and receptions. The majestic Bradley Hall, houses the world's largest Tiffany dome. The G.A.R. Rotunda is a more intimate space. The area opens to the stately G.A.R. Memorial Hall, which boasts a 30-foot-high ceiling and tremendous arches. The theater offers a proscenium stage, as well as lighting and sound equipment. Also available for rental are two functional meeting rooms.

You must supply your own caterer. Liquor is allowed with liability insurance. There are 550 chairs, 30 small and 30 large round tables, and 20 buffet tables available. All party supplies, kitchen equipment, and meeting equipment must be brought in. Wedding ceremonies are not allowed.

CHICAGO HISTORICAL SOCIETY

1601 N. CLARK STREET
CHICAGO, IL 60614
(312) 642-5035 EXT. 216, FAX (312) 266-2077
WWW.CHICAGOHISTORY.ORG
E-MAIL EVENTS@CHICAGOHISTORY.ORG

CONTACT Ally Allman, corporate events

CAPACITY Atriums, 350 banquet, 500 reception; Portrait Gallery, 90 banquet, 200 reception; East Lobby, 50 banquet; Uihlein Plaza, 600 banquet, 800 reception; Wrigley Gallery, 250 reception; Big Shoulders Café, 60 banquet, 110 reception; Arthur Rubloff Auditorium, 440 theater style.

RENTAL FEE $4,250–$9,250; for weddings: peak season, $3,800; off-peak, $2,850–$3,600; Café, conference rooms, and auditorium range from $50–$1,500.

DISCOUNTS For members and nonprofit organizations.

HOURS Monday–Sunday, 8 A.M.–5 P.M. and 5:30 P.M.–midnight.

PARKING Discounted parking for 440 cars.

Courtesy of the Chicago Historical Society

When your guests arrive at the Chicago Historical Society's main entrance, greet them in a three-story atrium lined with dozens of artifacts from the museum's collection. Its Arthur Rubloff Auditorium is a fully operational theater that can handle a shareholders' meeting, a training session, a concert, or other gathering. Conference rooms and the auditorium come equipped with audiovisual equipment. For smaller events there is the Big Shoulders Café.

Rental fees include coat check, security, maintenance, plus the assistance of the Society's staff. Charges for food, drink, and service are separate and must be arranged with one of the Society's caterers.

CUNEO MUSEUM AND GARDENS

1350 N. MILWAUKEE AVENUE
VERNON HILLS, IL 60061
(847) 362-3042, FAX (847) 362-4130
WWW.LAKE-ONLINE.COM/CUNEO

CONTACT Special events manager
BEST FEATURE European-style mansion.
BEST PARTY Filming site for *My Best Friend's Wedding* with Julia Roberts.
CAPACITY: Mansion, 65 banquet; tent and grounds, 400 reception; pool room, 70 banquet, 100 reception.
RENTAL FEE Call for fees.
HOURS Tuesday–Saturday, 6 P.M.–12 A.M.; closed January.
PARKING Space for 200 cars on grounds; larger events require valet parking.

This 32-room Venetian-style mansion was built in 1914 for Commonwealth Edison founder Samuel Insull and purchased in 1937 by John Cuneo, printing magnate and art collector. In 1991 the

Photograph by Barry Dowe, courtesy of Cuneo Museum and Gardens

mansion was converted into a museum, boasting an outstanding collection of 17th-century tapestries, fine Italian Old Master paintings, and period continental furniture. Large groups can dine and dance on the museum grounds that cover 75 acres and feature a pool (no swimming allowed), outdoor stage, formal gardens, and fountains. A smaller

party may wish to enjoy a formal dinner in the frescoed dining rooms.

Choose from their list of preferred caterers. The museum hosts only one event at a time. Ceremonies are permitted on the property. There is no air-conditioning in the museum and no smoking is allowed.

DUSABLE MUSEUM OF AFRICAN-AMERICAN HISTORY

740 E. 56TH PLACE
CHICAGO, IL 60637
(773) 947-0600, FAX (773) 947-0677
WWW.DUSABLEMUSEUM.ORG

CONTACT Tracey Williams, special events manager
CAPACITY Harold Washington Skylight Gallery, 200 reception; Illinois Black Legislative Auditorium, 466 theater; main lobby and new auditorium, 400 reception; original auditorium, 200 reception, 100 theater; meeting rooms, 30–50.
RENTAL FEE From $500–$3,500 for 3 hours with a per hour charge for additional time.
DISCOUNTS For nonprofit organizations.
HOURS Flexible.
PARKING Lot; street.

Founded in 1961, DuSable Museum was the first nonprofit museum dedicated to

Photograph by Steve Matteo

the collection, documentation, preservation, study, and dissemination of the history and culture of African-American descendants. In 1993 the Harold Washington Wing was opened with a 466-seat auditorium, a sculpture garden, and four galleries were completed, adding much more space for private events.

The museum has a list of approved caterers, but you may bring in your own if they are licensed by the City of

Chicago. Kitchen facilities are available. Serving equipment must be brought in, but a variety of audiovisual equipment, video conferencing, and satellite conferences can be rented from the museum. All events are expected to harmonize with the character and mission of the museum. Weddings are not allowed, however wedding receptions can be held after museum hours. Wheelchair accessible.

THE FIELD MUSEUM

1400 S. LAKE SHORE DRIVE
CHICAGO, IL 60605
(312) 665-7600, FAX (312) 665-7601
WWW.FIELDMUSEUM.ORG
E-MAIL ASMETANA@FMNH.ORG

CONTACT Alan Smetana, special events manager

CAPACITY Entire museum, 3,000 banquet, 5,000 reception; Stanley Field Hall, 2,000 banquet, 3,000 reception; balcony, 500 banquet, 1,500 reception; Daniel F. and Ada Rice Wildlife Research Station, 140 banquet, 300 reception; James Simpson Theatre, 900; Montgomery Ward Lecture Hall, 150.

RENTAL FEE Call for a quote.

HOURS 6 P.M. until your party ends.

PARKING Arranged with Soldier Field Joint Ventures.

The Field Museum overlooks the Chicago skyline and Lake Michigan. Upon entering Stanley Field Hall guests are greeted by gleaming white marble interiors, sky-

Courtesy of The Field Museum

lit vaulted ceilings and stately columns—complete with a 40-foot brachiosaurus, the world's largest mounted dinosaur, and a magnificent grand staircase. Guests are free to explore the museum's exhibits. For seminars, there is a 915-seat theater with state-of-the-art audiovisual systems.

The museum is handicapped accessible.

Caterers must be selected from the museum's list. Kitchen facilities are available, but you must bring in your own equipment. The museum staff will work closely with you. Audiovisual equipment is available.

FRIENDSHIP PARK CONSERVATORY

395 ALGONQUIN ROAD
DES PLAINES, IL 60018
(847) 298-3500

CONTACT Pat Pezen

CAPACITY Entire building with courtyard, 200; banquet room, 30–120 banquet, 150 theater style.

RENTAL FEE Entire building, $145 per hour, five-hour minimum; banquet room, $75–$95 per hour, depending on date/time of event and how room is divided; atrium photos, $75 per hour, one-hour maximum, open hours only.

DISCOUNTS For nonprofit organizations.

HOURS Flexible; daily.

PARKING Two adjacent lots.

This modern atrium and meeting space with its year-round flower beds always has something in bloom. The long foyer and reception area welcomes guests with a wall of floor-to-ceiling windows and

Courtesy of Friendship Park Conservatory

glass doors that look south onto a sheltered courtyard. The bright and airy atrium is located at the west end of the foyer. The room's lush floral displays are often used as a backdrop for wedding photos or small ceremonies. A large banquet room at the building's east end overlooks mature perennial flower beds. Each room can be used individually or you can create a personalized event that flows from one area of the building to another. The surrounding park can also be used for spring and summer events.

Choose from one of several caterers or for an extra $40 bring your own approved licensed and insured caterer. The conservatory provides all beverage services and can provide different bar set-ups. Tables, chairs, and meeting equipment are provided at no charge; but linens must be brought in. There is a small kitchen with a stove, oven, refrigerator, microwave, and coffeemakers. The site is handicapped accessible, and audiovisual equipment is available.

GARFIELD PARK CONSERVATORY

300 N. CENTRAL PARK AVENUE
CHICAGO, IL 60624
(312) 746-5100 OR (312) 742-PLAY
WWW.CHICAGOPARKDISTRICT.COM
E-MAIL PERMITS@CHICAGOPARKDISTRICT.COM

CONTACT Shaundra Johnson
BEST FEATURE A landmark conservatory with thousands of blooms.
BEST PARTIES Weddings, corporate events, and citywide festivals.
CAPACITY Entire conservatory, 1,500; Horticulture Hall, 500; Jensen Room, 100; Entry Pavilion, 200; Community Rooms, 75; Sensory Garden (outdoor), 300.
RENTAL FEES Private or non-profit, weekdays, $50–$750 (4 hours), weekends $75–$1,200; corporate events, weekdays, $200–$600 (4 hours), weekends $300–$1000.
DISCOUNTS Nonprofit rates available.
FOR THE KIDS The Elizabeth Morse Genius Children's Garden (indoors); Sensory Garden (outdoors).

Photograph by Brook Collins, courtesy of Chicago Park District

HOURS Daily 9 A.M.–5 P.M.; can be extended.
PARKING Free lot for 300.

The Garfield Park Conservatory is one of the world's largest gardens under glass. Lush rainforest, the desert cactus, and velvety moss create the perfect backdrop for any special event. Experience the sights and fragrances of a wide variety of flowers and plants, all in natural settings.

Spacious rooms feature stone paths that wind through breathtaking gardens. The Conservatory is handicapped accessible.

The Conservatory was designed by celebrated landscape architect, Jens Jensen, in 1906. It was considered revolutionary at the time because the building emulated a "great Midwestern haystack." This landmark facility attracts a host of events each year.

HAROLD WASHINGTON LIBRARY CENTER

400 S. STATE STREET
CHICAGO, IL 60605
(312) 747-4130
WWW.CHIPUBLIB.ORG

CONTACT Event coordinator
CAPACITY Winter Garden, 550 banquet, 650 reception; Grand Lobby, 650 receptions only; Auditorium, 385; video theater, 70; Complex Lobby, 150 reception; various meeting rooms, 25–200.
RENTAL FEE Call for pricing. Varies by day of use, and all rates are based on a four-hour use period.
DISCOUNTS For nonprofit organizations.
HOURS Varies, no later than midnight.
PARKING Several nearby lots and garages.

The Chicago Public Library's Harold Washington Library Center is the largest municipal library building in the world.

Courtesy of Harold Washington Library Center

Its Winter Garden, the architectural centerpiece of the library, is the ideal setting for special events. The glass-domed ceiling rises 52 feet above and is surrounded in five different types of marble from Italy and Turkey. The Grand Lobby is a three-story rotunda available for receptions, and the Auditorium is a 385-seat theatre ideal for meetings, dances or concerts. The library is wheelchair accessible.

You may choose caterers from the library's preferred list, or you may bring in your own with library approval. A prep kitchen is available. Banquet tables and chairs are provided. Audiovisual equipment is available for a fee.

INTERNATIONAL MUSEUM OF SURGICAL SCIENCE

1524 N. LAKE SHORE DRIVE
CHICAGO, IL 60610
(312) 642-6502, FAX (312) 642-9516
WWW.IMSS.ORG
E-MAIL INFO@IMSS.ORG

CONTACT Director of programs and events, extension 3130
CAPACITY Second floor with four rooms, 100 banquet, 150 reception, 80 theater.
RENTAL FEE Suggested minimum donation of $1,050 for three hours and $350 for every subsequent hour, plus $200 custodial fee.
HOURS Flexible.
PARKING Valet; limited lot parking.

Modeled after Marie Antoinette's French château, the museum is the home to shocking and educational medical exhibits from around the world. Detailed paintings of primitive surgery, human skulls, and surgical instruments will attract your guests' attention and provide interesting conversation topics. All events are held on the second floor. Upon request guests can tour the exhibits on the first, third, and fourth floors. No food or drink is allowed on these floors.

You should arrange your own catering. The museum will suggest caterers who are familiar with the site. The caterer must provide tables, chairs, linens, dishes, etc. Limited number of folding chairs and some audiovisual equipment is available. There is no smoking. Audiovisual equipment is available on site. Events are limited to medically related organizations; no weddings permitted. Wheelchair accessible.

Courtesy of International Museum of Surgical Science

IRISH AMERICAN HERITAGE CENTER

4626 N. KNOX AVENUE
CHICAGO, IL 60630
(773) 282-7035, FAX (773) 282-0380
WWW.IRISHAMHC.COM

CONTACT Conor O'Keeffe, operations manager
CAPACITY Auditorium, 700; social center and bar, 300 banquet; Fifth Province Lounge and Bar, 200 banquet; McGinty Room, 100 banquet; Shanachie Room, 130 banquet; meeting and dining rooms, 4–130 banquet.
RENTAL FEE $25–$700 depending on the number of people, room, and day and time of event.
FOR THE KIDS Kids are welcome up to 10 P.M.
HOURS Sunday–Thursday, 8 A.M.–10 P.M.; Friday and Saturday, 8 A.M.–midnight.
PARKING Two adjacent free lots.

Courtesy of Irish American Heritage Center

The Irish American Heritage Center hosts meetings, luncheons, receptions, and dances. The Fifth Province Pub has a wonderful atmosphere with a distinctive Irish flair. The slate-top bar and working fireplace provide an intimate backdrop for weekend entertainment featuring Irish musicians. The building is handicapped accessible.

All liquor must be purchased through the center. Kegs and bottles can be ordered individually or a bar plan that includes liquor as well as bartenders can be arranged. You may choose your own a caterer or bring in your own food. If needed, a large institutional kitchen is available for an additional fee. With the exception of a big-screen TV there is no audiovisual equipment available.

JOHN G. SHEDD AQUARIUM

1200 S. LAKE SHORE DRIVE
CHICAGO, IL 60605
(312) 692-3274, FAX (312) 939-3793
WWW.SHEDDAQUARIUM.ORG

CONTACT Denis Frankenfield, events/catering
CAPACITY Entire aquarium, 550 banquet, 1,200 reception; Oceanarium mezzanine, 800 reception; Oceanarium's outdoor terrace, 120 banquet, 500 reception; Caribbean Reef Rotunda, 250 banquet, 400 reception; Soundings restaurant, 120 banquet, 200 reception; Bubblenet restaurant, 220 banquet, 350 reception; Phelps Auditorium, 276 theater.
RENTAL FEE 50–100 guests, $3,000; 101–400 guests, $3,000 plus $10 per guest above 100; 401–1,500, $6,000 plus $5 per person above 400.
HOURS 7 P.M.–midnight, daily.
PARKING Adjacent lots.

Water your imagination at the spectacu-

Photograph by Edward G. Lines, Jr., courtesy of John G. Shedd Aquarium

lar Oceanarium featuring the world's largest indoor marine mammal pavilion and aquarium. Entertain your guests for cocktails and hors d'oeuvres along the Oceanarium's mezzanine level which overlooks the Pacific Northwest coastal habitat. Dine and dance in the aquarium and Coral Reef Rotunda among jewel-like displays of tropical fish.

All food and beverage is catered by the aquarium's catering office and kitchens. Rental fees do not include table linens, centerpieces, dinner tables, chairs, or coat check. These must be rented separately. The Aquarium must approve all events and is not available for political events or religious meetings and ceremonies. There are strict restrictions for music, photography, and entertainment.

KOHL CHILDREN'S MUSEUM

165 GREEN BAY ROAD
WILMETTE, IL 60091
(847) 256-6056, FAX (847) 853-9154

CONTACT Special events coordinator
BEST FEATURE Interactive exhibits for the young and the young-at-heart.
CAPACITY Two-story museum exhibit area, 100 banquet, 300 reception, 150 theater
RENTAL FEE $750–$2,000+.
FOR THE KIDS Children's birthday parties available during museum hours. Contact the registrar at (847) 256-3000 ext. 328 or 329.
HOURS Exhibit area, 5 P.M.–midnight.
PARKING Adjacent lot and street parking.

The hands-on exhibits at the Kohl Children's Museum offer a whimsical setting and a variety of possibilities for special events. Guests can experience the magical world of the computer in the StarMax Technology Center by Motorola, tour a Phoenician sailing ship,

Courtesy of Kohl Children's Museum

prepare meals in the royal kitchen, and search for treasure in the Long Ago and Far Away area. That's not all. You can make a splash in H2O, a dynamic water play environment; climb aboard a CTA train car; or dance to a different tune in Recollections, a computer-generated image system. Children's parties are held in a separate room, which can be decorated according to your preference.

A list of approved caterers is provided by the museum. There are a limited number of tables and chairs; extras must be brought in. There is no audiovisual equipment available. Deliveries are only allowed on the day of the event, and smoking is not allowed in the museum. One adult must be present for every five children.

LINCOLN PARK ZOO

2001 N. CLARK STREET
CHICAGO, IL 60614
(312)742-2300, FAX (312) 742-2306
WWW.LPZOO.COM
E-MAIL GROUPSALES@LPZOO.ORG

CONTACT Group sales department
CAPACITY Entire zoo, 2,500 banquet, 15,000 reception; Main Mall, 1,200 banquet, 3,000 reception; Kovler Lion House, 360 banquet, 600 reception; Regenstein Small Mammal-Reptile House, 200 banquet, 350 reception; Helen Brach Primate House, 200 banquet, 400 reception; Pritzker Children's Zoo, 120 banquet, 250 reception; Matthew Laflin Memorial Bldg., 130 banquet, 250 reception; Farm-in-the-Zoo, 500 banquet, 800 reception; Park Pavilion, 260 banquet, 450 reception; Big Cats Café, 250 banquet, 350 reception.
RENTAL FEE Evenings, $2,500-$15,000; Daytime meetings/picnics, $600+.
HOURS Evening events 6 P.M.–1 A.M.; daytime meetings/picnics 8 A.M.–5:30 P.M.

Photograph by Dugan Rosalini, courtesy of Lincoln Park Zoo

PARKING Paid lot; valet on request.

The Lincoln Park Zoo offers nine separate facilities that can be used for special events. At the Main Mall, guests can enjoy the seals and the sea lions in their outdoor pool. (A tent is necessary for this area and may be rented.) The Pritzker Children's Zoo has fantastic animal exhibits and a zoo nursery. For a formal event, the Matthew Laflin Memorial Building has been beautifully restored with a marble foyer and banquet room.

You must choose from the zoo's list of preferred caterers and suppliers. Menu packages and prices vary. The zoo staff will work closely with you to plan your event. Audiovisual equipment is available for some of the facilities. Religious and partisan political events are not permitted.

MUSEUM OF BROADCAST COMMUNICATIONS

CHICAGO CULTURAL CENTER
78 E. WASHINGTON STREET
CHICAGO, IL 60602
(312) 629-6019, FAX (312) 629-6009
WWW.MBCNET.ORG

CONTACT Julia Langfelder, events coordinator
CAPACITY Entire museum, 400 reception; Radio Studio, 70 banquet, 175 reception; TV Studio, 50 banquet, 75 reception; Brickhouse Gallery, 100 banquet, 175 reception.
RENTAL FEE Monday–Thursday, $500 per hour; Friday–Sunday, $600 per hour. Daily, $175 set-up and $350 cleanup fees.
DISCOUNTS 20 percent discount for corporate members and nonprofit organizations.
FOR THE KIDS Contact the museum's education department at 312-629-6014.
HOURS Flexible.
PARKING Nearby garage.

Courtesy of Museum of Broadcast Communications

Located in the Chicago Culture Center, the museum has five rooms available for private events. Each room gives your guests the chance to mingle among the legends of television and radio broadcasting. The exhibits are up and running throughout the party and can be tailored to your groups' individual needs. Your guests can anchor their own newscast or DJ a radio show and take home a souvenir tape.

The museum offers a recommended catering list. Additional amenities and services included in the rental fee are available upon request. Extensive audiovisual equipment is available, including VCRs, overhead projector and screens, cassette and CD recorder, TV monitors, ISDN line hookup for video conferencing, and even radio remote broadcasting. It's all included in the rental fee.

MUSEUM OF CONTEMPORARY ART

220 E. CHICAGO AVENUE
CHICAGO, IL 60611
(312) 280-2660 (GENERAL LINE) OR (312) 397-3855 (RENTAL OFFICE), FAX (312) 397-4095
WWW.MCACHICAGO.ORG

CONTACT Rental department

CAPACITY Second floor and sculpture garden, 300 banquet, 100–1,000 reception; Kanter Meeting Center, 70 banquet 100 reception or theater style; studio theater, 300.

RENTAL FEE Second floor and sculpture garden, $3,400–$5,500 (with access to third and fourth floor exhibitions add $500); Kanter Meeting Center, $500 for four hours or $750 up to eight hours; studio theater, $3,000 for four hours.

DISCOUNTS 25 percent discount for nonprofit organizations.

FOR THE KIDS Contact the education department.

HOURS Four-hour rental periods.

PARKING Garage on Chicago Avenue.

Photograph by Jim Prinz, courtesy of Museum of Contemporary Art

The Museum of Contemporary Art's dramatic spaces will make your event a memorable one. A breathtaking atrium welcomes visitors. The café is a large yet intimate space. The MCA's terraced sculpture garden is ideal for outside receptions. Groups can wander through spacious galleries that display works from Franz Klein to Andy Warhol to Alexander Calder.

Fabulous fares will be provided by Wolfgang Puck Catering. For after-hours events, the rental fee includes coat check, security, maintenance, engineer, and a rental staff member. Audiovisual equipment must be brought in. The MCA is handicapped accessible.

MUSEUM OF SCIENCE AND INDUSTRY

57TH STREET AND LAKE SHORE DRIVE
CHICAGO, IL 60637
(773) 684-9844 EXT. 2207, FAX (773) 684-3510
WWW.MSICHICAGO.ORG

CONTACT Special events/catering department

CAPACITY Entire museum, 600 banquet, 5,000+ reception or buffet dinners; Henry Crown Space Center, 150 banquet, 300 reception; various meeting spaces, 25–200.

RENTAL FEE Varies.

FOR THE KIDS Science made fun for kid's parties.

HOURS 6:30 P.M.–11 P.M., additional charge to extend party to midnight.

PARKING Indoor parking garage.

Housed in the classic Greek-inspired Palace of Fine Arts, the only building remaining from the 1893 Columbian Exposition, the Museum of Science and Industry is the nation's largest and most popular museum of contemporary science and technology. Sip cocktails around the Boeing 727, and then dine in the elegant rotunda. Have sub sandwiches outside the German U-505 submarine, or drive a 20-ton, state-of-the-art combine in the museum's farm exhibit. Follow petroleum on its journey from crude oil to the products we use every day. Jump into the Internet! The Museum of Science and Industry is an unforgettable location for any occasion.

The museum provides a variety of menu options. The executive chef will create a menu suited to your needs. Audiovisual equipment is available on site. The museum is handicapped accessible.

Courtesy of Museum of Science and Industry

Newberry Library

60 W. Walton Street
Chicago, IL 60610
(312) 255-3595, fax (312) 255-3513

Contact Director of events
Capacity East Hall, 275 banquet, 400 reception; lobby, 275 reception; Fellows' Lounge, 60 banquet, 100 reception; conference room suites, 15–30.
Rental Fee $325 per hour plus $125 per hour cleanup; conference rooms, $50 per hour.
Hours Evenings after 5:30 P.M.; Sundays anytime.
Parking 45-car lot in rear of building.

Photograph by Edward Fox, courtesy of Newberry Library

The Newberry Library is one of Chicago's most charming places to host a special event. The lobby has been restored to its original 1893 grandeur. The capitals of the columns were replaced and an art nouveau chandelier hangs from the 20-foot ceiling. The broad marble staircase is a popular site for wedding ceremonies and pictures. The East Hall has large windows that overlook a park and Michigan Avenue. Ideal for banquets, receptions, concerts, and lectures, the hall accommodates up to 275 comfortably. For smaller groups the Fellows' Lounge on the second floor has original oak paneling, rich carpet, and turn-of-the-century elegance with comfortable furnishings, Steinway Grand, and antique grandfather clock.

By prior arrangement, an event may be enhanced by viewing some of the Newberry's rare book treasures or by a tour of the building. Guards and a coat check are provided. You may bring your own caterer. Liquor and live music are allowed. Chairs, tables, and a dance floor are available at reasonable rates.

Scholl College of Podiatric Medicine

1001 N. Dearborn Street
Chicago, IL 60610
(312) 280-2909, fax (312) 280-2997

Contact David McKay, exhibit coordinator
Capacity Main floor lobby, 40 banquet, 150 reception.
Rental Fee $500 for three hours.
Hours Monday–Friday, 7 A.M.–11 P.M.; Saturday, 9 A.M.–5 P.M.
Parking Nearby pay lots.

Courtesy of Scholl College of Podiatric Medicine

Scholl College was founded in 1912 by Dr. William M. Scholl, whose lengthy career bridged the worlds of business, foot care, and education. The marble lobby that welcomes you to the Feet First exhibit has been restored, complete with copies of the original 1920s furnishings and adornments. Perfect for cocktail receptions, intimate dinner parties, and other special events, this lobby features walls of beige marble, an inlay terrazzo floor, and a hand-painted ceiling. The permanent exhibit, Feet First, invites visitors to touch and examine an oversized skeletal model of the human foot, teaching them to appreciate one of the most complex mechanisms in the human body and is perfect for company "kick-offs" or "putting you best foot forward" motivational parties.

You may choose you own caterer or the college can provide a list. Tables, chairs, linens, and serving equipment must be brought in. Limited audiovisual equipment is available. There is no smoking allowed. The college is handicapped accessible.

South Shore Cultural Center

7059 S. Shore Drive
Chicago, IL 60649
(312) 747-2486 or (312) 742-PLAY

Contact Nancy Toledo

Best Parties South Shore has hosted many of Chicago's most prestigious weddings.

Capacity Robeson Theater, 600 theater only; Dining Room, 300 banquet, 400 theater; Solarium, 150 banquet, 300 theater; Oak Room, 40 conference, 50 theater; Conference Room, 25 banquet, 35 theater.

Rental Fee Receptions, fundraisers, banquets on Monday–Thursday nights, $750– $1,000 (4-hour period); Friday– Sunday nights, $1,200–$1,500; smaller meetings on weekdays, $50–$150 per hour, $100–$750 per day.

Discounts 50 percent with nonprofit documentation (501C3) from the IRS.

Hours Sunday–Wednesday 9 A.M.–12 A.M.; Thursday–Saturday 9 A.M.–1 A.M.

Parking Free parking for 250 cars.

Photograph by Brook Collins, courtesy of Chicago Park District

The South Shore Cultural Center, a 65-acre park with a golf course, tennis courts, a bathing beach, and an impressive building, originated as the South Shore Country Club. In 1905, Lawrence Heyworth, President of the downtown Chicago Athletic Club, envisioned an exclusive club with a "country setting." Architects Marshall and Fox, later known for the Drake Hotel, designed the Mediterranean Revival style club.

Today, the splendor of South Shore Cultural Center includes ornately crafted ceilings and speckled marble columns, and is completely handicapped accessible. To the north of the building, the Grand Ballroom overseas a spectacular view of Chicago's lakefront. Clients must select from the South Shore's pre-approved list of caterers.

Spertus Institute of Jewish Studies

618 S. Michigan Avenue
Chicago, IL 60605
(312) 322-1781, fax (312) 922-6406
www.spertus.edu

Contact Bonnie Sohn, building coordinator

Best Feature Art gallery attached to auditorium.

Capacity Bederman Auditorium, 220 banquet, 400 theater; Lebeson Gallery, 150 reception, 70 theater; classrooms, 30–75; conference room, 20 banquet.

Rental Fee $50–$350 depending on the room.

For the Kids Children's museum with the ArtiFact Center, contact (312) 322-1747.

Hours Monday–Thursday, 8 A.M.–10 P.M.; Friday, 8 A.M.–6 P.M.; Sunday, 8:30 A.M.– 5 P.M.

Parking Reduced rates available at four nearby garages.

Courtesy of Spertus Institute of Jewish Studies

The Spertus Museum of Jewish Studies is one of the city's best-kept secrets, which is a pity because it has a lot to offer for private parties and events of all kinds. The Krensky Conference Room, with a large meeting table and a view of Grant Park, is perfect for business seminars. For larger gatherings there is the Bederman Auditorium which has a 15 x 30-foot stage and a baby grand piano. Connected to the auditorium is the Lebeson Gallery, where art exhibits are displayed. For children's parties, there is the ArtiFact Center, a hands-on archaeology exhibit located in the basement of the museum.

Food and serving equipment must be brought in—kosher catering only. The museum has a list of accepted kosher caterers. Kitchen facilities are available. Liquor is allowed with approval. Some audiovisual equipment including a podium and microphone are available. The center is handicapped accessible.

TERRA MUSEUM OF AMERICAN ART

664 N. MICHIGAN AVENUE
CHICAGO, IL 60611
(312) 664-3939 OR (773) 549-5300 (CATER-ING), FAX (312) 664-2052

CONTACT Stephanie Leese, director of community relations

CAPACITY Entire museum, 500; private meeting room, 150.

RENTAL FEE Negotiable, based on day of event and size of group; non-profit special rate.

FOR THE KIDS Studio workshop space for family-related art programs.

HOURS Based on availability.

PARKING Four public lots nearby.

This five-story marble facade on Michigan Avenue was recognized by the American Institute of Architects for outstanding architecture. The museum's permanent collection highlights American art from the late 18th century to about 1940, featuring Impressionism. Traveling exhibitions with national recognition will enhance your guests' experience. The landing on the second floor is available for food and beverage service and the floor-to-ceiling windows make the passing parade on Michigan Avenue part of the setting. The museum is ideal for cocktail receptions and sit-down functions for up to 60 guests. The museum is handicapped accessible.

Elegant Edge Distinctive Catering provides all food and beverage service. Guests have access to the entire facility, but food and beverages are restricted to the second floor landing. Weddings, showers, political or religious events, fundraisers, and other events of a personal nature are not permitted. Limited audiovisual equipment is available. There is no smoking allowed.

Photograph by Wayne Cable, courtesy of Terra Museum of American Art

RESTAURANTS

Angelina Ristorante

Ann Sather

Berghoff Restaurant, The

Bistro 110

Blackhawk Lodge

Cheesecake Factory, The

Cité at the Top of Lake Point Tower

Club Lucky

Como Inn

Daily Bar & Grill

Dining Room at Kendall College, The

Ed Debevic's

Eli's Cheesecake World

Eli's the Place for Steak

Everest: A Lettuce Entertain You Restaurant

Fritzl's Country Inn

Gino's East

Goose Island Brewing Company

Grillroom Chophouse & Wine Bar, The

Harry Caray's Restaurant

House of Blues

Hudson Club

Jackson Harbor Grill

King James' Barbeque

Le Colonial

Maggiano's Little Italy

Magnum's Prime Steakhouse and White Star Lounge

Merc's Restaurant

Mia Torre

Mike Ditka's Restaurant

Mrs. Levy's Delicatessen

Nick's Fishmarket—Rosemont

Nikos

O'Brien's Restaurant & Bar

P. J. Clarke's: A Lettuce Entertain You Restaurant

Palette's Restaurant

Palm Restaurant, The: At the Swissotel Chicago

Quincy Grille on the River

Reza's

Salvatore's Ristorante

Scoozi!

Shaw's Crab House

Signature Room at the 95th, The

Spiaggia, Private Dining Rooms of

Star of Siam

Terrace Restaurant, The

Va Pensiero Restaurant

Wild Onion

Zodiac Restaurant at Neiman Marcus

ANGELINA RISTORANTE

3561 N. BROADWAY
CHICAGO, IL 60657
(773) 935-5933

CONTACT Zack Pass, owner and general manager

BEST FEATURE Sicilian café atmosphere.

CAPACITY Main room with bar, 70 banquet, 100 reception; side room, 50 banquet, 75 reception.

RENTAL FEE $500–$2,000 depending upon number of people, time, and date of event.

HOURS Sunday–Thursday, 5:30 P.M.–10 P.M.; Friday–Saturday, 5:30 P.M.–11 P.M.; other times by arrangement.

PARKING Valet; street.

Courtesy of Angelina Ristorante

This traditional southern Italian trattoria whisks you into the classic atmosphere of a Sicilian café. Angelina offers sophisticated cooking and relaxed, friendly service amidst a bustling and vibrant urban residential location in Lakeview, between Lake Shore Drive and Wrigley Field. Plan a gathering for a small group during their regular business hours or rent your own room for a private dinner that your guests will remember. The main dining room has mustard-colored, hand-painted stucco walls with shelves full of empty wine bottles.

Angelina Ristorante specializes in true southern Italian cooking. Assemble your meal from the regular menu, or let the chef and staff create your own customized meal. An extensive wine list complements the variety and quality of the hearty fare.

ANN SATHER

929 W. BELMONT AVENUE
CHICAGO, IL 60657
(773) 348-2378, FAX (773) 348-1731
WWW.ANNSATHER.COM

CONTACT Scott Roubeck, director of catering

BEST FEATURES Old World charm; cinnamon rolls to die for.

CAPACITY 320 banquet, 600 reception.

RENTAL FEE Based on food and beverage consumption; for noncatered events, $35–$2,600.

DISCOUNTS Will work with any budget; discounts for nonprofit organizations.

HOURS Sunday–Thursday, 7 A.M.–9 P.M.; Friday and Saturday, 7 A.M.–10 P.M.; flexible for events.

PARKING Free lot.

Photograph by Steve Matteo

Ann Sather whisks you away to the Old World charm of Scandinavia. Decorative hand-painted murals and paintings reflect the traditions and styles of Sweden. Hardwood floors, stained-glass windows, and atrium skylights enhance the high, vaulted ceilings and spacious dining rooms. The banquet rooms are located on the second floor and come complete with a full bar, a stage for musicians or speakers, and excellent cuisine. Known for their melt-in-your-mouth cinnamon rolls, this is an excellent site for your next business breakfast or bridesmaids' brunch.

The restaurant caters all events. (They are also available for off-site catering.) Their prices begin at $10 per person and complete packages including an open bar begin at $35 per person. But they will work with any budget. The restaurant needs a 72-hour notice to arrange for audiovisual equipment. The banquet rooms are handicapped accessible.

THE BERGHOFF RESTAURANT

17 W. ADAMS STREET
CHICAGO, IL 60603
(312) 427-3170, FAX (312) 427-6549
WWW.BERGHOFF.COM

CONTACT Catherine Hartman, banquet
manager
BEST PARTY Annual Oktoberfest, the "wurst
party of the year."
CAPACITY 30–300.
RENTAL FEE Varies.
HOURS Flexible.
PARKING Discounted at nearby garage.

The Berghoff is a symbol of tradition in
Chicago. From the restaurant's begin-
nings as a café featuring Berghoff beer
to today's full-service restaurant, The
Berghoff has become a favorite destina-
tion. The annex party rooms have the
same appeal as the main floor dining
rooms with stained-glass windows, photos from the Berghoff family collection

Courtesy of The Berghoff Restaurant

of the 1893 World's Colombian
Exposition, and tuxedo-clad waitstaff.

The Berghoff caters events with cuisine
that combines traditional German
favorites and contemporary American
fare. Special events encompass every-

thing from power lunches for 25 to lavish wedding receptions for 250. There
are several packages available and the
menu can be customized. Audiovisual
equipment can be arranged through the
restaurant. Wheelchair accessible.

BISTRO 110

110 E. PEARSON STREET
CHICAGO, IL 60611
(312) 266-3110 OR (312) 335-5036,
FAX (312) 664-6822
WWW.BISTRO110.COM

CONTACT Lisa Nadle
BEST FEATURE Exceptional wood-fired
cuisine in an authentic bustling bistro
atmosphere.
BEST PARTY Sunday jazz brunch.
CAPACITY 150 banquet, 500 reception.
RENTAL FEE Based on food and beverage
consumption.
HOURS Flexible.
PARKING Valet.

Just steps from Michigan Avenue, and
across from historic Water Tower
Square, Bistro 110 is a charming location for any gathering. A fashionable,
friendly restaurant accented with shiny
copper and contemporary watercolor
murals, Bistro 110 continues the French

bistro tradition with an
American accent. Known for
its fabulous oven-roasted
whole garlic served with
crusty French bread, Bistro
110 specializes in hearty
wood-burning, oven-roasted
cuisine, flavorful pasta dishes, salads, sandwiches, and
extraordinary desserts. The
restaurant has an extensive
French-American wine list
to complement your meal.

Up to 200 guests can easily
be accommodated for social
or corporate events, afternoon lunches, Sunday
brunches, or elegant din-
ners. Up to 500 people can
be accommodated for receptions. An attentive planning
staff will coordinate every
detail. Audiovisual equipment can be rented through
the restaurant. Wheelchair
accessible.

Photograph by Mark Ballogg, courtesy of Bistro 110

BLACKHAWK LODGE

41 E. SUPERIOR STREET
CHICAGO, IL 60611
(312) 280-4080 OR (312) 335-5036,
FAX (312) 664-6822
WWW.BLACKHAWKLODGE.COM

CONTACT Lisa Nadle, event planner
BEST FEATURE An authentic rustic lodge atmosphere.
BEST PARTY Sunday bluegrass brunch.
CAPACITY 150 banquet, 300 reception.
RENTAL FEE Based on food and beverage consumption.
HOURS Flexible.
PARKING Valet.

Rustic elegance in the heart of a metropolitan city, Blackhawk Lodge celebrates tradition in a gracious setting—just steps away from Michigan Avenue. With its knotty pine panels, timber walls, wicker furniture, fireplace, and new front porch, the Blackhawk Lodge evokes a comfortable atmosphere for any occasion.

Famous for regional American cuisine, including grilled, barbecued, and oven-roasted specialties, Blackhawk Lodge was awarded a coveted three-star rating by the *Chicago Tribune*.

Cozy, yet elegant areas may be reserved for a holiday feast, wedding festivities, or business dinners. The restaurant can accommodate 300 guests indoors. The chef will customize each menu to suit the occasion. Signature items include bourbon-barrel smoked tenderloin and seared peppercorn-crusted yellowfin tuna with wasabi potatoes. Desserts such as Tennessee cornbread pudding and Georgian pecan tart inspire indulgence. The restaurant's event planner can arrange for rental of audiovisual equipment. Wheelchair accessible.

Courtesy of Blackhawk Lodge

THE CHEESECAKE FACTORY

374 OLD ORCHARD CENTER
SKOKIE, IL 60077
(847) 329-8077, FAX (847) 329-8246

CONTACT Restaurant manager
CAPACITY Private party room, 20–32 banquet.
RENTAL FEE Based on food and beverage consumption.
HOURS Monday–Thursday, 11:30 A.M.–10 P.M.; Friday and Saturday, 11:30 A.M.–midnight; Sunday, 10 A.M.–10 P.M.
PARKING Plenty on-site.

If the idea of hosting your next event at The Cheesecake Factory makes your mouth water, you will be pleased to know the Skokie location has a private dining room. A minimum of 20 people is required to rent the room and it can hold a maximum of 32. With its surreal Alice in Wonderland-like decor and festive atmosphere The Cheesecake Factory will make any event something to remember.

The menu is eclectic and includes much more than just cheesecake. You can select anything from a crusted filet of salmon to a Cajun jambalaya pasta to Thai chicken pizza. There is a set-up fee of $50 that includes white linen tablecloths and candles on the tables. A non-refundable deposit of $250 is required for all private events. A 20 percent service charge is added to the final bill. If you choose to bring in wine or champagne, there is a $5 corkage fee per bottle. There is a 50 cents per person charge to serve a cheesecake purchased at the restaurant and a $1 per person to serve a cake that is brought in.

Courtesy of The Cheesecake Factory

CITÉ AT THE TOP OF LAKE POINT TOWER

505 N. Lake Shore Drive, 70th Floor
Chicago, IL 60611
(312) 644-4050, fax (312) 644-4066

Contact Michael Ideson, director of catering
Best Feature Circular restaurant features incredible views of the city and lakefront.
Best Party Chicago International Film Festival's anniversary party for the Alfred Hitchcock film *Vertigo*; guests included Roger Ebert, Dwight Yokam, Billy Zane, and Smokey Robinson.
Capacity 70th floor circular restaurant, 10–200 banquet, 250 reception.
Rental Fee Flexible, based on size of party and food and beverage consumption.
Hours Daily, dinner from 5:30 P.M.; Sunday champagne brunch, 11 A.M.–3 P.M.
Parking Valet parking in the building.

A landmark restaurant located on Lake Michigan at Navy Pier, Cité features views of Chicago's majestic skyline from

Courtesy of Cité at the Top of Lake Point Tower

the 70th floor of Lake Point Tower. This is perhaps the most romantic setting in Chicago. The Cristalle Room, showcasing the city like no other private room, is a success for dazzling parties, receptions, and corporate functions.

Cité can accommodate 10-200 guests. The Cristalle Room can hold up to 80 guests for a private dinner. Catered events are priced at $35 per person for luncheons, $45 per person for dinners (with a minimum of 30 people). Private rooms can be reserved for the Sunday Champagne Brunch as well. Food and beverage minimums apply.

CLUB LUCKY

1824 W. Wabansia Avenue
Chicago, IL 60622
(773) 227-2300, fax (773) 227-2236
www.clubluckychicago.com
E-mail clublucky@ameritech.net

Contact Jim Higgins, co-owner
Best Features Traditional Italian food served family style; handmade pastas.
Best Party Martini contest.
Capacity Cocktail lounge, 30 banquet, 60 reception; main dining room, 130 banquet, 250 reception; private dining room (the Club Room), 35 banquet, 50 reception.
Rental Fee Based on food and beverage consumption.
Hours Flexible; open daily for lunch and dinner.
Parking Valet; parking lot; street parking.

This casual Italian restaurant is reminiscent of a supper club and cocktail lounge from the 1940s. The atmosphere is informal, portions are generous, and

Courtesy of Club Lucky

the prices are reasonable. What more do you need for your next party or special occasion? The rich red Naugahyde booths and a long Chicago bar in the cocktail lounge immediately remind you of a different time. The 1940s decor continues throughout the restaurant—from the antique stainless steel martini shakers to the lighting fixtures that resemble satellites in orbit.

The restaurant caters all events, and can find a menu to fit your budget. Dinners range from $12–$30 per person, lunches from $6–$15 per person, and hors d'oeuvre receptions from $10–$25 per person. Cocktails are $4–$7 each. A jukebox, sound system, and VCR with three monitors are available. You may bring your own entertainment. The restaurant is not handicapped accessible.

COMO INN

546 N. MILWAUKEE AVENUE
CHICAGO, IL 60622
(312) 491-6050, FAX (312) 421-4322

CONTACT Catering coordinator
BEST FEATURE Famous landmark; in business since 1924.
CAPACITY 13 private banquet rooms, 15–250 banquet, 500 reception.
RENTAL FEE Based on food and beverage consumption.
DISCOUNTS Private parties on Friday night and on Sundays receive a 10 percent discount.
HOURS Monday–Saturday, 11:30 A.M.–midnight; Sunday noon–11 P.M.
PARKING Free lots; valet available.

Each of the 13 private banquet rooms at the Como Inn has a unique decor and whimsical atmosphere—from a 19th-century Florentine library to a contemporary hall that leads into the bright, modern Yolandas Room. The walls of the each room are adorned with a variety of items—large white fish, golden cupids, oil paintings, and grapevines. With this much variety, there is a room perfect for all types of events.

The Como Inn provides all the food and drink. Lunches start at $9.95 per person, dinners at $13.95 per person, and all-inclusive wedding packages at $52.50 per person. There are several bar packages available. A variety of meeting equipment is provided or can be rented for a small charge.

Courtesy of Como Inn

DAILY BAR & GRILL

4560 N. LINCOLN AVENUE
CHICAGO, IL 60625
(773) 472-1601
WWW.DAILYBAR.COM

CONTACT Kim Veber, Claire Perry, or Heather Zomer
CAPACITY Private room, 20–50.
RENTAL FEE None.
HOURS Monday–Friday, 4 P.M.–2 A.M.; Saturday, Noon–3 A.M.; Sunday, Noon–1 A.M.
PARKING Street; valet by request.

Located in the Lincoln Square neighborhood, the Daily Bar & Grill's private dining room features leather sofas and armchairs, deep red walls, red velvet drapes, hardwood floors with oriental rugs, a private bar, and soft candlelight. The restaurant offers a variety of menu and bar options, and is the perfect spot for a casual cocktail gathering on an informal dinner.

Daily Bar & Grill handles all aspects of catering for private parties. Food buffets range from $9.95–$14.95 per person, and includes anything from burgers and chicken sandwiches to Southwestern style buffets. Bar packages range from $15–$25.

Photograph by Spare Time, Inc., courtesy of Daily Bar & Grill

THE DINING ROOM AT KENDALL COLLEGE

2408 ORRINGTON AVENUE
EVANSTON, IL 60201
(847) 866-1399, FAX (847) 866-1379

CONTACT The dining room receptionist
BEST FEATURE Excellent food at affordable prices.
CAPACITY Dining room, 65 banquet; additional room, 65 banquet.
RENTAL FEE Based on food and beverage consumption.
HOURS Lunch is served Monday–Friday, noon to 1:30 P.M.; dinner from Tuesday–Saturday, 6 P.M.–8:00 P.M.; closed during term breaks.
PARKING Street; lot.

Courtesy of the Dining Room at Kendall College

The Dining Room is a student-operated establishment that serves as a culinary learning environment for the School of Culinary Arts at Kendall College. The spacious two-level dining room was completely refurbished in 2001 and features a glass-enclosed kitchen. There is an adjoining banquet room that can be used in conjunction with the dining room for larger parties.

A three-course lunch is $16.00 per person. Dinner prices vary. The Dining Room does not sell alcohol, but you may bring your own liquor. There is a $5 corkage fee. Some audiovisual equipment is available for a fee. The Dining Room is handicapped accessible and is a smoke-free environment.

ED DEBEVIC'S

640 N. WELLS STREET
CHICAGO, IL 60610
(312) 664-1707

CONTACT Cyndi Gompper-Butler, sales and catering manager
CAPACITY Entire restaurant, 300; The Porch, 150; Elvis Presley Room, 45; Route 66 Room, 30.
RENTAL FEE Based on food and beverage consumption; a room rental charge may apply for Friday–Sunday events.
FOR THE KIDS Great fun for kids' parties.
HOURS Sunday–Thursday 11 A.M.–10 P.M.; Friday and Saturday, 11 A.M.–11 P.M.
PARKING Valet.

Courtesy of Ed Debevic's

The loud, sassy, dancing waiters and waitresses at Ed Debevic's will entertain you and your guests. There are three rooms that are perfect for private functions. You can pay homage to the King in the Elvis Presley Room, get your kicks in the Route 66 Room, or have a bash with 150 of your closest friends on The Porch.

Diner-style food is Ed's specialty. You can order off the menu or choose one of the party packages. Ed's American Meal includes your choice of a hamburger, hot dog, grilled chicken sandwich, or a grilled cheese, plenty of fries, and the world's smallest sundae for $10.25 per person. The Elvis Presley Special includes three appetizers, beer and wine, anything off the menu, Ed's dessert table, decorations, and a photographer for $24 per person.

ELI'S CHEESECAKE WORLD

6701 W. FOREST PRESERVE DRIVE
CHICAGO, IL 60634
(773) 205-3800, FAX (773) 205-3801
WWW.ELICHEESECAKE.COM

CONTACT Tour and special event coordinator
CAPACITY Café, 50.
RENTAL FEE None.
FOR THE KIDS Cake decorating and tours are fun for kid's events.
HOURS Monday–Friday, 7 A.M.–6 P.M.; Saturday, 9 A.M.–5 P.M.; Sunday, 11 A.M.–5 P.M.
PARKING Ample spaces.

Photograph by Steve Matteo

Eli's Cheesecake made its public debut in 1980 at the first Taste of Chicago food festival. Since then, this mouth-watering dessert has become a Chicago favorite. Eli's Cheesecake World is a 62,000-square-foot bakery where they bake almost every imaginable version of cheesecake—from the original plain variety to the triple chocolate truffle.

A behind-the-scenes tour of the bakery, a cake decorating contest, or a dessert tasting can be part of the entertainment at Eli's. This is a great spot for kid's parties; you can fill them up with sugar, then return them to their parents!

The bakery provides all food and beverages. Menu items include soup and sandwiches. The staff will work with you to customize your menu. There is no smoking in the facility.

ELI'S THE PLACE FOR STEAK

215 E. CHICAGO AVENUE
CHICAGO, IL 60611
(312) 642-1393, FAX (312) 642-4089
WWW.ELICHEESECAKE.COM

CONTACT Justin Bender, executive chef
CAPACITY Party room, 75 banquet and reception.
RENTAL FEE None.
HOURS Flexible, from 11 A.M.
PARKING Nearby garage with discounted rates.

Photograph by Steve Matteo

In 1966, when Eli M. Schulman opened The Place for Steak, who would have guessed that it was not his steaks but his rich and creamy cheesecake that would eventually make the restaurant a success? You can make your next event a hit by treating your guests to a taste of this to-die-for dessert in Eli's private dining room. The room is located on the second floor of the restaurant and is decorated

in shades of green with white leather banquet chairs. There is a balcony that overlooks the Eli M. Schulman Playground at Seneca Park and the Museum of Contemporary Art. The restaurant is handicapped accessible.

Eli's will cater all events. The menu is full of mouth-watering dishes so you

should try and resist the temptation to head straight for the dessert table. Lunches start at $7.50 per person and dinners at $17.95 per person. For parties of 40 or more, the staff will work with you to arrange an inclusive package. Most audiovisual equipment must be rented.

EVEREST

A Lettuce Entertain You Restaurant

440 S. LaSalle Street
Chicago, IL 60605
(312) 663-8920, fax (312) 663-8802

Contact Catering Sales
Best Feature Views of the city's financial district.
Capacity Entire restaurant, 125 banquet, 150 reception; six private rooms, 8–72 banquet, 20–125 reception.
Rental Fee Call for rates.
Hours Flexible for private events.
Parking Free in lot; complimentary valet.

Acclaimed cuisine and excellent views are what makes this restaurant stand out as a great place to wow a client, celebrate a birthday, or host a reception. The restaurant's River Room has windows that reveal a dramatic view from 40 floors above the city's financial district. The decor is in neutral tones with wood credenzas and Audubon murals. Everest received four-star reviews from the *Chicago Tribune*, the *Chicago Sun-Times*, and *Chicago Magazine*.

Everest's Chef Jean Joho grew up in Alsace, France. His inventive cuisine draws on these roots. There are almost 300 Alsace wines on the extensive wine list. Breakfasts are from $16.50 per person for a continental breakfast to $32.50 per person for the Chicago Stock Exchange Breakfast. Lunches start at $30 per person. A five-course dinner menu is $75 per person and up. Audiovisual equipment is available upon request. Everest is wheelchair accessible.

Courtesy of Everest

FRITZL'S COUNTRY INN

377 N. Rand Road
Lake Zurich, IL 60047
(847) 540-8860, fax (847) 540-8869
www.fritzl.com

Contact Peter, owner
Best Feature European cuisine.
Best Parties Octoberfest; New Year's Eve gala.
Capacity First room, 20 banquet, 40 reception; second room, 50 banquet, 70 reception; third room, 150 banquet, 175 reception.
Rental Fee No charge if food and beverages are served. If no food is served, $25–$300 depending on room.
For the Kids Children's party discounts available.
Hours Tuesday–Saturday, 4–10 P.M.; Sunday, 3 P.M.–9 P.M.; flexible hours for private parties.
Parking Ample.

The facilities at Fritzl's Country Inn are

Courtesy of Fritzl's County Inn

perfect for weddings, rehearsal dinners, showers, and Christmas parties. The rooms are decorated in hunter green and oak woodwork; white linens and fresh flowers add an elegant touch. The banquet room has high ceilings, large chandeliers, and a dance floor. Fritzl's has been hosting events for more than 12 years.

The restaurant caters all events. Dinners are from $13.95–$19.95 per person. Packages including an open bar, four-course meal, fresh flowers, and linens, range from $21.95–$27.95 per person. A cash bar is also available. Some audiovisual equipment is available, including a microphone and podium and projection screens. The restaurant is handicapped accessible.

GINO'S EAST

633 N. WELLS STREET
CHICAGO, IL 60610
(312) 266-5421, FAX (312) 943-9589
WWW.GINOSEAST.COM

CONTACT Erica Prenger, group sales director
BEST FEATURE Award-winning, Chicago-style, deep dish pizza.
CAPACITY Rooms accommodate 30–100. (Private room space varies in suburban locations—St. Charles, Oak Lawn, Rosemont, Orland Park, Rolling Meadows.)
RENTAL FEE Based on consumption, day, and time.
FOR THE KIDS Gino's East will help with magicians, DJ's, etc.
HOURS Monday–Thursday, 11 A.M.–10 P.M.; Friday and Saturday 11 A.M.–midnight; Sunday 12 P.M.–10 P.M.
PARKING Valet.

Courtesy of Gino's East

Rated #1 by *Chicago Magazine* and the *Chicago Tribune*'s Readers' Poll, the original Gino's East is a legend with local Chicagoans, national celebrities, and visitors from around the world. Your guests can inscribe graffiti messages on the walls without getting in trouble, or check out celebrity autographs from David Letterman, Ronald Reagan, Jack Nicholson, and others. Gino's has been the host for school groups, awards banquets, corporate meetings, rehearsal dinners, baby showers, and retirement parties.

Private and semi-private rooms are available. Room charges vary. Pizza party packages begin at $8.75 per person. Bar packages are also available, as is off-site catering. Gino's is handicapped accessible.

GOOSE ISLAND BREWING COMPANY

1800 N. CLYBOURN AVENUE
CHICAGO, IL 60614
(312) 915-0071 OR (773) 832-9040 EXT. 231
3535 N. CLARK STREET
CHICAGO, IL 60657
(773) 832-9040 EXT. 231, FAX (773) 832-9053
WWW.GOOSEISLAND.COM

CONTACT Catering sales and special events
CAPACITY At the Clybourn location: Hop Room, 40 banquet, 50 reception; Beer Cellar, 25 banquet, 60 reception; Patio, 50 banquet, 70 reception; Loft, 20 banquet, 30 reception; The Great Hall, 70 banquet, 100 reception. All rooms have a 25-guest minimum. At the Wrigleyville location: entire facility, 400 reception.
RENTAL FEE Based on food and beverage consumption.
HOURS Flexible.
PARKING Free lot.

Photograph by Steve Matteo

Goose Island is named after an island on the Chicago River where, at one time, geese were raised. Guests here can watch a sporting event or video presentation on the large screen TV in the Beer Cellar, or sip beer and munch on Goose Island's famous homemade potato chips on the Patio. The Wrigleyville location boasts the same Goose Island hospitality and beer and is the perfect location for large receptions or other special events.

There are several private party menus available, priced from $15–$40 per person. Try the Blonde Ale three-course dinner, the Cellar Appetizer Buffet, the Tailgate, or the Brew Master. Of course, your guests will get to munch on Goose Island's famous homemade pub chips. Customized menus are an option. Both locations are handicapped accessible. Goose Island has a VCR and monitors available for your use.

THE GRILLROOM CHOPHOUSE & WINE BAR

33 W. MONROE
CHICAGO, IL 60603
(312) 222-0627
WWW.RDGCHICAGO.COM

CONTACT Margaret O'Donnell, director of sales
BEST FEATURE Located in the heart of downtown.
BEST PARTY Grand Opening Benefit for the Greater Chicago Food Depository.
CAPACITY Entire restaurant, 300; private room, 40.
RENTAL FEE Based on date and time.
HOURS Based on function.
PARKING Valet.

This classic Chicago chophouse features a wide range of choices that include steaks, chops, pasta, and seafood. The Grillroom is conveniently located in the heart of the downtown area. Walk to theaters, office buildings, hotels, shopping, museums, and more. The main dining room seats over 300 with a private dining room that has a 40-seat capacity.

Warm, neutral colors, hardwood floors, a marble cocktail lounge, accents of brass, mood lighting, and lots of tall, leather booths create a clubby feel that has a universal appeal. The Grillroom is handicapped accessible.

Photograph by Steven Becker Photography, courtesy of the Grillroom Chophouse & Wine Bar

HARRY CARAY'S RESTAURANT

33 W. KINZIE STREET
CHICAGO, IL 60610
(312) 828-0966, FAX (312) 828-0962
WWW.HARRYCARAYS.COM
E-MAIL MONICA@HARRYCARRYS.COM

CONTACT Monica Volini, director of catering
CAPACITY East and West rooms combined, 220 banquet, 400 reception; either room alone, 70 banquet, 100 reception; MVP Suite, 70 banquet, 100 reception.
RENTAL FEE MVP Suite, $150; East Room, $75; West Room, $75.
HOURS Monday–Saturday, 8 A.M.–2 A.M.; Sunday, 11 A.M.–midnight.
PARKING Valet, $8 per car.

Perfect for a variety of events, Harry Caray's private rooms are decorated with authentic baseball memorabilia and artifacts. The highlight of the East Room is a floor-to-ceiling mural of Wrigley Field and the Chicago skyline. The West Room contains the original antique bar from Arlington Park Racetrack. The MVP Suite features hardwood floors, an old-fashioned tin ceiling, leather furniture, and natural lighting. Harry's private office is attached to the MVP Suite and can be used for meetings or small dinners.

Harry Caray's, known for both Italian favorites and steak and chops, supplies all food and beverage. Bar options include cash bar, consumption basis, or package bars. Outside cakes, decorations, and entertainment are allowed. Harry Caray's has a wireless microphone and podium for use at no charge. Additional audiovisual equipment is provided on a rental basis. Wheelchair accessible.

Courtesy of Harry Caray's Restaurant

House of Blues

329 N. Dearborn Street
Chicago, IL 60610
(312) 923-2015 or (312) 923-2000,
fax (312) 923-2041
www.hob.com

Contact Kirsten Hiner, Director of Sales
Capacity Entire site, 1,800 reception;
Restaurant, 200 banquet, 400 reception;
semi-private rooms, 100 banquet, 100
reception; Music Hall, 1,000 reception.
Rental Fee Varies according to day of the
week and season.
Hours Daily, 11:30 A.M.–2 A.M.
Parking Valet available.

Courtesy of House of Blues

Chicago's premiere restaurant and concert venue is located in the Marina City Complex, and consists of four levels: an innovative multimedia restaurant with two semi-private rooms, a three-story music hall inspired by the famous Estate Theatre "Estavovski" in Prague, and two levels of private opera skyboxes.

Guests of the HOB will find a fusion of a Mississippi Delta juke joint with a classical opera house of the late 1920s.

All catering is done in-house. The sales and catering department can provide menu packages for group lunches, dinners, and receptions. Signature items include seafood jambalaya, étouffée, BBQ ribs, and corn bread with maple butter. Decadent desserts include bread pudding and chocolate fudge brownies. The venue is handicapped accessible. Audiovisual equipment is available.

Hudson Club

504 N. Wells Street
Chicago, IL 60610
(312) 467-1947 or (773) 472-1601
www.thehudsonclub.com

Contact Kim Veber, director of special
events; or Claire Perry or Heather Zomer,
special events sales managers
Best Features Innovative American cuisine,
large wine list.
Capacity Entire facility, 400 reception;
Metropolis Room, 48 banquet, 85 reception;
Velvet Lounge, 40 reception.
Rental Fee No room rental fee.
Hours Flexible.
Parking Valet.

Courtesy of Hudson Club

This is a chic 1940s-style supper club features a décor throughout of lush velvets, deep mahogany woods, brushed aluminum, and soft, intimate candlelight. The Metropolis Room is perfect for sit-down dinners, while the Velvet Lounge makes a cozy setting for cocktail parties.

All food and beverage is provided by the club. Several menu options allow you to choose between a large assortment of hors d'oeuvres, appetizers, salads, entrees, and desserts. Also, with 100 different wines by the glass, bottle, or in a "flight" taster portion, the Hudson Club is the perfect location for a wine tasting or similar event. Upon request, the club will provide anything from flowers and decorations to audiovisual equipment. The restaurant is handicapped accessible.

JACKSON HARBOR GRILL

6401 S. LAKE SHORE DRIVE
CHICAGO, IL 60649
(773) 288-4442, FAX (773) 288-3567

CONTACT Paula Saks, catering manager
CAPACITY Boat Room, 70 banquet, 100 reception; upstairs dining room, 50 banquet, 70 reception; main dining room, 30 banquet, 50 reception; outdoor porch, 30 banquet, 40 reception; outdoor tent capacity, 300+.
RENTAL FEE Varies with day of the week and season.
HOURS Daily; flexible.
PARKING Up to 100 cars in adjacent lot.

Courtesy of Jackson Harbor Grill

Transport your guests to a magical getaway in a century-old Coast Guard Station located on the shore of Lake Michigan. The largest area available for private events is the Boat Room, which has a rustic and warm environment with oak paneling and 20-foot high doors that open directly onto Lake Michigan. The main level dining room and the romantic adjacent porch area offer a unique indoor/outdoor atmosphere, while the upstairs dining room offers quiet elegance. The facility is not handicapped accessible.

The grill's selection of menu items is flexible. They will prepare everything from simple hors d'oeuvres to a multi-course dinner. The restaurant has an extensive beer and wine list. Fresh cut flowers and entertainment can also be arranged. The grill does not have audio-visual equipment available.

KING JAMES' BARBEQUE

1200 HAWTHORNE
WEST CHICAGO, IL 60185
(630) 231-6262, FAX (630) 231-6280

CONTACT Catering manager
BEST FEATURE Picnic grounds on four acres of land.
CAPACITY Restaurant and bar, 125 banquet; outdoor area, 500 banquet
RENTAL FEE Quoted on a per person basis.
FOR THE KIDS Outdoor fun for children's parties.
HOURS Restaurant and bar available anytime except Friday evenings; outdoor grounds, May–October, daily.
PARKING Lots on premise.

Courtesy of King James' Barbeque

For an all-you-can-eat barbeque picnic, this is the spot. Situated on four acres of woodland, King James' Barbeque is perfect for company picnics, informal wedding receptions, and family reunions. The restaurant and bar area, located in a rustic cedar-sided building with a stone chimney, blends into the natural setting and makes a great place to hole up if the weather isn't cooperating. The outdoor grounds have a volleyball court, a horseshoe pit, and plenty of picnic tables where you can just relax and enjoy the surroundings.

An old-fashioned pig roast is a popular choice but many other types of meat are slow roasted: Texas-style beef brisket, sausage, ribs, and chicken. Included in the per person price is a full buffet setup (tables, serving equipment, buffet table coverings, skirting, dinnerware, napkins) and personnel to maintain the buffet. Service upgrades to stainless or silver dinnerware, cloth tablecloths, and additional service personnel are available for a charge. Buffet lines are kept open for a minimum of one hour and meals are all-you-can-eat.

Le Colonial

937 N. Rush Street
Chicago, IL 60611
(312) 255-0088, fax (312) 255-1108

Contact Wendy Kopen or Joe King
Best Feature Candle-lit terrace overlooking Rush Street.
Capacity Dining room, 95; lounge, 60.
Rental Fee Based on food and beverage consumption, availability.
Hours Daily, noon–11 P.M.
Parking Valet available.

Le Colonial is a French Vietnamese restaurant located in the heart of Chicago's Gold Coast. It recaptures the beauty, romance, and spirit of colonial French Southeast Asia from the 1920s. The ground-level dining room has louvered wall panels, tile floors, lazy-moving ceiling fans, and vintage Vietnamese black and white photos. Upstairs, guest enjoy light fare and cocktails at the 30-person mahogany bar, or in the lounge, which offers overstuffed sofas, Oriental rugs, exotic plants, and antique furnishings.

The restaurant offers authentic French-Vietnamese cuisine such as Chao Tom (grilled shrimp wrapped around sugar cane), Ca Chien Saigon (crisp-seared red snapper), Suon Nuong (rack of lamb with saffron rice and grilled vegetables), and Bo Sate (sautéed filet mignon with sate spice, yams and string beans). The staff will assist you in selecting from this truly unique menu.

Le Colonial's enclosed terrace, which overlooks the bustle of Rush Street, is available for year-round dining. It opens completely during the summer months to provide the finest in al fresco dining.

Photograph by Steincamp/Ballogg Chicago, courtesy of Le Colonial

Maggiano's Little Italy

A Lettuce Entertain You Restaurant

516 N. Clark Street
Chicago, IL 60610
(312) 644-4284, fax (312) 644-1027
Maggiano's Banquets
111 W. Grand Avenue
Chicago, IL 60610
WWW.MAGGIANOS.COM
E-MAIL MG47BANQUETS@MAGGIANOS.COM

Contact Jeannie Rautenberg, Rebecca Hinterlong, Laura Hoffman, banquet managers
Capacity Entire Wine Cellar, 210 banquet, 300 reception; Barolo and Belaggio rooms combined, 160 banquet, 200 reception; bar only, 50 banquet, 100 reception. Entire Grand Banquet, 300 banquet, 400 reception; Antinori and Amarone rooms, 130 banquet, 175 reception; Barbera and Orvieto rooms, 30 banquet, 50 reception.

Photograph by Steve Matteo

Rental Fee None, price based on food and beverage minimums.
Hours Open daily, 8 A.M. to 1 A.M.
Parking Valet; street; nearby public lots.

Maggiano's features an uncanny resemblance to one of New York's traditional Little Italy localities. Maggiano's recently added a separate banquet facility at 111 W. Grand, but the restaurant has its own banquet accomodations, the Wine Cellar. The room accommodates intimate family gatherings, blow-out galas, or anything in between.

The emphasis is on family-style service, but there are also breakfast, buffet, and cocktail options. Consumption-based bars, as well as bar packages, can be arranged. Parties can be personalized through the use of custom designed invitations, linens, and centerpieces. Full audiovisual selections, fax, and photocopying services are also available.

MAGNUM'S PRIME STEAKHOUSE AND WHITE STAR LOUNGE

225 W. ONTARIO STREET
CHICAGO, IL 60610
(312) 337-3836, FAX (312) 337-1836
WWW.ACEPLACES.COM

CONTACT Lucy Cook, corporate director of catering
BEST FEATURE Excellent cuisine.
CAPACITY 5 private dining rooms, 10–150 banquet; White Star Lounge, 100–400 reception.
RENTAL FEE Based on food and beverage consumption.
HOURS Dining rooms, anytime; White Star Lounge until 10 P.M.
PARKING Valet; nearby lots.

Courtesy of Magnum's Prime Steakhouse and White Star Lounge

Located in the heart of the River North restaurant and entertainment district, Magnum's has become a mecca for steak aficionados. The private dining rooms feature fireplaces, built-in bars, etched mirrors, and custom artwork. The White Star Lounge, which is adjacent to Magnum's, is a hot dance club that is great for a cocktail reception. Classic disco and dance hits from the 70s and 80s are complemented by a state-of-the-art lighting and video show. Retro furnishings and decor create a comfortable upscale atmosphere for up to 400 guests. White Star's VIP rooms can be reserved for smaller parties.

Magnum's serves USA prime aged steaks, seafood, and continental fare. Dinner packages start at $22.95 and up. A cocktail and hors d'oeuvres reception starts at $25 per person. Magnum's also caters events held at White Star. Audio-visual equipment is available for rent. Both sites are handicapped accessible.

MERC'S RESTAURANT

605 EAST 111TH STREET
CHICAGO, IL 60628
(773) 468-6372, FAX (773) 468-4234

CONTACT James Huckabee, owner
CAPACITY Entire restaurant, 130 banquet; main floor, 80 banquet; second floor dining area, 50 banquet.
RENTAL FEE Depends on time of day and number of guests.
DISCOUNTS Ten percent to qualifying parties.
HOURS Tuesday–Saturday, 11:30 A.M.– 2:30 P.M.; Thursday, 5 P.M.–9 P.M.; Friday and Saturday, 5 P.M.–9 P.M.
PARKING On the street.

Courtesy of Merc's Restaurant

Built in 1881, this renovated mansion has original working fireplaces, tapestry carpeting, and claret window swags. A cherry-wood staircase leads to the second floor, which has a cozy parlor and a private dining room.

For more intimate gatherings, The Retreat features French-American cuisine. All catering is done on-site. Entree prices range from $6–$10 per person for lunch and $15–$20 for dinner; buffet prices range from $14.95–$22.95. Group service prices range from $14–$24, and hors d'oeuvre buffets run $12.95–$15.95. An open bar is $12 per person; other bar options include cash bar and actual consumption billing. Plate charges and corkage fees are assessed for all outside bakery goods and liquor. A podium is available; other meeting equipment may be brought in with permission. Smoking and children's parties are not permitted. The Retreat is not wheelchair accessible.

MIA TORRE

Sears Tower

233 S. Wacker Drive
Chicago, IL 60606
(312) 993-1923, fax (312) 993-2763

Contact Ann Provenzano, event planner
Best Feature Lively atmosphere within Sears Tower building.
Capacity 125 banquet, 250 reception.
Rental Fee Based on food and beverage consumption.
Hours Flexible.
Parking Garage across from the Franklin Street entrance.

Courtesy of Mia Torre

Inspired by the energy and convivial atmosphere of the Palio horserace in Sienna, Italy, Mia Torre is the perfect site for a celebration. The spirited decor will enhance any event. The interior is rich with stucco textures and bright, lively colors. A painted garden trellis, brick stone floors, and a faux sky paint-ing recreate the charm of relaxed outdoor dining characteristic of the Italian countryside. The site is handicapped accessible.

The cuisine is authentic regional Italian with a festive flair, and features innovative salads, gourmet pizzas, contemporary pastas, panini sandwiches, rotisserie specials, and tempting desserts. An extensive yet affordable Italian/American wine list is available to complement any meal. A creative menu will be custom designed by the experienced event planners. You may reserve the entire restaurant or just a semiprivate area. Audiovisual equipment is available for rental.

MIKE DITKA'S RESTAURANT

100 E. Chestnut Street
Chicago, IL 60611
(312) 587-8989, fax (312) 587-8980

Contact Zak Dich or Heather Sampognaro
Best Feature Da Coach's sport's souvenirs.
Capacity Hall of Fame Room, 110 banquet, 80 classroom, 50 conference; Cricket Rooms, 45 banquet, 30 classroom, 25 conference; Board Room, 32 banquet, 28 classroom, 25 theater.
Rental Fee Based on food and beverage consumption.
Hours Daily, 7:30 A.M.–2 A.M.
Parking Valet, public lots nearby.

Courtesy of Mike Ditka's Restaurant

Mike Ditka's Restaurant is spearheaded by Mike Ditka himself, former head coach of the Chicago Bears and Hall of Fame player, under the auspices of Chicago restaurateur, Joe Carlucci. There are four rooms available for functions: Hall of Fame Room, Board Room, Cricket "A," and Cricket "B." The sports items, paintings, and photographs that decorate the walls and are sure to spark conversation among your guests. Located next door to the Tremont Hotel, the restaurant can accommodate groups of 10-300. Even if you choose a white tablecloth setting, Mike Ditka's main-tains a casual yet sophisticated feel.

The restaurant provides an American bistro menu for all events. Menu specialties include the Duck Cigar and Da Coach's Pork Chop. Mike Ditka's also boasts game-winning steaks, fish, pasta, and first-string desserts. The restaurant is handicapped accessible.

MRS. LEVY'S DELICATESSEN

233 S. WACKER DRIVE
CHICAGO, IL 60606
(312) 993-1923, FAX (312) 993-2763
WWW.LEVYRESTAURANTS.COM

CONTACT Ann Provenzano, event planner
BEST FEATURE Celebrity wall of fame, old-fashioned soda fountain.
CAPACITY 200 banquet, 250 reception.
RENTAL FEE Based on food and beverage consumption.
HOURS Flexible.
PARKING Garage across from the Franklin Street entrance.

As Chicago's most authentic deli, Mrs. Levy's Delicatessen offers a range of creative dining capabilities. Celebrity photographs line the walls and oldies tunes have toes tapping upon entrance. Mrs. Levy's also features an old-fashioned soda fountain, reminiscent of classic diners of days past. Presided over by the deli's matriarch, Mrs. Levy herself, the deli is ideally suited for bar/ bat mitzvahs, reunions, birthday parties, company events, or other celebrations. The deli is wheelchair accessible.

Homemade soups and imaginative sandwiches are the specialties of Mrs. Levy's. Flexible event menus offer options like the famous ruben, "higher-than-sky" triple decker sandwiches, or one of the many healthy creations. Entrees can be topped off with a spectacular fountain concoction, created with chocolate almond crunch or chocolate peanut butter truffle. Mrs. Levy's offers a selection of premium ice creams and desserts sure to tempt the tastes of any guest. Audiovisual equipment is available for rental.

Courtesy of Mrs. Levy's Delicatessen

NICK'S FISHMARKET— ROSEMONT

O'Hare International Center

10275 W. HIGGINS ROAD
ROSEMONT, IL 60018
(847) 298-8200

CONTACT Catering manager
BEST FEATURE Three 450-gallon aquariums.
CAPACITY Entire restaurant, 250 banquet; private dining room, 36 banquet, 50 reception; semiprivate, 150 banquet.
RENTAL FEE Based on food and beverage consumption.
HOURS Dinner only; Sunday–Thursday, 5:30 P.M.–10 P.M., Friday and Saturday, 6 P.M.–11 P.M.
PARKING Complimentary valet.

Courtesy of Nick's Fishmarket

The luxurious burgundy leather booths and commissioned artwork at Nick's Fishmarket create a polished atmosphere. The decor is highlighted by three 450-gallon saltwater aquariums built into the walls. Adjacent to the front dining area is a lounge with a 40-foot wine cellar, marble bar, cocktail tables, and stage and dance floor. You can rent the entire restaurant for large parties or a private dining room for events of up to 50 guests.

Nick's provides food and beverages.

Seafood is the focus of the menu. Fresh catches such as opakapaka and mahi-mahi are flown in directly from Hawaii. Shellfish offerings include live Maine lobster, lobster tail, and fresh Florida stone crabs. The wine list has more than 200 domestic and imported wines. There is same-day storage for flowers and wedding cakes that you bring in. Nick's does not serve lunch.

NIKOS

7600 S. HARLEM AVENUE
BRIDGEVIEW, IL 60455
(708) 496-0300, FAX (708) 458-4400

CONTACT Nick Vern
BEST FEATURE Flaming entrees.
CAPACITY Two rooms, each 350 banquet, combined 750 banquet; cocktail lounge, 100 banquet; Fireside Room, 80 banquet.
RENTAL FEE Based on food and beverage consumption.
HOURS Flexible.
PARKING Free valet.

Photograph by J & J Photography and Printing Services, courtesy of Nikos

This restaurant in Chicago's southwest suburbs has banquet facilities that can accommodate up to 750 people for a sit-down dinner. The two banquet rooms are decorated in mauve and light-colored wood with numerous mirrors, silk flowers, oil paintings, and a parquet dance floor. A tall wooden staircase leads into each of the rooms and makes for a grand entrance. An art deco cocktail lounge is available for private parties with up to 100 guests or for semiprivate parties with fewer guests.

The restaurant provides all food and beverage. Some of the more outstanding menu options are the flaming entrees (Steak Diane and The Poseidon Adventure) and the flaming deserts (Cherries Jubilee, and Strawberry and Bananas Aloha). Ice sculptures, cakes, invitations, limousines, and any other extras your party might require can be arranged by Nikos' catering coordinator. Prices vary seasonally and monthly, so it is best to contact the restaurant for a quote.

O'BRIEN'S RESTAURANT & BAR

1528 N. WELLS STREET
CHICAGO, IL 60610
(312) 787-3131, FAX (312) 787-9434

CONTACT Catering manager
BEST FEATURE Live piano nightly.
CAPACITY Oak Room, 120 banquet, 250 reception; Garden Café, 80 banquet, 150 reception; boardroom, 20 banquet, 40 reception.
RENTAL FEE Based on food and beverage consumption.
HOURS Monday–Thursday, 11 A.M.–10:30 P.M.; Friday and Saturday, 11 A.M.–12:30 A.M.
PARKING Free lot.

Courtesy of O'Brien's Restaurant & Bar

Located in the heart of Old Town, O'Brien's offers casual elegance with continental cuisine. The Oak Room is ideal for meetings, formal dinners, and cocktail receptions. The room is located on a private floor with a separate bar. During the summer months, the Garden Café is a delightful spot for an outdoor event. The Café is decorated with teak furniture and a gazebo bar.

O'Brien's offers prime steaks, fresh seafood, and lighter fare options. A menu will be personalized for your event. You may bring in your own entertainment or enjoy the piano player, who performs nightly. Special transportation services include a limousine, the O'Brien's Trolley, double-decker buses, a white Rolls Royce, and a horse-drawn carriage. A VCR, TV, and microphone sound system are available.

P. J. Clarke's

A Lettuce Entertain You Restaurant

1204 N. State Parkway
Chicago, IL 60610
(312) 664-1650
www.leye.com

Contact Ginny Schodasch, catering sales
Best Feature One of Chicago's favorite watering holes.
Best Party Birthday party for Woody Harrelson.
Capacity Clover Room, 56 banquet, 125 reception; second and third floors, 125 reception; entire restaurant, 500.
Rental Fee $150.
Hours Flexible to 2 A.M.
Parking Limited on street; lot across the street.

Photograph by Steve Matteo

With a relaxed, unpretentious atmosphere, this restaurant is perfect for less formal occasions. The Clover Room, located on the third floor, features a turn-of-the-century oak bar, separate dining area, two TVs and a VCR, and a small outdoor patio overlooking State Street. The room can be set for cocktail receptions, sit-down dinners, or meetings. The second and third floors are also available for private parties with around 250 guests.

P. J. Clarke's features a classic American grill with dishes like Bourbon Marinated Pork Chops ($16.95), New York Strip Steaks ($21.95), and Mustard Charred Salmon ($18.95). A BBQ buffet with dessert is $19.95 per person. Liquor packages are $10 per person for a one-hour open bar with house brands and $14 for premium brands. Audiovisual equipment, special linens, centerpieces, and other extras can be arranged for an additional charge. The restaurant is not handicapped accessible.

Palette's Restaurant

1030 N. State Street
Chicago, IL 60610
(312) 440-5200, fax (312) 943-9477

Contact Heinz Kern, owner
Capacity Main dining room, 158 banquet; bar area, 90 banquet; private party room, 100 banquet; entire facility, 275 reception.
Rental Fee Negotiable.
Hours Monday–Thursday, 5–10 P.M.; Friday–Saturday, 5–11 P.M.; Sunday 5–10 P.M.
Parking Valet, discount with validation.

Photograph by Steve Matteo

Palette's, a restaurant serving innovative American cuisine, was designed by Serbian artist Boban Ilic. In the center of the main dining room a 14-foot wrought iron sculpture of the mythological figure Icarus reaches for the Michelangelo-style fresco on the ceiling. Palette's long bar area with eclectic velvet sofas and chairs can accommodate as many as 90 persons. A mahogany-paneled private dining room with an elegant crystal chandelier and original paintings is perfect for a prenuptial dinner, corporate holiday party, or an intimate wedding of up to 100 people. The main dining room seats 158 and can be configured for smaller groups.

Palette's takes a contemporary approach to both its decor and its cuisine. The restaurant caters all events and will tailor the menu to your needs.

The Palm Restaurant

At the Swissotel Chicago

323 E. Wacker Drive
Chicago, IL 60601
(312) 616-8141, fax (312) 616-3717
www.thepalm.com

Contact Ann Marie
Capacity Private dining room, 64 banquet, 100 reception; boardroom, 16 banquet.
Rental Fee Based on food and beverage consumption.
Hours Daily, 11:30 A.M.–11 P.M.; other times by arrangement.
Parking Valet; $6 with restaurant validation.

Photograph by Peter Vanderwarker, courtesy of The Palm Restaurant

Previously located in the Mayfair Hotel the legendary Palm Restaurant reopened in the Swissotel in September of 1996. Recommended for its huge prime steak and jumbo Nova Scotia lobsters, The Palm is also known for its Wall of Fame, featuring caricatures of celebrities and local VIPs. The Palm has a speakeasy atmosphere. The private dining room boasts a fantastic view of Lake Michigan and Navy Pier. The boardroom can be used for both social and business events and comes with a TV, VCR, fax, and telephone capabilities. The Palm is handicapped accessible.

All food and beverage is provided by the restaurant. Dinners start at $52 per person and lunches at $21 per person. Customized menus can be arranged to meet any specifications. The Palm can provide flowers, special linens, and musical trios at your request for an additional charge.

Quincy Grille on the River

200 S. Wacker Drive
Chicago, IL 60606
(312) 627-1800, fax (312) 627-1029
www.quincygrille.com

Contact Diane Reichle, general manager and director of catering
Best Feature Outdoor park and riverfront view.
Capacity Main dining room, 175 banquet, 300 reception; outdoor park, 300 reception.
Rental Fee Based on food and beverage consumption and setup required.
Hours Daily by arrangement.
Parking Nearby lots; valet available.

Courtesy of Quincy Grille on the River

Located directly on the Chicago River, the club offers a dramatic view of the steady stream of sailboats and tourist boats below. The picture windows evoke the feeling of being on a cruise ship. The main dining room has a granite-topped bar and a grand piano. The understated decor provides a neutral yet elegant backdrop for any type of event. A small private party room for up to 20 guests is perfect for meetings, luncheons, or seminars. The outdoor park and terrace—complete with waterfall and the Sears Tower as a backdrop—are spectacular and are perfect for cocktails, receptions, or even a wedding ceremony.

Quincy Grille will customize a menu for your event. Lunches range from $15–$25 per person; dinners $25 and up per person; breakfast is also available. Bar packages are available on a per-drink basis or per hour. The club can arrange flowers, audiovisual equipment, entertainment, and other extras, or you can provide them.

REZA'S

432 W. ONTARIO STREET
CHICAGO, IL 60610
(312) 664-4500
5255 N. CLARK STREET
CHICAGO, IL 60640
(773) 561-1898

CONTACT Joe or Reza Toulabi, owners

CAPACITY Ontario location: entire restaurant, 800 banquet, 1,000 reception; private and semiprivate dining areas, 20–450 banquet. Clark location: entire restaurant, 100 reception.

RENTAL FEE Based on food and beverage consumption.

HOURS Daily, 11 A.M.–midnight; later by arrangement.

PARKING Ontario location: nearby lot; valet for a fee. Clark location: street.

Photograph by Steve Matteo

Reza's on Ontario Street is well equipped for company parties, birthdays, rehearsal dinners, and more. Reza's is known for its excellent cuisine and microbrewery where they make their own brand of Persian beer. The huge brewing kettles are displayed in a glass area behind the bar and serve as an interesting backdrop for your event.

All events are catered by the restaurant. Reza's features Persian, Mediterranean, and vegetarian dishes. Included in the per person prices are nonalcoholic drinks, bamye (pastry), pita bread, relish trays, rice, and soup. Three-hour bar packages are available. All menu options can be served either family- or buffet-style. The Ontario location offers free shuttle service to and from anywhere in downtown Chicago.

SALVATORE'S RISTORANTE

525 W. ARLINGTON PLACE
CHICAGO, IL 60614
(773) 528-1200, FAX (773) 528-1272
WWW.SALVATORES-CHICAGO.COM

CONTACT Shirley Davis, catering director; or Sherife Jusufi, general manager

BEST FEATURE Italian country mansion atmosphere.

BEST PARTIES Weddings, rehearsal dinners, corporate functions.

CAPACITY Three rooms, 15–260 banquet, 400 reception.

RENTAL FEE $100–$400.

DISCOUNTS In January and February.

HOURS Flexible.

PARKING Valet; two nearby lots.

Courtesy of Salvatore's Ristorante

Salvatore's northern Italian restaurant is housed on the ground floor of a nostalgic hotel built in the roaring 20s. From the grand lobby entrance with its black and white marble floor to mahogany paneled rooms surrounded by French windows and an enchanting patio, Salvatore's evokes a sense of grandeur. The Pasta Vino Room is a bright and airy space that overlooks the courtyard and can accommodate 60 guests for dinner and 100 for cocktails. The largest of the rooms is the Classico Room, which is perfect for a sit-down dinner with up to 165 guests. The West Room is equipped with an antique baby grand piano that can be used for your event.

The restaurant caters all functions. Dinner packages including wine are available for about $54 per person. A dinner extravaganza with a four-hour premium bar service is $80 per person. Audiovisual equipment is available for rental. The washrooms at Salvatore's are not handicapped accessible.

Scoozi!

410 W. Huron
Chicago, IL 60610
(312) 943-5900, fax (312) 943-8969
Contact Melissa Marcus, catering sales
Best Features Festive and lively, opera singers.
Best Party Tomato Fest.
Capacity Entire restaurant, 320; semi-private room, 50.
Rental Fee Call for rates.
For the Kids Pizza Parties every Sunday.
Hours Flexible for private events.
Parking Valet.

Scoozi! re-creates the atmosphere of an Italian Renaissance trattoria with earthy hues and a warmly lit interior. It boasts an open floor plan with 30-foot ceilings and an authentic wood-burning oven. The restaurant, located in the heart of Chicago's River North Art Gallery District, is handicapped accessible.

Scoozi!'s semi-private dining room features a 70-foot-long wine wall separating the guests from the main dining room. This allows guests the luxury of privacy without losing any of the energy and excitement the restaurant has to offer.

Photograph by Steinkamp/Ballog Chicago, courtesy of Scoozi!

Shaw's Crab House

1900 E. Higgins Road
Schaumburg, IL 60173
(847) 517-2722, fax (847)517-1188
www.shawscrabhouse.com
E-mail shawscatering133@aol.com

Contact Catering sales
Capacity 10–200.
Rental Fee Based upon food and beverage consumption.
Hours Flexible for private events.
Parking Free.

A vibrant, hand-painted mural accentuates the dramatic grand staircase leading to second-level private dining and board rooms at Shaw's Crab House. These rooms are available for functions with seating for 10–100, and are complete with a full bar and reception area. They feature wood-trimmed walls with a 1940s feel and décor, and offer the convenience of in-house audiovisual equipment, including Internet access.

Courtesy of Shaw's Crab House

Private dining menus include fresh fish, crab, lobster, shrimp, chicken, and prime steak, and a wide selection of hors d'oeuvres and appetizers.

Lunches start at $20 per person, and dinners are $35 and up. Shaw's Pastry Chef will also customize the dessert menu for your event, from key lime pie to crème brûlé.

THE SIGNATURE ROOM AT THE 95TH

875 N. MICHIGAN AVENUE
CHICAGO, IL 60611
(312) 787-9596 OR (630) 968-7778
(WOODRIDGE), FAX (312) 280-9448
WWW.SIGNATUREROOM.COM

CONTACT Tricia Bryant
CAPACITY Can accommodate events from 30–1,000.
RENTAL FEE Based on food and beverage consumption.
FOR THE KIDS A special children's buffet at the Sunday brunch.
HOURS Restaurant, Monday–Saturday, 11 A.M.–2:30 P.M. and 5–10 P.M. (until 11 P.M. on Friday and Saturday); Sunday 10:30 A.M.–2:30 P.M. and 5 P.M.–10 P.M. Lounge, Sunday–Thursday, 11 A.M.–12:30 A.M. (featuring live jazz 8 P.M.–midnight), Friday and Saturday, 11 A.M.–1:30 P.M.
PARKING In the building or at nearby garages.

Courtesy of The Signature Room

Located on the 95th floor of the John Hancock Center, the Signature Room's floor-to-ceiling windows offer incredible views of the city. The restaurant also has a state-of-the-art banquet facility in Woodridge, the Signature Room at Seven Bridges, that can accommodate events up to 1,100. Both facilities are handicapped accessible.

Whether you are planning an event for 30 or 1,000, the staff will assist you in customizing a menu that will have guests tempted from the first hors d'oeuvre to the last delicate pastry. Entertainment, audiovisual equipment, ice sculptures, flowers, special linens, and other extra touches can be arranged. Private dining rooms are also available.

SPIAGGIA, PRIVATE DINING ROOMS OF

980 N. MICHIGAN AVENUE, 3RD LEVEL
CHICAGO, IL 60611
(312) 280-3300, FAX (312) 943-9337
WWW.SPIAGGIARESTAURANT.COM

CONTACT Joan Kim, Susan Fishbein, or Robyn Pfeffer, event planners
BEST FEATURE Excellent cuisine and spectacular view.
CAPACITY 200 banquet, 500 reception.
RENTAL FEE Based on food and beverage consumptioh; room fees applicable to certain events.
HOURS Flexible.
PARKING Garage in the building.

When a business event calls for a warm, yet prestigious setting, the Private Dining Rooms of Spiaggia offer superb cuisine in a spectacular setting. Located one floor above the four-star Spiaggia restaurant, the Private Dining Rooms offer five separate rooms that can be combined in many configurations to meet specific needs. This site offers a dramatic view of Lake Michigan quite unlike any other in the city. When this view is paired with the award-winning cuisine of chef Tony Mantuano, an event becomes complete.

Chef Mantuano possesses a passion for simple, sophisticated foods. This is reflected in a menu custom designed for each event. A resident wine expert will also recommend just the right bottle to complement menu choices. The special event team can assist in any aspect of planning, from entertainment recommendations to providing state-of-the-art audiovisual equipment. The restaurant is handicapped accessible.

Courtesy of Spiaggia

STAR OF SIAM

11 E. ILLINOIS STREET
CHICAGO, IL 60611
(312) 670-0100, FAX (312) 222-4100
WWW.STAROFSIAM.COM

CONTACT Eddie Dulyapaibul, chef/owner
BEST FEATURE Industrial chic.
CAPACITY Banquet room, 120 banquet, 150 reception; main floor dining room, 125 banquet.
RENTAL FEE Banquet room, $50.
HOURS 11 A.M.–11 P.M.
PARKING Street; nearby public lot; valet.

Courtesy of Star of Siam

One of the most popular Thai restaurants in the River North area, Star of Siam is appropriate for anything from birthday parties to large private meetings. The interior features an open look with carpeted bench seating and sunken island seating for small groups. The main floor has the look of a loft with a high ceiling supported by oak beams and lined with exposed russet-red heating ducts.

The restaurant supplies all food and beverage. Family-style lunches are from $13–$15 per person. Family-style dinners that include appetizers, noodle dishes, entrees, rice, dessert, and nonalcoholic drinks are from $15–$20 per person. If alcohol is included in the package, it will cost from $20–$30 per person. You can bring in baked goods and a sound system is available. The restaurant is not handicapped accessible.

THE TERRACE RESTAURANT

Wilmette Golf Course

LAKE AVENUE AND HARMS ROAD
WILMETTE, IL 60091
(847) 256-9626 OR (847) 256-9628
WWW.WILMETTEPARK.ORG

CONTACT Banquet coordinator
BEST FEATURE Overlooks the Wilmette Golf Course.
CAPACITY 25–200.
RENTAL FEE Based on food and beverage consumption.
HOURS Flexible.
PARKING Free on site.

Courtesy of the Terrace Restaurant

The Terrace Restaurant is located within the park-like environs of the beautiful Wilmette Golf Course. The clubhouse features wood-paneled walls and a pastel color scheme that blends easily with any theme. The site includes a large room with a fireplace, and a piano is available upon request. An adjoining room with picture windows offers airy views of the Wilmette Golf Course.

The Terrace's friendly, courteous staff prepares and serves all food. The restaurant offers a full array of private party services for groups from 25–200. This site is great for everything from sports banquets to bridal showers, from bar/bat mitzvahs to retirement dinners. Weddings are their specialty. Audiovisual equipment is available on-site.

VA PENSIERO RESTAURANT

1566 OAK AVENUE
EVANSTON, IL 60201
(847) 475-7779, FAX (847) 475-7825
WWW.VAPENSIERO-CATERING.COM

CONTACT Patrick Igo, director of catering
BEST FEATURE Regional Italian cuisine in an intimate setting.
CAPACITY Verdi Room, 90; Solera Room, 72; Ivory Room, 60; Grand Parlour, 52; additional rooms available for smaller groups.
RENTAL FEE $100–$650, depending on the room.
HOURS Flexible.
PARKING Valet available; limited street.

Courtesy of Va Pensiero Restaurant

Tucked within the historic Margarita European Inn (see separate listing), Va Pensiero's intimate Verdi Room features an Enoteca (wine library), a working fireplace, and classic architecture. A foyer adjoins the Verdi Room with the main dining room; both rooms can be utilized together for larger functions. If the weather permits, a terrace is available for parties of 40. Most rooms are handicapped accessible.

Va Pensiero features regional Italian cuisine, a full selection of liquor, extensive wine list, and personalized service. You can select from the extensive catering menu or they will customize one for you. Brunch and lunch prices range from $30–$65 per person including tax and service charge. Dinner prices range from $65–$125 per person including tax and service charge. Audiovisual equipment is available for rental.

WILD ONION

3500 N. LINCOLN AVENUE
CHICAGO, IL 60657
(773) 871-5113 OR (773) 871-5555

CONTACT Ramsey Yokana, owner
BEST FEATURE Eclectic bistro-style cuisine.
CAPACITY Entire Restaurant, 150 banquet, 200 reception; four semiprivate dining rooms, 20–60 reception; patio, 50 banquet, 100 reception.
RENTAL FEE Based on food and beverage consumption.
HOURS Flexible.
PARKING Ample street parking, valet available.

Courtesy of Wild Onion

This loft-inspired storefront has exposed brick walls, polished hardwood floors, and high beamed ceilings. A popular dining site in the Roscoe Village area, Wild Onion features eclectic bistro-style cuisine and can accommodate groups of 10 to 200. There are two large dining rooms at the front of the restaurant and two smaller rooms in the back for intimate parties. When the weather permits, the outdoor patio can be used for events with up to 100 guests.

You may choose from the menu or make a special request. Entrees start at $8.95 per person. Appetizer buffets start at $11.95 per person. Sit-down dinner packages are $14.95–$28.95 per person. Private bar for all functions. There is no audiovisual equipment available.

ZODIAC RESTAURANT AT NEIMAN MARCUS

737 N. MICHIGAN AVENUE, 4TH FLOOR
CHICAGO, IL 60611
(312) 642-5900 EXT. 2365,
   FAX (312) 642-9622

CONTACT Laurie Jaffe, general manager of restaurants

BEST FEATURE Etched glass ceiling.

CAPACITY Entire restaurant, 200 banquet, 300 reception.

RENTAL FEE Based on food and beverage consumption; frequently waived.

HOURS Private parties anytime; lunch à la carte service 11 A.M.–4 P.M., Monday–Saturday.

PARKING Self-parking lot in building.

Photograph by Steve Matteo

Situated next to the gourmet food and wine department of Neiman Marcus, this unique specialty retailer venue offers an elegant fine dining setting with a relaxed atmosphere. Guests enter the salmon-colored foyer, decorated with French Steinlen posters, peach walls, and dark wood paneling. The green marble bar is full service, with a wine list featuring domestic and European vintages. The main dining room boasts a magnificent rectangular ceiling overhanging of etched glass. Two smaller dining rooms provide additional space for pre-dinner receptions or for smaller parties.

The restaurant caters events with breakfasts from $7.95 per person, lunches from $14.95 per person, a basic appetizer buffet is $10.95 per person, and dinners from $21.95 per person. Audiovisual equipment is available. Special requests are welcome and the general manager/catering director will handle every detail from printed menus to decorations, music, and photography.

SHIPS AND TRANSPORTATION

Anita Dee I and *II*

Chicago from the Lake

Chicago Transit Authority

Chicago's First Lady and *Chicago's
    Little Lady*

Odyssey Cruises

The Spirit of Chicago

Wagner Charter Company:
    The Buccaneer

Wagner Charter Company:
    The Jamaica

Anita Dee I and II

Docked at Navy Pier

Administrative Offices:
2000 N. Racine Avenue
Chicago, IL 60614
(773) 281-1300, fax (773) 281-1371
www.anitadee.com
E-mail info@anitadee.com

Contact Sales department
Best Feature Modern decor, and full service equipment.
Best Party Reception for the president of Chile and U.S. dignitaries.
Capacity *Anita Dee I*, 50–149 reception; *Anita Dee II*, 150–400 reception.
Rental Fee *Anita Dee I*: $750–$1,050 per hour (3-hour minimum). *Anita Dee II*: $1,000–$2,000 per hour (4-hour minimum). Rates vary according to day of the week, time of day, and season.
Hours Flexible; afternoon and evening.
Parking Navy Pier parking garage. Navy Pier trolley shuttle service available.

Courtesy of Anita Dee

The 140-foot *Anita Dee II* (pictured), has three levels. The first level offers a spacious lounge deck with stylish leather couches, a baby grand piano, and a semicircular bar that extends outside to the rear deck. The elegant dining deck is equipped with a bar and a silver banquette for your buffet. The upstairs observation deck runs nearly the length of the ship, and boasts the most breathtaking view of the skyline imaginable. The 90-foot *Anita Dee I* is decorated in a classic nautical style. The enclosed main deck is split into two regions, both with wood-paneled walls and ceiling. The lounge area has deep leather couches running along the walls and navy blue carpeting. Cushioned window seats line the back walls, and there is a wooden bar and a small wood dance floor as well. The roof observation deck also offers a wooden bar and dance floor.

Our event coordinators will assist you in determining the goals of your event, as well as in selecting caterers, entertainment, themes, decorations, flowers, and transportation. Audiovisual equipment is not available. The *Anita Dee II* is not fully handicapped accessible.

Chicago from the Lake

Docked at North Pier

455 E. Illinois Street, Slip Level
Chicago, IL 60611
(312) 527-2002, fax (312) 527-2313
www.chicagoline.com

Contact Sales manager
Capacity *Fort Dearborn* and *Innisfree*, 200 reception; *Marquette*, 55 reception.
Rental Fee *Fort Dearborn* and *Innisfree*, $800 per hour Sunday–Thursday, $900 per hour Friday, Saturday, and holidays; *Marquette*, $500 per hour Sunday–Thursday, $600 per hour Friday, Saturday, and holidays.
Hours May 1–October 31, weather permitting.
Parking Limited discounted parking in public lots; no street parking.

Chicago from the Lake has three ships available for evening private events. The *Fort Dearborn*, the *Innisfree*, and the

Courtesy of Chicago from the Lake

Marquette are docked at River East Plaza, at the historic North Pier Docks. The *Fort Dearborn* and the *Innisfree* are 65-foot two-decked boats with open top decks that can be covered during inclement weather. The *Marquette* is a 58-foot single-deck ship that is perfect for smaller events. You can entertain and inform your guests with a 90-minute architectural or historical narration ($150 extra).

A list of recommended caterers is available. Beverage service is provided by the ship. A beer, wine, and soft drink bar is $12 per person for two hours. A two-hour premium bar is $16 per person. A 10 percent amusement tax is added to vessel rental charges. The *Fort Dearborn* and the *Innisfree* have a minimum headcount of 150 passengers for Friday, Saturday, and holiday events.

CHICAGO TRANSIT AUTHORITY

MERCHANDISE MART PLAZA, ROOM 411
CHICAGO, IL 60654
(312) 664-7200 EXT. 4126

CONTACT Train rental
BEST FEATURE Urban mobility.
CAPACITY Train cars, 80–90 banquet per car (must use at least two cars).
RENTAL FEE $1,044 for four hours.
HOURS Weekdays anytime but 6:30 A.M.–9:30 A.M. and 3:30 P.M.–6:30 P.M.; weekends anytime.

Courtesy of Chicago Transit Authority

Searching for an unusual party atmosphere? Try one that moves; rent a CTA train. Make a birthday, wedding, graduation, or company promotion a one-of-a-kind event. Trains on all of the CTA's lines are available for up to seven-hour rentals. You can stop at every station or just ride the whole way.

Trains can be decorated any way that you wish and you should supply any food that you want. You can even ask your favorite caterer to hop aboard. Liquor is restricted to wine and champagne. Two tables and two bars can be rented for an additional $105. There are no electrical sockets, so radios must be battery-powered. You need to pay in full and supply an itinerary at least three weeks in advance. Bathrooms stops will be included.

CHICAGO'S FIRST LADY AND CHICAGO'S LITTLE LADY

MICHIGAN AVENUE & WACKER DRIVE
CHICAGO, IL 60601
MAILING ADDRESS:
P.O. BOX 68
PALATINE, IL 60078
(847) 358-1330, FAX (847) 991-5255
WWW.CRUISECHICAGO.COM

CONTACT Sales Staff
CAPACITY *First Lady*: Private dining salon, 75 banquet, 225 reception (150 for weddings); *Little Lady*, 10–100.
RENTAL FEE $800–$950 per hour (evenings) plus food and beverage costs.
DISCOUNTS Available early spring and late fall.
HOURS Evenings, May 1–November 1.
PARKING At Executive Plaza Hotel, Illinois Center, and Hyatt Regency, all located on Wacker Drive.

Courtesy of Chicago's First Lady

Chicago's First Lady is a custom, vintage-designed dining cruise ship, reminiscent of the former presidential yacht *Sequoia*. The carpeted, climate-controlled main deck salon has several sky lights and is decorated in burgundy, hunter green, brass, and mahogany. The salon has a full-service bar and galley as well as a piano and dance floor area. The open-air deck also has a bar and dance floor and provides additional space for viewing the sunset and city lights or even a wedding ceremony. For groups of 10–100, *Chicago's Little Lady* is the perfect choice. A miniature version of *Chicago's First Lady*, the *Little Lady* is also available each evening for private entertaining.

Two custom caterers provide a wide variety of food cooked on board to fit your taste and budget. Entertainment options may include live bands, a D.J., or commentary provided by the Chicago Architecture Foundation.

ODYSSEY CRUISES

Docked at Navy Pier

600 E. GRAND AVENUE
CHICAGO, IL 60611
(630) 990-0800 FOR GROUPS OF LESS THAN
16, (312) 321-7620 FOR GROUPS OF 16+,
FAX (312) 321-7630
WWW.ODYSSEYCRUISES.COM

CONTACT Katie Kennedy, director of sales
CAPACITY Entire ship, 700 banquet; Emerald
Deck, 500 banquet; Sapphire Deck, 250
banquet; Topaz Deck, 133 banquet; Sky
Deck, 200 banquet.
RENTAL FEE Based on food and beverage
consumption and number of passengers.
HOURS Flexible when renting the entire ship.
Individual decks available during regular
cruise hours: daily lunch and dinner cruises,
Friday and Saturday midnight cruises. The
ship operates April 1–December 31 and is
available other times with restrictions.
PARKING Pay lots at Navy Pier and North
Pier.

Courtesy of Odyssey Cruises

With nautical breezes, creative menus, attentive service, and incredible skyline views, this luxury yacht offers an excellent setting for a party. Three comfortable, enclosed, climate-controlled decks provide an atmosphere reminiscent of the classic ocean liners. Guests can wander the enclosed decks, catch a breeze on any of the three outside observation decks, or visit the captain on the bridge.

Prices range from $30–$95 per person and include a three- to four-course seated meal. Weekday lunches are $35 per person; weeknight dinners are $79 per person; Sunday jazz brunches are $45 per person and Friday and Saturday night dinner cruises are $82 and $95 per person respectively. Moonlight cruises are subject to availability and are $32 per person. Prices for children are half the adult rate. Children under 3 are free. The *Odyssey II* is wheelchair accessible and equipped with a state-of-the-art sound system and audiovisual equipment. No smoking is allowed inside the dining areas.

THE SPIRIT OF CHICAGO

Docked at Navy Pier

MAILING ADDRESS:
455 E. ILLINOIS STREET, SUITE 461
CHICAGO, IL 60611
(312) 836-7899 FOR INDIVIDUALS,
   (312) 321-1241 FOR GROUPS OF 20+

CONTACT Carol Markay, sales director
BEST FEATURE Lakefront cruise ship with
entertainment.
CAPACITY Entire ship, 600 banquet or reception; main deck, 220 banquet, 250 reception; second deck, 200 banquet, 200 reception; third deck, 136 banquet, 150 reception; observation deck, 100 banquet or reception.
RENTAL FEE Based on packages or food and
beverage options.
HOURS Please inquire about party cruise
hours and charter options.
PARKING Self-parking access on north side of
Navy Pier; nearby hourly lots serviced by
free Navy Pier trolley shuttles.

Dine, dance, applaud a Broadway-style show, view Chicago's breathtaking skyline, or just relax while your party cruises on Lake Michigan. The three-deck ship has spacious outdoor strolling decks and climate-controlled interiors designed with huge panoramic windows, dance floors, and full-service bars. The ship is handicapped accessible.

The Spirit of Chicago offers complete cruise packages featuring live entertainment, spectacular sightseeing, and full-course meals prepared by the ship's renowned galley chefs. Packages range from $30 per person to $110 per person and include discounts for groups of 20–600. The ship's group party planners will help you customize your event with special themes, extensive bar and menu options, audiovisual capabilities, and flexible floor plans.

Courtesy of The Spirit of Chicago

Wagner Charter Company

The Buccaneer

Docked on Lower Wacker Drive
Mailing Address:
2N076 Linda Avenue
Carol Stream, IL 60188
(630) 653-8690, fax (630) 653-8979
www.wagnercharter.com
E-mail cruising@wagnercharter.com

Contact Chad or Mike, cruise sales directors
Best Features Customized private charters and theme parties.
Best Party Venetian night cruise.
Capacity 58 banquet, 145 reception.
Rental Fee $375 per hour in spring and fall, $525 per hour for a Friday or Saturday evening in July or August.
Discounts Call for current discounts or incentives.
For the Kids Pirate Adventure cruises are available, starting at $12 per person; birthday packages are also available.

Courtesy of Wagner Charter Company

Hours Late April to mid-October, 24 hours a day, seven days a week.
Parking Three nearby parking garages.

Aye-aye Mate! Chicago's only pirate ship, this 100-foot-long boat, features trompe l'oeil cannons and gun ports, murals, an authentic mermaid bow spirit, and a skull and crossbones flag. The main deck can be opened or closed for comfort in a variety of weather conditions and has ample room for dancing or seated dining. At the stern, a convenient three-sided bar provides quick service. Below deck, *The Buccaneer*'s lower lounge is perfect for buffet presentations. This fantasy ship is perfect for all types of occasions, from kids' theme parties to corporate events.

For food and beverage service, Wagner Charter Company's exclusive caterer offers total flexibility. Standard menus are provided or the cruise coordinator can design a custom menu. A casual buffet starts at $5.00 per person. Bar packages start at $12.75 per person. Complete packages start at $18.95 per person.

Wagner Charter Company

The Jamaica

Docked on Lower Wacker Drive
Mailing Address:
2N076 Linda Avenue
Carol Stream, IL 60188
(630) 653-8690, fax (630) 653-8979
www.wagnercharter.com
E-mail cruising@wagnercharter.com

Contact Chad or Mike, cruise sales directors
Best Features Customized private charters and theme parties.
Capacity 176 banquet, 215 reception.
Rental Fee $600 per hour in spring and fall; $900 per hour for a Friday or Saturday evening in July and August.
Discounts Call for current discounts or incentives.
For the Kids Any cruise can be customized into a fun kid's party with complete decor and entertainment.
Hours March 1–December 31, 24 hours a

Courtesy of Wagner Charter Company

day, seven days a week.
Parking Three nearby garages.

For a spectacular nautical setting and an ever-changing view of the Chicago River's breathtaking canyon of skyscrapers, plan a party aboard *The Jamaica*. This 105-foot-long yacht has an upper deck for dancing under the stars and a main salon with wraparound picture windows allowing a magnificent view, even on chilly days. With more than 43 years of experience, Wagner Charter is Chicago's oldest charter company.

The Jamaica offers every amenity, including custom catering and decor, starting at $5.00 per person for a casual buffet. Bar packages start at $12.75 per person with a cash bar available. Spacious dance floors and a wide variety of entertainment options are also available. Complete packages start at $23.95 per person.

THEATERS, COMEDY CLUBS, AND DINNER CLUBS

Arts Center of Oak Park

Center for Visual and Performing Arts

Chicago Theatre, The

Civic Opera House

Copernicus Foundation Gateway Theater

Old Town School of Folk Music

Paramount Arts Center

Park West

Puppet Parlor Theatre

Rialto Square Theatre

Second City, The

Symphony Center

Tommy Gun's Garage

Arts Center of Oak Park

200 N. Oak Park Avenue
Oak Park, IL 60302
(708) 366-3981, fax (708) 366-6909

Contact Chatka Ruggiero, owner
Capacity Auditorium, 700; lobby, 150 reception; Great Room and Hemingway museum, 250 reception, 150 theater.
Rental Fee Auditorium $350; Great Room with Hemingway Museum, $150; lobby, $150. These are minimum fees.
Discounts For nonprofit organizations.
Hours Flexible.
Parking On-street parking, and two city lots one block away.

Glorious amber light streams through the many caramel-hued glass windows of this stately, neoclassic structure built in 1914 as a Christian Science church. Now the lobby, second floor auditorium, lower level Great Room, and Ernest Hemingway Museum are available for community, business, and nonprofit events. Massive pillars in the auditorium support an 18 x 36-foot concert stage, and an ornate grill masks the pipes of an organ. The auditorium has six dressing rooms, a grand podium, a sound system, and a Baldwin grand piano. The Great Room is an attractive 4,500 square-foot carpeted room with a podium, sound system, kitchen, and grand piano.

Select a caterer from their list. With the center's approval, you can also bring in your own caterer. The center is ideal for meetings, concerts, receptions, lectures, seminars, and buffets. Sit-down dinners and wedding receptions are discouraged. Eight rectangular tables, 10 round tables, and 120 chairs are available at no charge. The entire building is air-conditioned. The museum is handicapped accessible, but the auditorium is not.

Courtesy of Arts Center of Oak Park

Center for Visual and Performing Arts

1040 Ridge Road
Munster, IN 46321
(219) 836-1950
www.cvpa.org
E-mail cvpa@iname.com

Contact Banquet manager
Capacity Dining room, 450 banquet, 600 reception; gallery, 250 banquet, 350 reception; theater, 450; other rooms, 30–80.
Rental Fee No rental fee with food/beverage service.
Discounts Specials for weekday events.
Hours Daily until midnight.
Parking On-site for 350 cars; valet available.

A cultural mecca and a versatile site for social events and corporate functions, this modern fine art center features a dining room, a 450-seat theater, and a spacious art gallery. The Center is surrounded by well-manicured grounds and scenic wooded areas; the floor-to-ceiling windows bring to full view the beautiful landscape. At the entrance, there is a sunny atrium that leads to a dramatic winding staircase.

All events are catered by the Center. Dinner prices range from $27–$42 per person. A four-hour bar package is $13 per person. Lunch prices range from $12–$21 per person and breakfast is available. Hors d'oeuvre receptions may be hosted in the dining room, lobby, and occasionally in the gallery. Audiovisual equipment is available. The facility is handicapped accessible.

Courtesy of Center for Visual and Performing Arts

THE CHICAGO THEATRE

175 N. STATE STREET
CHICAGO, IL 60601
(312) 263-1138 OR (614) 469-1045,
   FAX (312) 263-9505
WWW.CAPA.COM

CONTACT Debbie Rosenthal
CAPACITY Auditorium, 3,500 theater; theater lobbies, 880 banquet, 2,500 reception; main lobby and mezzanine lobby, 200 banquet, 700 reception.
RENTAL FEE Call for rates.
HOURS Flexible.
PARKING 3,000 spaces at a special group rate.

Photograph by Barry Rustin, courtesy of the Chicago Theatre

The Chicago Theatre has long been considered a distinctive civic ornament. You can rent the auditorium and lobby areas of this historic landmark for almost any type of event—from a live concert to a small reception. Announce your event in more than 3,640 lights on the marquee. The elegant Grande Lobby was inspired by the Palace of Versailles. The auditorium has a 70-foot proscenium that frames the stage. The theater is handicapped accessible.

Choose from the theater's list of preferred caterers. A full complement of audiovisual equipment and technical support offers maximum flexibility for your event. An intricate three-color house lighting system with dimmers is provided. In addition, there is a 40 x 60-foot movie screen, 56+ line sets, and a complete set of drapes.

CIVIC OPERA HOUSE

20 N. WACKER DRIVE
CHICAGO, IL 60606
(312) 419-0033

CONTACT Bob Skehan, special events manager
BEST FEATURE Grand foyer.
CAPACITY Rice Grand Foyer, 300 banquet, 700 reception; mezzanine, 100 banquet, 200 reception; Opera Club, 75 banquet, 125 reception; Graham Room, 200 banquet, 300 reception; Malott Room, 50 banquet, 75 reception.
RENTAL FEE $250–$7,500 depending on space used.
HOURS Flexible.
PARKING Nearby lots; valet.

The shimmering, newly renovated Daniel F. and Ada L. Rice Grand Foyer is an elegant and spacious site for entertaining on a grand scale. The art deco design and hand-detailed ornamentation that adorn the ceiling make a spectacular impression. The William B. and Catherine Graham Room comprises five adjoining rooms, all located on the mezzanine level of the Civic Opera House. Each room is set apart by a series of graceful arches, allowing the large room to retain a sense of intimacy. Also located on the mezzanine level is the Malott Room, which is graciously appointed with rich, comfortable furnishings that resemble a drawing room.

Civic Opera House will provide a list a caterers from which to choose. All food, beverage, and rental of tables, chairs, linens must be handled by the caterer. Audiovisual equipment is available for a fee. Opera/theatrical events have a priority, so availability is limited.

Courtesy of Hedrich-Blessing Photography, courtesy of Civic Opera House

Copernicus Foundation Gateway Theater

5216 W. Lawrence Avenue
Chicago, IL 60630
Theater rental: (773) 777-9438, banquet and meeting rooms: (773) 777-8898

Contact Theater: Dennis Wolkowicz; banquet and meeting rooms: Ellen Wierzewshi

Best Feature Excellent acoustics in the theater.

Capacity Theater, 2,000 theater; banquet hall, 150 banquet and reception; three meeting rooms, 30–150 banquet and reception.

Rental Fee Call for rates.

Hours Flexible.

Parking On-site free lot.

The Copernicus Foundation's Gateway Theater was Chicago's first theater built for sound films and even today it offers near-perfect acoustics. The Gateway was

designed by Rapp & Rapp, who also designed the well-known Chicago Theatre. The inside of the theater has a Roman feel with ornate columns and great arches. The immense lobby features a sweeping staircase which leads to the balcony. Part of the lobby has been remodeled into meeting rooms and a banquet facility. The rooms are somewhat plain, but the banquet hall has the original vaulted ceiling, chandeliers, and a dance floor.

You must bring in your own caterer. Be aware that food and drink is not allowed in some parts of the building. Most audiovisual equipment must be brought in. The site is handicapped accessible and there is no smoking in the theater.

Photograph by White Eagle Studio, courtesy of the Copernicus Foundation Gateway Theater

Old Town School of Folk Music

4544 N. Lincoln Avenue
Chicago, IL 60625
(773) 728-6000

Contact Allyson Kennis, extension 3337

Best Feature Versatile concert space.

Capacity Concert Hall, 300 hall.

Rental Fee $1,750 for the Concert Hall for an evening.

Hours Friday, Saturday, and Sunday, after 5 P.M.

Parking Valet; limited on street

The Old Town School of Folk Music has been a Chicago institution for over 40 years. Located in the beautiful Lincoln Square neighborhood since 1998, the Old Town School is a musical home to over 5,000 students a week ranging in age from six months to senior citizen. It also hosts 60+ concerts a year in the American Airlines Concert Hall with such diverse artists as Roger McGuinn,

Patti Smith, Femi Kuti, and Stacey Earle. The concert hall features state-of-the-art sound, lighting, video projection, and video recording systems. The Old Town School is handicapped accessible.

The décor is warm and casual, featuring 1930s-era WPA murals above the stage and in the upper lobby. The Old Town School of Folk Music would make a unique and memorable location for your next event.

Courtesy of Old Town School of Folk Music

PARAMOUNT ARTS CENTER

23 E. GALENA BOULEVARD
AURORA, IL 60506
(630) 896-7676

CONTACT Jeff Wells, operations coordinator

CAPACITY Paramount Theatre, 1,888 theater; North Island Center Atrium, 300 reception; Copley Theatre, 216 theater; Meyer Ballroom, 350 banquet, 500 reception; Marquee Room, 100 banquet, 150 reception.

RENTAL FEE Paramount Theatre, $2,000–$2,500; Copley Theatre, $30–$60 per hour.

HOURS Flexible.

PARKING Nearby public lots; limited street.

The Paramount Arts Center is appropriate for elegant get-togethers, private performances, and business meetings. The theater is associated with North Island Center, which is located across the street and is a perfect spot for smaller parties or receptions.

Hollywood Casino Aurora Catering

Courtesy of Paramount Arts Center

caters all functions for North Island Center. For events at the Paramount you may use Hollywood or your own caterer. Paramount will provide all liquor. Audiovisual equipment is available and both theaters have backstage dressing rooms. The Paramount also offers ticket and promotion services. Eating and smoking are not allowed in the theaters.

PARK WEST

322 W. ARMITAGE AVENUE
CHICAGO, IL 60614
(773) 929-5959 OR (312) 440-9191
WWW.PARKWESTCHICAGO.COM

CONTACT Theresa Altgilbers or Scottie Patrick, special events director

BEST FEATURE State-of-the-art audiovisual capabilities.

CAPACITY 750 banquet, 1,000 reception.

RENTAL FEE $6,000 commercial/private rental; $3,300 nonprofit organizations.

HOURS Flexible

PARKING Limited on the street; valet is available.

This versatile, high-tech facility can be used for corporate meetings and presentations, client receptions, fundraisers, and much more. The 11,000-square-foot facility with five tiered levels, large balconies, seven bars, and comfortable booths is both beautiful and practical in design. If live entertainment and dancing is what you're looking for, there is a 1,200-square-foot dance floor and stage set beneath a magnificent domed ceiling. Recent renovations include 24 video monitors and four large screens. The facility is handicapped accessible.

Catering can be provided by Park West, but outside caterers are welcome. All liquor is provided by Park West; drink prices start at $4.50. Technical labor is nonunion at a rate of $30/hr. per person. One hundred person minimum is necessary to rent the facility.

Courtesy of Park West

PUPPET PARLOR THEATRE

1922 W. MONTROSE AVENUE
CHICAGO, IL 60613
(773) 774-2919 OR 989-0308
E-MAIL RALPHKIPNESS@DOTPLANET.COM

CONTACT Ralph Kipniss, president
BEST FEATURE Puppet shows.
BEST PARTIES *Les Petites Follies* and *Opera Highlights* with marionette personalities. $12 per person; minimum 12.
CAPACITY 70 banquet; birthday parties up to 30.
RENTAL FEE Birthday parties $12 per person.
DISCOUNTS Group rates on weekdays for 30 or more.
FOR THE KIDS Great for kid's parties.
HOURS Showtimes are Saturday and Sunday, 2 P.M.; adult opera, Friday, 7:30 P.M.; reservations required. Admission $8 per person; $15 per person for adult operas.
PARKING On street.

The house lights dim, a miniature

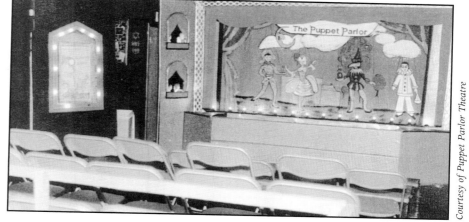

Courtesy of Puppet Parlor Theatre

orchestra pit rises, the Papatini lifts his baton, and the overture begins at the Puppet Parlor Theatre. The theater, patterned after European marionette theaters, is a unique, intimate setting for your next party. The shows run about an hour and twenty minutes and change throughout the year. After the show, banquet tables are set up and the party continues. There are also classes on puppet and marionette making, costume making, and staging a puppet produc-

tion. Not just for children's events, the Puppet Parlor will introduce all ages to the art of puppetry.

You may bring decorations and cake and ice cream to suit your theme. The theater will serve fruit punch and popcorn. (No other food is allowed.) There are no kitchen facilities. Liquor is allowed for adult groups. Some audiovisual equipment is available. There is no smoking. Handicapped accessible.

RIALTO SQUARE THEATRE

102 N. CHICAGO STREET
JOLIET, IL 60432
(815) 726-7171

CONTACT Nancy Bertnik, director of programming
CAPACITY Theatre, 1,900; Rotunda, 400 banquet, 1,000 reception.
RENTAL FEE Theatre and Rotunda, $4,300 for Saturday (plus production and staff costs); Rotunda only, $1,135 for Saturday.
DISCOUNTS For nonprofit organizations.
HOURS Flexible.
PARKING Nearby public lots.

The Rialto, designed in the roaring 20s, is an opulent vaudeville/movie palace that has hosted Benny Goodman, Jack Benny, and Charlie Chaplin. The Rialto stages various live performances throughout the year, but the theater is available for private performances and parties. Spanning an entire city block,

the theater's lobby includes an elaborate walkway fashioned after the Hall of Mirrors at Versailles. The Rotunda is a magnificent space designed after the Parthenon, which the boasts the largest chandelier in the United States. Two curving staircases on opposite sides of the Rotunda seem specially designed for a grand entrance from the balcony.

Bring your own caterer or they can suggest one. The Rialto handles all liquor. Tables are provided, but other equipment must be brought in. Various audiovisual equipment is available, and (for a fee) a staff to operate it. The theater is handicapped accessible.

Photograph by Fender & Donisch, courtesy of Rialto Square Theatre

THE SECOND CITY

1616 N. WELLS STREET
CHICAGO, IL 60614
(312) 664-4032, FAX (312) 664-9837
WWW.SECONDCITY.COM

CONTACT Director of sales
BEST FEATURE World-famous improvisational comedy.
CAPACITY Mainstage, 340 theater; ETC theater, 180 theater.
RENTAL FEE Mainstage, $4,200; ETC, $2,130 on Tuesday–Thursdays and Sundays; higher prices for private Friday and Saturday shows.
HOURS Flexible hours for private events.
PARKING Public lots in Pipers Alley and Treasure Island; $1 discount with validated parking stub.

Photograph by Jennifer Girard, courtesy of The Second City

Add some laughs to your next company outing or private party with the help of the hilarious improvisational comedy troupe at The Second City. Upon its opening in December of 1959, The Second City achieved instantaneous success. The comedy club has been the starting point for such well-known actors as John Candy, Gilda Radner, Ed Asner, and Chris Farley. They remain committed to developing the finest improvisational actors and continue to receive rave reviews. Private events can be hosted in the Mainstage theater or in the ETC theater.

You are welcome to arrange an outside caterer or The Second City can prepare a light fare. Drinks are $2.00–$6.50 each. Deliveries must be made after 9:30 A.M. Most meeting equipment must be rented. However, a sound system, microphones, and screens are available. Handicapped access through ETC entrance only.

SYMPHONY CENTER

220 S. MICHIGAN AVENUE
CHICAGO, IL 60604
(312) 294-3260, FAX (312) 294-3329
WWW.CSO.ORG
E-MAIL GREDENIUS@CSO.ORG

CONTACT Greg Redenius, Symphony Center rental events manager
CAPACITY Orchestra Hall, 2,521; Grainger Ballroom, 210 banquet, 350 reception, 300 theater; Buntrock Hall, 300 banquet, 500 reception, 375 theater; Rotunda (six levels), each level 80 banquet, 200 reception.
RENTAL FEE Armour Stage, $5,000–$6,000; Grainger Ballroom, $1,500–$3,500; Buntrock Hall, $2,000–$3,000.
HOURS Flexible.
PARKING Public lots nearby; limited street.

Courtesy of Symphony Center

Home to the Chicago Symphony Orchestra, this turn-of-the-century landmark building can accommodate a variety of events, such as weddings and receptions in the Grainger Ballroom and Buntrock Hall, hors d'oeuvres in the Rotunda, corporate meetings or dinner and dancing on the Armour Stage. The Grainger Ballroom features 35-foot vaulted ceilings hung with original chandeliers, gold trimmed and mirrored walls, draped windows overlooking Michigan Avenue, and updated lighting and sound systems. The fifth floor lobby has a tremendous view of the Art Institute's south garden.

Catering, including alcohol service, is provided by Applause Foodservices, Inc. Prices vary according to customer needs. Chairs and banquet-style tables can be provided. Extensive audiovisual equipment including lecterns, microphones, and projection screens are available for an additional fee. Smoking is not permitted.

TOMMY GUN'S GARAGE

1239 S. STATE STREET
CHICAGO, IL 60605
(312) 461-0102, FAX (312) 461-9553
WWW.TOMMYGUNSGARAGE.COM

CONTACT Sandy Mangen
BEST FEATURE Roaring speakeasy setting.
CAPACITY Entire theater, 190 banquet, 250 reception.
RENTAL FEE $1,500 and up.
HOURS Flexible.
PARKING Evenings and weekends free; $5 per car during weekdays.

Courtesy of Tommy Gun's Garage

Enter this roaring 1920s dinner theater through da rear entrance and slip "Gloves" da password. Be careful not to forget, see, or you might end up wearing sche-ment schoes, see, and sleeping with the fishes, see. Tommy Gun's is an audience interactive musical comedy revue complete with gangsters, flappers, and bullet holes in the walls. The room features a 1928 Model A car, a replica of the St. Valentine's Day Massacre Wall, and memorabilia from the 20s. Your guests will have a fabulous time while they are transported back in time.

The in-house caterers will prepare your buffet or sit-down lunch or dinner. A full-service bar with reasonably priced drink packages is available. Dinner entrees range from $16–$22 per person. The minimum charge to book the room for a private event is $1,500 plus bar. A VCR, wireless microphone, stage, tape deck, and stage lighting is available. The site is handicapped accessible.

General Resources

Chicago Convention and Tourism Bureau
  2301 S. Lake Shore Drive,
  Chicago, IL 60616
  (312) 567-8500
  www.chicago.il.org

Chicago Office of Tourism
  78 E. Washington Street,
  Chicago, IL 60602
  (312) 744-2400
  www.ci.chi.il.us/CulturalAffairs/
  OfficeofTourism

City of Chicago
  Mayor's Office of Special Events
  121 N. LaSalle Street, Ste. 703,
  Chicago, IL 60602
  (312) 744-3315
  w5.chi.il.us/SpecialEvents

Crains Chicago Business magazine
  www.crainschicagobusiness.com

DuPage Convention and Visitors Bureau
  915 Harger Road, Ste. 240,
  Oak Brook, IL 60523
  (800) 232-0502
  www.dupagecvb.com

EventSource, The Event Planning Search
  Engine
  www.eventsource.com

Greater Woodfield Convention and Visitors
  Bureau
  1430 Meacham Rd.,
  Schaumburg, IL 60173
  (800) 847-4849
  www.chicagonorthwest.com

Hotel-Motel Association of Illinois
  www.hotel-motel-illinois.com

Illinois Restaurant Association
  (800) 572-1086 or (312) 787-4000
  www.illinoisrestaurants.org

International Special Events Society
  www.ises.com

League of Chicago Theaters
  228 S. Wabash, Suite 300,
  Chicago, IL 60604
  (312) 554-4800
  www.theaterchicago.org

Meeting Professionals International, Chicago
  Area Chapter
  (847) 657-6745
  www.mpicac.org

National Speakers Association, Illinios
  Chapter
  (630) 971-1600
  www.nsa-il.org

Oak Brook Area Association of Commerce
  and Industry
  One Tower Lane, Suite LL20,
  Oak Brook Terrace, IL 60181
  (630) 572-0616
  www.obaci.com

Rosemont Convention Bureau
  9301 W. Bryn Mawr Avenue,
  Rosemont, IL 60018
  (847) 823-2100
  www.rosemont.com/bureau.html

Bridal-Specific Resources

Association of Bridal Consultants
  www.bridalassn.com

Association of Certified Professional Wedding Consultants
  (408) 528-9000
  www.acpwc.com

Chicago Wedding Online
  www.chicagoweddingonline.com

Wedding Bells—Chicago
  www.weddingbells.com/unitedstates/
  stores/chicago.html

Wedding Spot—Chicago
  www.weddingspot.com/chicago

Transportation

RTA Travel Information Center
  (312) 836-7000
  www.rtachicago.com

Charter Buses

Adventure Charters, Inc.
  (800) 942-9363
  www.dispatchone.com

American Sightseeing Chicago
  (312) 251-3100

Aries Charter Transportation, Inc.
  (888) 305-8700

Celebrity Coach, Inc.
  (708) 418-3103

Chicago Gray Line
  (312) 251-3107

Chicago Trolly Company
  (312) 663-0260 or (773) 648-5000

Coach One, Inc.
  (773) 468-2000
  www.coachone.com

Continental Air Transport
  (888) 2-THEVAN
  www.airportexpress.com

Dynasty First Class Transportation
  (773) 826-5020

Embassy Coach Lines
  (708) 849-8034

Fonseca Coach Lines, Inc.
  (708) 352-6960

Joy Motor Coach
  (708) 371-2723

Lambers Bus Lines
(800) 822-3550

Mid-America Charter Lines, Inc.
(847) 437-3779
www.bus-charter.com

Midwest Transit System
(708) 448-7822

Neal's Coach Line
(708) 331-4660

Phoenix Charter Transport, Inc.
(312) 666-3309

Pontarelli Limousine & Group Charters
(312) 226-5466

Robinson Coach Company
(847) 866-1958

Treasured Tours
(773) 734-2345

Van Galder Bus Co.
(608) 752-5407

Walters Bus Service, Inc.
(773) 785-9176

Limousine and Classic Car Services
All American Limousine
(877) 992-0902
www.allamericanlimo.com

American Limousine
(630) 920-8888
www.americanlimousine.com

Amm's Limousine
(773) 792-1126
www.amlimo.com

Boston Coach
(800) 672-7676

Carey Limousine Service
(773) 763-0009

Chicago Flag Luxury Sedan and Limo/
Tours/Shuttle
(312) 944-4476

Chicago Limousines
(800) 540-1750
www.chicagolimo.com

Delaware Cars & Limousine
(800) 222-8370 or (312) 337-2800
www.delawarecars.com

The Limo Center, Ltd.
(800) 654-5459 or (312) 829-1000

Mahogany Limousine Service
(773) 784-7716

Metropolitian/Dav-El Limousine
(800) 437-1700 or (312) 808-8000

My Limousine of Chicago, Inc.
(888) 540-0442
www.mylimoofchicago.com

O'Hare Midway Limousine Service, Inc.
(847) 234-4550

Smart Cars, Inc.
(847) 299-3600

Valet Parking
Valet Parking Service
(312) 332-1134

LOCATIONS WITH OUTDOOR FACILITIES AND GARDENS

LOCATIONS THAT ACCOMMODATE 500 OR MORE GUESTS

Chicago

ALPHABETICAL LISTING OF LOCATIONS

ADVERTISERS' INDEX

ACCOMMODATIONS

CATERING

a work of art...

artistic events

BY CARLYN BERGHOFF CATERING, INC.

...*f*or your palette

www.carlynberghoffcatering.com | 3 1 2 . 4 3 2 . 0 2 0 0

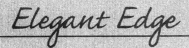

LET REGENCY CATERERS BRING ELEGANCE TO YOU.

Hyatt Regency Chicago, the largest property in the Hyatt chain operates 365 days a year with over 1600 talented employees, including an award winning culinary team of 100 professionally trained chefs and 150 certified wait staff.

Our successful off-premise catering wing, Regency Caterers, opened ten years ago and has planned thousands of events to rave reviews.
Hyatt offers years of experience that translates into successful events that won't be forgotten.
We'll create cutting edge menus and our event experts will take care of every detail, from arranging for valet parking to "good night" coffee and cookies!

Hotel rooms will also be available for your guests who may want to spend the evening in Chicago. You've got the Hyatt name on it.

Chicago's Cultural Center

PROFESSIONAL ADVANTAGES

- Expert recommendation on decor, specialty linen, entertainment, invitations and photography
- Quality china, glassware and silverware
- Fully insured, licensed and bonded
- An array of equipment to fit your special needs
- Competitive pricing

CUSTOM SERVICES

- Award winning chefs
- Professional service staff
- Custom designed menus
- Creative theme parties
- Complete bar service
- Extensive Wine Cellar
- Kosher catering supervised by The Chicago Rabbinical Council
- Valet parking
- Limousine transportation to and from events
- Custom event planners
- Hyatt Regency Chicago overnight accommodations
- Checkroom & restroom attendants
- Complete liquor liscensing and insurance

SITES

- Civic Opera House
- The Field Museum of Natural History
- The Chicago Cultural Center
- The Harold Washington Library
- The Chicago Children's Museum
- Chicago's First Lady Yacht

REGENCY
CATERERS
BY HYATT

For further information call Regency Caterers by Hyatt.
Phone: 312-616-6800
Fax: 312-616-6904

John Reilly Photography

BBJ Linens *Nothing but the best for your guests*

BBJ Linens provides an extensive selection of high quality rental specialty linens. From chair covers and dazzling custom designs to brocades, metallics and tapestries, we bring "that something extra" to your special event. Call us today for more information. *You set the theme, we'll fulfill the dream!*

Servicing customers nationwide.   Phone 847-328-8400 or 800-722-0126 Fax 847-329-8405

Chicagoland's first choice for party rentals...

Hall's Rental Service Inc.
6130 W. Howard
Niles, IL 60714
T: 847.929.2222
F: 847.929.2223
Visit our new website:
www.hallsrental.com

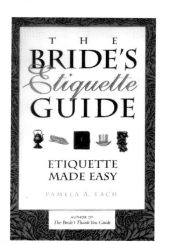

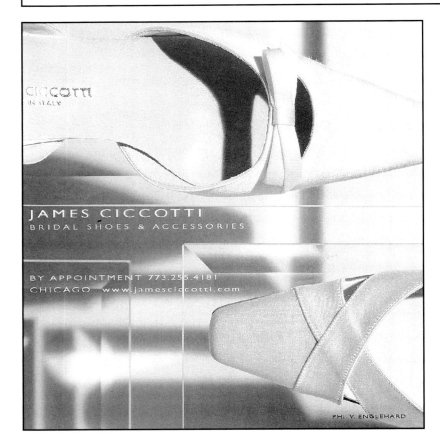

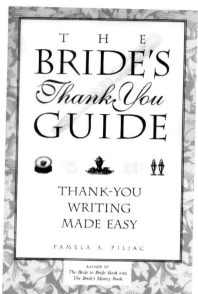

SECOND EDITION

CHICAGO
Special
EVENTS
Sourcebook

EDITED BY LINDA LUTTON

The comprehensive guide to locations in Chicago and suburbs for MEETINGS,
PARTIES, WEDDINGS, and other SPECIAL OCCASIONS

Return
Engagement

If you would like to purchase an
ad in the next
Chicago Special Events Sourcebook,
contact

Ad Sales Rep
c/o Chicago Review Press
814 North Franklin Street
Chicago, IL 60610

or call **312.337.0747**
www.ipgbook.com

CHICAGO
REVIEW
PRESS

SERVICE
IS US
INC.
Providing Waitstaff,
Bartenders and Culinary
Professionals

Serving Chicagoland
Since 1989

5347 North Clark Street
Chicago, IL 60640

Phone: 773-784-2225
Fax: 773-784-6128

Now Online at:
http://member.aol.com/SIUINC2/index.html

Orchestra of the Americas^{SM}

The Great American Dance Orchestra

Rhythm, Romance, Elegance, Excitement ... in the tradition of
Ellington, Basie, Sinatra, Tito Puente, Gloria Estefan, Gipsy Kings,
Aretha, Stevie Wonder, Earth, Wind & Fire, Barry White, Donna Summer,
Santana, Rolling Stones, Temptations, Steely Dan, Stevie Ray Vaughn, et al.

Impeccable References • Unmatched Versatility • Guaranteed Satisfaction

Smaller groups available for ceremony, cocktails, dinner, awards presentations, etc.

773.334.1532 • BacchusGrp@Compuserve.com

New York • Chicago • Los Angeles • San Francisco • Miami • Orlando • New Orleans

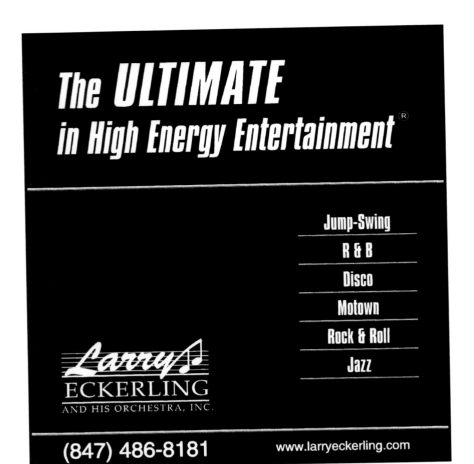

224

Would you like your establishment to be considered for the next *Chicago Special Events Sourcebook?*

Contact the

Sourcebook Editor
^{c}/o Chicago Review Press
814 North Franklin Street
Chicago, IL 60610

www.ipgbook.com

CHICAGO
Special
EVENTS
Sourcebook